DNA of the Spirit is like a banquet table generously laid before us by its sponsors, inviting us to trust the call of the new energies increasingly available to us. More than to find our place at the table, the invitation is also to come into the kitchen and the gardens and to learn to grow the ingredients and to prepare the meal for ourselves. The saints, angels, masters, and sages of all the ages — even the fabric of life itself — are ready to give counsel and instruction in a way that is readily accessible and permeated with complete love. The presence of all the contributors was evident in the reading, meaning that the book itself is a powerful conduit of transmission. We are meant to dialogue with eternity and realize the fullness of the soul.

> — Robert D. Waterman, EdD, author,
> developer of Noetic Field Therapy,
> founder and president of the
> Quimby Amenti Foundation
> (www.Mystery-School.com)

I have known Rae Chandran for quite a few years, and I know him to be a dedicated spiritual man. He is dedicated to serving the needs of others and of being honest and true to himself and to those he serves. He can be counted on to give you his best advice and his best opinions when asked for. I would say this is a man you can believe in when it comes to what he does and how he does it. Good life to you all.

> — Robert Shapiro, author, professional
> trance channel, mystic educator

DNA of the Spirit brings together new spiritual understanding about our DNA strands. Rae Chandran is a powerful channel who is doing groundbreaking spiritual work on DNA and its relation to karma, ascension, and our multidimensional selves. The central message of this book is about how humanity successfully crossed a powerful threshold in 2012. The possibilities of a Golden Age are now before us. New tools to prepare for this new era, including healing Earth, are explained within. I recommend this book highly for all spiritual seekers who are looking for a clearer understanding about humanity's next evolutionary step!

— David K. Miller, author,
professional channel, founder of
the Group of Forty
(www.GroupofForty.com)

DNA
OF THE SPIRIT

VOLUME 1

A practical guide to reconnecting with your divine blueprint

CHANNELED BY **Rae Chandran**
with Robert Mason Pollock

This book is dedicated to all the brothers and sisters of this beautiful planet who are on the path of self-discovery.
—Saint Germain, July 30, 2013

DNA OF THE SPIRIT

VOLUME 1

A practical guide to reconnecting with your divine blueprint

CHANNELED BY **Rae Chandran**
WITH **Robert Mason Pollock**

LIGHT Technology
PUBLISHING

For more information about special discounts for bulk purchases, please contact Light Technology Publishing Special Sales at 1-800-450-0985 or publishing@LightTechnology.net.

ISBN-13: 978-1-62233-013-3
Published and printed in the United States of America by:

PO Box 3540
Flagstaff, AZ 86003
800-450-0985
www.LightTechnology.com

Table of Contents

Foreword

I first met Rae Chandran during December 2012 in Aswan, Egypt. Rae leads tours of sacred sites in Egypt, Israel, and Greece, and I had booked a tour with him. We bonded immediately, and some months later, we started collaborating on this book.

My spiritual practices and beliefs had become fairly static before meeting Rae. I had spent more than twenty years in a mystery school and spiritual community, and although I had left the community ten years before meeting Rae, I was still working with the same paradigms I had formed years before. My last book, *Navigating by Heart*, summarizes those beliefs and practices.

During our July 8, 2012, channeling session, Saint Germain described how Rae and I might introduce ourselves to the readers of this book. Saint Germain said I was emerging from a cocoon, and this is true. After years of living in a closed community of like-minded people, I found that my social and coping skills had atrophied, and being out in the world had become pretty scary. So for the first few years, I sought ways to live safely. I have an energy-healing practice, and I teach workshops from time to time. I also live a fairly introverted life with a lot of alone time. Apparently, all this is about to change.

Working on this book has opened my eyes to the spiritual and energetic changes that are happening on planet Earth. The year 2013 was the first year of a dimensional shift in consciousness. Humanity has grown in consciousness immensely, warranting the release of ancient truths and practices from the mystery schools of Egypt and elsewhere. Our bodies are changing so that they can support crystalline (or Christ) consciousness. Opportunities for ascension are here. We are laying the groundwork for two generations of new children to manifest some of these changes.

Rae and I did not write the material presented in this book. Rae is an incredibly clear channel, but the masters and archangels whose words you will read are the true authors. I am a wordsmith. My job was to organize, edit, and clarify.

My other job was to learn. I learned to stop thinking of DNA in terms of inherited physical characteristics and to see it as an information library for my soul. My DNA contains the history of me, lifetime after lifetime. It is a record of the attitudes, karma, and emotional predispositions I brought into this lifetime and a blueprint (or lesson plan) for my self-improvement. It is also a record of my existence from the moment of my creation as a starbeing to my present incarnation.

This information is written in each cell of my body, as it is in yours. And there are practices I can do — and energetic connections I can make — to raise my consciousness and activate additional strands of DNA. This leads to further spiritual empowerment, heightened awareness, and deeper connections to the Creator and to beings who work from the inner planes to support humanity.

There is much material in this book that is new to me. My practices had not included the use of sounds, toning, or symbols. It did not include connecting energetically to the earth, to other celestial bodies, or to animals. And dragons were totally off the charts! But I am an open-minded person, and eventually, I ceased to be astonished by the material I was editing and started practicing some of it.

You will find that you will relate to some of what is in this book, and other practices will not resonate with you. That is as it should be. I particularly resonated with asking to be taken to the Arcturian healing temple to have my pineal gland cleared and activated. I felt a lot of clarity with that work after a few days of very mild headaches. I have also worked on deepening my connection with Saint Germain, Akhenaton, and Yeshua. I can feel their support.

Rae and I don't see ourselves as special. We were asked to do a job, to present this material. We will practice some of it, and other pieces we will leave — or do in later years. I feel that the real work will be done by you, the readers. If a significant number of people work to prepare the way for the two generations of new children discussed in this book, miracles will become commonplace, Earth will be healed, and humans will be lifted above the conflict and scarcity that are so prevalent on our planet today. It is really up to all of us to manifest this new reality together.

Robert Pollock
Pittsfield, Massachusetts

You must believe that you are a quantum being — that you can
raise your vibration — to activate your 12-strand DNA.
— Saint Germain

Preface

I came from a background of deeply ingrained thought patterns and belief systems originating from the ancient Indian religions, so it was rather inconceivable a few years ago for me to even think of knowing God through any other means. But through a series of life-changing experiences, I was forced to confront this reality in a very stark way. This opened a deep curiosity within me to know more about God and life itself.

Through many trials and errors, I slowly started to discover myself and how I created my own life through my thinking processes, my belief systems, my actions, and my intentions. This led me to search more deeply within myself to find the greater cause of suffering not only in myself but also to find the cause of all the great sorrows of the world.

Through my many journeys into the deepest parts of myself, I was fortunate enough to meet many masters who guided me to go more deeply within to seek answers. Some of these masters were on the physical plane. Their guidance is etched deeply within my soul — Robert Shapiro, David Miller, and Lee Carroll (all from the United States); Natalie Glasson from the United Kingdom; the works of Neale Donald Walsch; and other masters from the inner planes, whose guidance helped me immensely (and still does) — Master Kuthumi, Master Saint Germain, Archangel Metatron, and King Akhenaton.

This book is a collaboration with the masters of the inner planes and with Robert Pollock on the physical plane. Meeting Robert in late 2012 was a turning point in the production of this book. Without Robert's cooperation and support, this project would not have taken root, and I immensely thank him for this. We were also supported energetically in this process by two beautiful beings of light from Israel — Mordechai Yashin and Fredaricka Yarom. We were also supported greatly by all the people who took the time to transcribe, edit, and go through all the materials in a timely fashion and with much grace. So in a big way, this project was truly a cocreative process.

Many of the messages contained in this book are practices that I have done and still do, and others are channeled for the first time. This book is meant to be a practical guide whereby you can practice what is mentioned in the book, for it is my belief that any material — whether channeled or guidance from any other source — must empower and uplift the reader to feel the energy of the words and the love they convey so that they feel expanded and uplifted. I believe that this book will satisfy these essences.

Finally, I wish to thank the Creator for gently guiding me and bringing me to the point of being able to bring these messages forth to support humanity. I also wish to thank my family for their support in this.

Namasté,
Rae Chandran
Tokyo, Japan

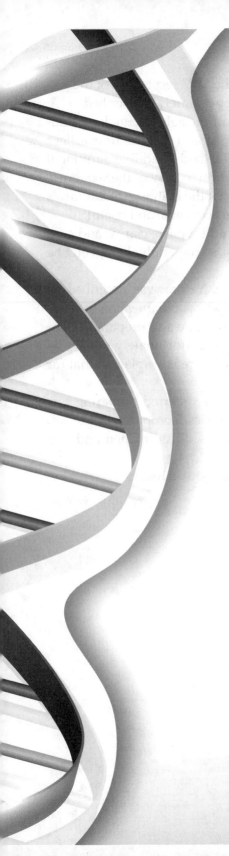

Acknowledgments

Many people helped make this book possible. Our team is from England, Scotland, Israel, four of the United States, Canada, Malaysia, and Japan. We stayed in touch through email, Skype, and DropBox.

The channeling sessions were in question-and-answer format conducted over Skype. Rae Chandran channeled the masters and archangels. Robert Pollock, Mordechai Yashin, and Fredaricka Yarom were the main questioners; between one and three of us were present at most of the sessions, and we were occasionally joined by Audrey Chin and Kenea Eakin.

Audrey and Kenea transcribed some of the sessions. Allison Dohrman, Jan Seward, Ellen Nairn, and Deonna Phillips transcribed others. Paul Vande-Burgh helped with the initial editing and countless technical details, such as getting DropBox to work. Paul also checked the finished manuscript against the MP3 recordings of the sessions to see that the information had been accurately transcribed.

Monica Markley is on the editorial staff of Light Technology Publishing. She reviewed the manuscript and posed a series of excellent and probing queries about the material. Rae and I had five additional sessions during 2014 with Archangel Metatron to answer these queries. This material appears in brackets throughout the manuscript. Monica's questions help make this book much more accessible and useful.

Liz Stell gave the manuscript its final edit, polish, clarity, and consistency. She also asked the right questions, so hopefully there won't be many puzzled readers.

Somewhere in the sessions, Fredaricka Yarom was described as the Librarian of the Universe. Whenever there was a question of reference or spelling, Fredaricka knew the answer. She also prepared extensive lists of questions for the sessions, and unfortunately there was not enough time for her to ask them all. So there is ample material for future volumes.

Gayle Averyt helped defray the costs we incurred preparing this material. Ari Greenberg helped with graphics, computer mysteries, and posed for the DNA mudra photographs. Russell Chen and Rae Chandran designed the cover.

Thank you, each of you, for making this book a reality.

List of Contributors

**Higher Beings Channeled
through Rae Chandran**

Abraham and Sarah, combined
Adama
Amma, the Divine Mother
Angelic Beings
Anna (Jesus's grandmother)
Archangel Gabriel
Archangel Metatron
Archangel Metatron and Saint Germain
Archangel Metatron and the Angelic Beings
Archangel Michael
Creator
Crystal Skull
Flamingoes
Gaia
Grandmother Spider
Juliano, from Arcturus
King Akhenaton
Lord Krishna
Lord Maitreya
Lord Melchizedek
Mahatma

Master Kuthumi
Master Thoth
Masters of DNA
Mother Mary
Oma, the Divine Mother of Divine Mothers
Orengi
Peacocks
Plant Species
Pleiadian Master
Pythagoras (Master Kuthumi)
Saint Germain
Saint Germain and Metatron
Samiel
Sananda
Sanat Kumara
Spirit of the Whales
Sri Bonato
Yeshua
Yeshua and Babaji
Zoosh

The Questioners:
Robert Pollock
Mordechai Yashin
Fredaricka Yarom
Audrey Chin
Kenea Eakin

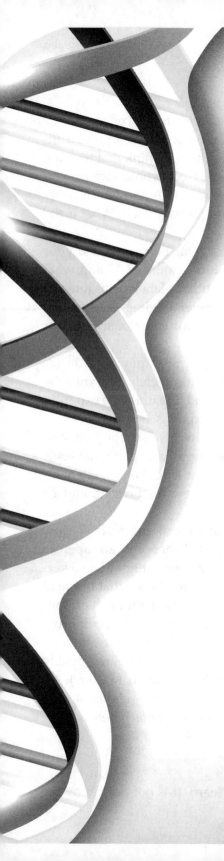

From Archangel Metatron

January 30, 2014

This is Metatron.

Hello.

Congratulations, dear brother [for completing the manuscript]. The train is just beginning to move. It has just started getting into gear. You are going to be very busy, so hold on to your hats. It will be a fun ride. You are at the controls.

We wish to talk briefly today. I have called DNA the core element of who you are. But who you are is still a mystery. DNA contains the history of you, but what about the creation itself? DNA contains not only the history of who you are but also who you were at the time of your creation and where you are going.

Could you explain more about who a person is at the time of his or her creation?

From the Creator, a sense of who you are, a part of the Creator itself: You are the Creator.

Can you say, "I am God?"

What I would say is that I am an aspect of the Creator. Is that correct?

Of course, it is correct, because human beings have a great diffi-culty saying, "I am God." It is too grand for them to think that they are God. When you finally get to see the face of God, whose face do you see? Yes, you — the golden one, the golden face. DNA contains not only this aspect, who you truly are, but also your journey itself. What is the journey? That is an interesting question.

DNA is not only the spiritual aspect of your being but also your entire journey and the potential for your future journey — and what that journey will be, either on this planet or other planets. This journey is imprinted on your DNA. It is not only understanding the spiritual aspect of your being but also the entirety of your consciousness: your past, your present, and your future.

Self-realized beings accept the grandness of who they are. You see the bigger picture and how your journey is completely tied into the journey of the universal self. When you expand, the universe expands. It is through your journey that the universe expands.

On a larger level, you affect the cosmos. In this concept, you start understanding your grandness. This is the true meaning of what Jesus said: "He who believes in Me, the works that I do, he will do also" [John 14:12, NASB]. He knew his past, he knew his present, and he knew his forward journey.

How can you understand this and make it a living reality? How can you activate it? It is through your DNA. When you are open to understanding your DNA, you also work with the energy of resurrec-tion itself. Every moment you live, you are dying. When that moment is over, it is finished. If you ask for resurrection every moment of your life, what happens, dear brother? You are continuously opening up, more and more, every moment. And you must ask for resurrection.

When you ask for resurrection in every moment, you are opening up a larger and larger aspect of yourself. This is what Master Jesus did. He was shown what to do in the next moment — moment after moment — throughout his life. This naturally happens when you are completely tuned into working with your DNA.

We are guided moment to moment?

Not guided, you will know. You will learn. It is not only knowing this in the present moment but also every present moment is an awakening to higher reality, higher understanding, and higher truth. Every moment becomes a grand moment of awakening to the expansion of the universe itself.

When you awaken, you are not only becoming a spiritual being but you are also expanding. Through your expansion, God is expanding. Since you are part of God, it is natural that when you expand, God expands, is it not? This is a gift to the universe.

When you awaken, this awakens the cosmos, everything in the cosmos, including Gaia. Your awakening expands Gaia's consciousness and the consciousness of the trees, animals, and plants. Then you are contributing what you truly came here for — the evolution of the species, of everything. Everything was created to expand and evolve. Otherwise, it would decay and die. Good day to you. This is Metatron.

In April 2014, during one of the five footnote sessions, Archangel Metatron asked that the following be put at the beginning of Volume 1:

This is a practical book, and two things are important in your practice. One is asking. The other is forming intentions. If you do not ask, it is not given at all. In the old energy, ignorance was bliss. In the new energy, ignorance is dangerous. People need to know about this. The old way of thinking is gone. The Creator will not come down and support you. You must cocreate through asking and support yourself with your constant work.

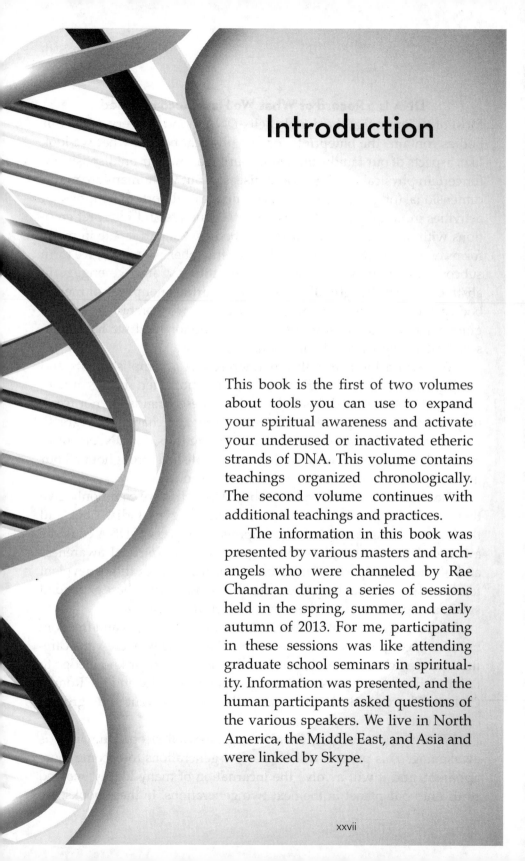

Introduction

This book is the first of two volumes about tools you can use to expand your spiritual awareness and activate your underused or inactivated etheric strands of DNA. This volume contains teachings organized chronologically. The second volume continues with additional teachings and practices.

The information in this book was presented by various masters and archangels who were channeled by Rae Chandran during a series of sessions held in the spring, summer, and early autumn of 2013. For me, participating in these sessions was like attending graduate school seminars in spirituality. Information was presented, and the human participants asked questions of the various speakers. We live in North America, the Middle East, and Asia and were linked by Skype.

DNA Is a Record of What We Have Accomplished

Most of us know that the double helix DNA found in every cell of our bodies contains the blueprints for our physical bodies: what we look like, aspects of our family and ethnic heritage, and our predispositions for certain physical conditions and diseases. But we humans are multi-dimensional (or quantum) beings; we engage in all sorts of nonphysical activities in nonphysical dimensions. We generate and interpret emotions with our nonphysical emotional bodies. We participate in many forms of mental activity: We decide, we remember, we reason, we form subconscious impressions, we develop attitudes, and we engage in abstract mental thought all by using our various nonphysical mental bodies. We can enter spiritual realms: We pray, we worship, we receive guidance from our consciences and our intuition, and we have transcendental experiences, dreams, and realizations.

We begin a lifetime with our nonphysical accomplishments and predispositions in place, and we have an additional ten strands of nonphysical DNA to record this information. These strands are not fixed; they record the changes we make as we grow and change (or regress). We carry this information forward into future lives, for DNA is information. It is a record of what we have accomplished throughout all our lifetimes from our creation as individualized souls.

The ancients understood more about DNA than we commonly give them credit. Seekers in the mystery schools of Egypt, India, Tibet, and the Essenes understood that the nonphysical aspects of DNA could be awakened and activated as they expanded their spiritual awareness and aligned all aspects of their consciousnesses with the benevolent forces of the universe. They knew that they would bring these expanded spiritual capabilities with them into their future lifetimes.

With enhanced spiritual connection come not only joy and freedom but also great prowess and knowledge. The ancients were very careful who they chose to teach, for they did not want their knowledge to fall into the wrong hands. With the rise of Christianity and the Roman Catholic Church in the West, these teachings either went underground or died out.

We are now emerging from a long spiritual sleep. Humanity is awakening. This process will take a few generations to become more apparent, and it will involve the incarnation of many highly evolved souls onto our planet in the next two generations. In these books, we call these souls the New Children. It is because of this great awakening that the spiritual guides of humankind (the masters, archangels, and lords of the spiritual hierarchy) believe that the time is right to release the information in this book. We have grown ready to receive it.

Tools for Raising Consciousness

The information in this book was channeled by Rae in a series of sessions during which Robert, Fredaricka, Mordechai, and others posed questions to the beings who worked with us to disclose the information. This book contains the transcriptions of nineteen sessions held during 2013. These sessions were seminars conducted by the masters. We submitted the manuscript of these sessions to Light Technology Publishing, and our editor, Monica Markley, suggested sections that needed clarification and elaboration. Rae and I held five additional sessions, mostly with Archangel Metatron, during March and April of 2014, adding about fifty pages of material to the book, which is sprinkled throughout the original transcriptions in [brackets].

During these sessions, many practices, tools, and techniques were revealed for raising consciousness and activating nonphysical strands of DNA. I felt truly honored to be asked to participate in the sessions. They opened my eyes to aspects of my spirituality I had never considered. Many of the practices are forms of meditation. Other practices and observances that are not meditative include ways to raise the energy of the food you eat and the water you drink, working with the consciousness of plants and animals, setting intentions, using sounds and toning, using symbols, and using mudras. You will probably not find every practice appealing; choose those that are. This is a smorgasbord with lots of choices, so use your discernment to choose what resonates with you.

Here are some suggestions: There are exercises (mudras and symbols) for each of the twelve layers of DNA. We were advised to practice these together, not to work on only one or two layers now and other layers later. Regular practice is important, and so is discipline. Keep in mind that discipline means regularity, not punishment.

Your efforts will be magnified if you include practicing with others ("For where two or three are gathered together in my name, there am I in the midst of them" [Matthew 18:20, KJB]). This could include working with likeminded friends or attending workshops to supplement your individual practice.

Other Books About DNA

The true authors of this material include Master Saint Germain, Master Sananda (who incarnated as Yeshua and whom we call Jesus), Master Kuthumi, King Akhenaton, Mother Mary, Anna (the grandmother of Yeshua), Archangel Metatron, Lord Melchizedek, Lord Maitreya, Sanat Kumara, Gaia, a Pleiadian master, and the Masters of DNA. Other disincarnate beings participated from time to time.

This is not the first book on 12-strand DNA. But it is the first we know of to comprehensively focus on 12-strand DNA activation: tools and techniques to change the nonphysical strands of DNA so that your energetic signature changes to reflect your spiritual progress.

Several authors have relayed channeled material about 12-strand DNA beginning in the 1990s. Each related a somewhat different facet of the history of human DNA and why the ten etheric strands were altered or deactivated. Barbara Marciniak wrote *Bringers of the Dawn* in 1992, channeling Pleiadians who seeded their 12-strand DNA to humans hundreds of thousands of years ago, only to have the planet overrun by entities who altered human DNA to manage and control our species. Anne Brewer wrote *The Power of Twelve* in 1998; subsequent revisions in 2000 and 2009 included some how-to material on DNA activation and channeled information from the Mesopotamian gods who were described in Zecharia Sitchin's books, beginning with *The 12th Planet*. In 2010, Lee Carroll issued the twelfth book in his Kryon series entitled *The Twelve Layers of DNA: An Esoteric Study of the Mastery Within*. This book includes Hebrew names and symbols for the twelve layers of DNA.

Becoming Masters

The central message of this book is very hopeful. It is about how humanity successfully crossed a threshold in 2012. The possibilities of a Golden Age are before us. Some of the tools to do this work are in this book. And other tools will follow in future books about healing Earth of the karma of human conflict and healing the animal kingdom of the karma of abuse by humans.

The material we were given on altering human DNA emphasizes the progress that humanity is making in awakening to our history of being controlled through fear; how humans have grown stronger through exposure to adversity; and how we are being groomed to assume roles as interplanetary explorers, freedom fighters, lightworkers, and citizens of the galaxy. Old fear-based paradigms can be replaced through expanded spiritual awareness, and we humans can become empowered to see ourselves as the quantum, interdimensional beings we truly are. We are capable of performing miracles. We are capable of healing Earth and the life forms she supports of the negativity and darkness we have generated. We are capable of becoming masters.

— Robert Pollock

Chapter 1

Mudras for Activating the Twelve Layers of DNA

April 10, 2013

Saint Germain, a Pleiadian Master, and Master Kuthumi

This is Saint Germain. All traditions have secret wisdom and secret knowledge. There is an ancient wisdom from the past that can support one's awakening into new consciousness.

Oral traditions have secret knowledge and wisdom that can now be revealed after passing the marker of December 2012. We can bring this forth because there was a mass awakening at that time, and now each person can come into a certain new truth. We feel people are now more receptive to the truth.

Before now, humanity was not ready to receive this truth. For example, you drive a beautiful car. But what would people say if that car was given to you 200 years ago, before people had any understanding of cars? They might say something like, "It's a product of the Devil" or, perhaps, "Maybe he made it with black magic." The same would be

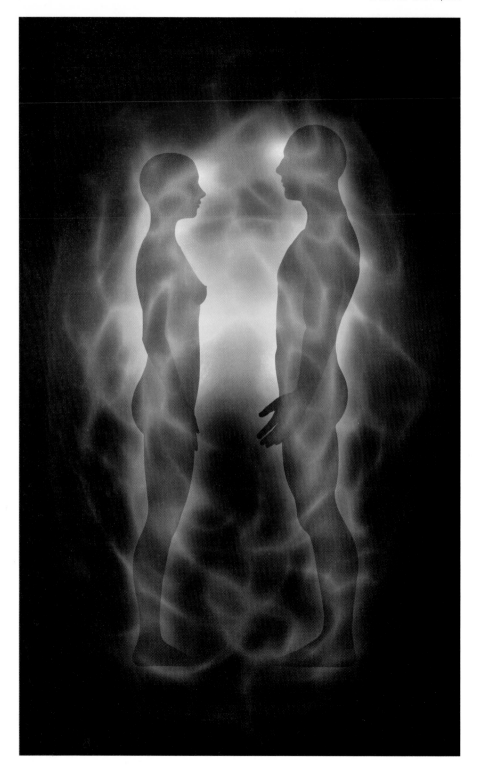

true with a simple calculator or so many other items we now consider commonplace. Humanity would not have comprehended them 200 years ago, but now you are ready to receive this ancient wisdom.

When humanity is ready, a thought form enters human sight. Human beings have been watching birds fly for thousands of years, but only in the last century have they found a way to fly. Why not before?

We believe it is the right time to bring forward many of the ancient truths and much of the ancient wisdom. But people are resistant to new ideas. Anything you bring forth may be seen as blasphemy, but as you know, many truths begin as false paradigms, fool's jokes, or blasphemy. Sometimes when you reveal a new truth, people say, "Oh, maybe we should come and check it out," but then often they never fully accept it.

These are ancient tools given by the ancient Egyptian masters who came from Atlantis as well as from Akhenaton, Lord Ra, Thoth, the Hathors, and many others. These are mystical teachings from the ancient past. King Tutmosis III, the warrior king, was Master Kuthumi. Many of the mudras were practiced by him on a daily basis. So I would like to tell you only one thing: Since people now have more acceptance of higher truths, present this material in any way you feel appropriate, but these are our thoughts on the subject.

Now, my dear family, I would like to present some highly evolved beings. They are particularly fond of this planet for they have seeded it with their own DNA. We are honored to have a great Pleiadian master here with us today.

※　　※　　※

The Twelve Layers of DNA

This is Pleiadian Master with Master Kuthumi. Greeting and blessings. In the ancient Egyptian way, we say *hi heem*. It means "greetings from the heart." Let our hearts beat together, for we are one with the Creator. Let us take a moment for the joining and mending of the heart and the melding of the energy. We have important information for you — important information for the world — at this time, for the world is awakening, living life faster, and the pace only gets faster and faster.

The true origin of humankind will be found within the next few years. All the old teachings, including Charles Darwin's theory of evolution, will be discarded, and it will be said that it served its purpose, for now we have found higher truth and new understanding. These new tools will allow each human being on the planet to connect with a very high energy from us, because we are you of the future. We have implanted our DNA in each and every one of you. This realization will cause a major awakening of consciousness on the planet.

In this context, we would like to present twelve mudras related to our DNA. As you know, DNA is basically messages or information that is to be activated with the raising of one's consciousness. It is an instruction manual waiting to be read. How you use it depends on how you accept it with your mind and how you activate it. We start by raising the consciousness. And these mudras, songs, breathing, and symbols affect consciousness so that they can naturally affect DNA.

In principle, there are twelve layers of DNA to mastery, and there are mudras to help you activate each layer:
- The first layer is the Tree of Life.
- The second layer is the Blueprint of Life.
- The third layer is the Present Consciousness Awakening.
- The fourth layer is Belief.
- The fifth layer is the Awakening Self.
- The sixth layer is the most sacred and divine layer: I Am That I Am.
- The seventh layer is Balance.
- The eighth layer is Truth.
- The ninth layer is Opening the Blind Eye and Seeing without Illusion.
- The tenth layer is Remembrance.
- The eleventh layer is Realization.
- The twelfth layer is God.

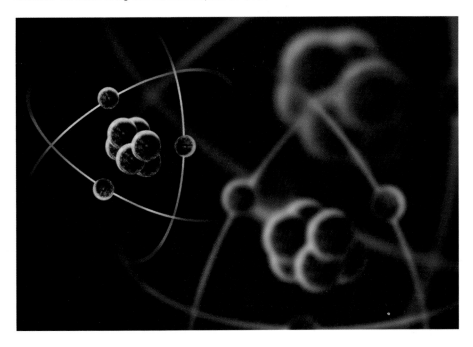

Using Mudras, Sounds, and Symbols

We have brought some mudras that, with practice, can help facilitate raising your consciousness. These mudras, along with sounds, breathing, and symbols, will surely lift one's consciousness over time. These can be the key to a new consciousness for the human being who practices them. Background music can support this work, such as the tone of *Om* or the music created by the great Atlantean musician Michael Hammer.

You may sit or stand when you do these mudras. Just breathe deeply. The only thing we ask is to close your eyes and be in a state of relaxed healing. The terminology we will use to describe our fingers is thumb, first finger (index finger), second finger (middle finger), third finger (ring finger), and fourth finger (pinky finger).

These mudras should be done as one set. They are mudras just for DNA. You cannot take one of these and do it on its own. They are done in a set of twelve mudras just for DNA.

You will see your energy much more intensely amplified if you use background music, especially the sound *Om*, Tibetan bowls, a crystal bowl, a metallic sound, a bell sound, or a gong sound. Experiment with this and come up with your own approach. People will need to adapt these tools to their own cultures.

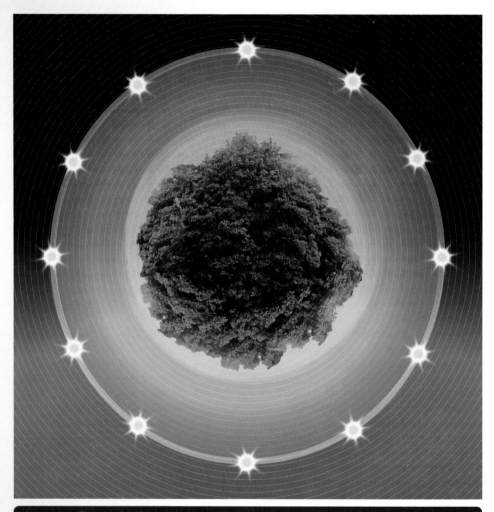

Layer 1: Tree of Life

The First Mudra: the Tree of Life

The chant for the Tree of Life mudra is *Om*. Practice this mudra for three to five minutes every day for fifteen days, and you will feel an opening in the heart area. Energy will start moving around your heart, circulating like a donut from the front of your heart and going around the back of your body and again flowing back to the heart. But there is not just one layer of energy. There will be multiple layers of energy in a donut shape with the colors of soft purple and soft gold.

You might experience a feeling of being uplifted. It is good to sit down when doing these because your energy could be very invigorated and must be built up slowly. This pose has more affinity with the female.

Figure 1: The thumb touches the tips of the second, third, and fourth fingers on both hands, and the tips of these fingers on both hands touch each other. The index fingers are not touching anything and are extended and pointing away from you. Hold both hands in front of your heart horizontally.

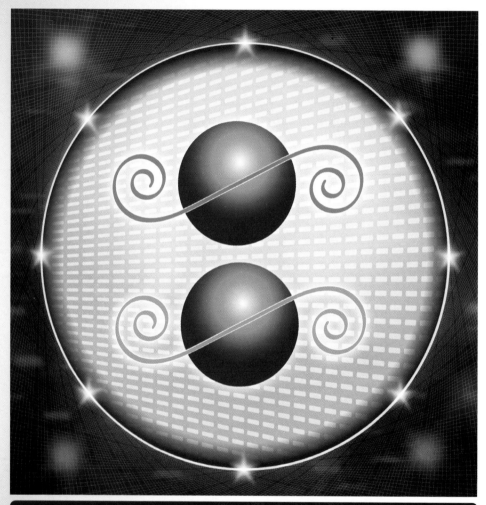

Layer 2: Blueprint of Life

The Second Mudra: the Blueprint of Life

The Blueprint of Life mudra generates the power to access the blueprint of your life. This is your truth that you have in your societies. You must pass this down to your own people in their own countries. I cannot emphasize often enough: You must adapt this work to the societies that use these techniques.

The chanted tone for this layer is "oooooooooo ooooooooooo," sliding upward two whole notes for the second "ooooooooooo." This generates the power to access the blueprint of your life. Many people feel that when they do this, energy of a pure white color flows from the brain down to the heart in a straight line; it creates a pathway for them to walk on in their lives. It helps them remember their blueprints, and it creates a good pathway for them to stay on for this lifetime.

 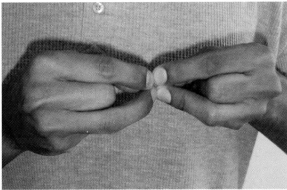

Figure 2: On both hands, the thumbs touch the first and third fingers (index and ring fingers). The second and fourth fingers (middle and pinky fingers) are closed, touching the palm. Hold both hands horizontally in front of the heart so that the tips of the index and ring fingers and the thumbs of both hands touch each other. Your fingers form the shape of a triangle.

Layer 3: Present Consciousness Awakening

The Third Mudra: the Present Consciousness Awakening

Layer three awakens your Present Consciousness: the desire to know more about yourself. Every soul will slowly start awakening to the desire to know more about itself at the chosen time. This desire comes from the activation of layer three. Usually, this is done unconsciously, but you can activate the third layer by asking and forming the intention.

For those of you who are not clear about your life journey and want to know why you are here and your higher purpose for being here, you can tap into this layer. Intent is a very powerful tool. When you ask for layer three to be activated, you will start to feel its consciousness streaming into you, along with the feelings and emotions associated with knowing more about yourself. This layer is a layer for self-discovery.

This mudra generates the energy of deep calmness, like an ocean — an all-encompassing, beautiful, serene, peaceful, calm ocean. You are the depth of the ocean yourself. The sound chanted for this layer is "aaaaaaaaaaaaaaa."

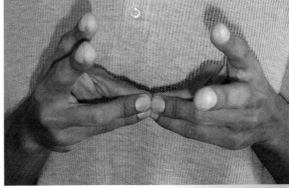

Figure 3: On both hands, the thumbs touch the third and fourth fingers (ring and pinky fingers). The index and the middle fingers are not touching and are extended. Bring both hands in front of your heart. You will see your hands form many small triangles.

Layer 4: Belief

The Fourth Mudra: the Belief Layer

Beliefs create a person's reality. Your thoughts, words, actions, and feelings all come from your belief system about yourself and about the world. Your beliefs were formed in this life and in past lives. Even your experiences are an inner reflection of your belief system.

Belief is the key to your life: What you believe, you create. If you believe that the world will treat you badly, then your life will reflect this. If you believe that life is all goodness, you will create goodness. Believe in the highest good for yourself.

There is much carryover from ancient times. You must break these old patterns. This is called ancient truth theory. Almost all humans can clear their consciousnesses of old beliefs and attitudes.

This mudra is really critical, so we have a special sound that can break down barriers, the sound that we know is a sound of God: "wwh-hoooooooooooomm." Raise the tone slightly at the end of sounding. You can also call on your personal angels at this time to help you.

When fully generated, your third chakra area will feel like a fire, burning many old patterns from the deep residual past. Do this tone for some time. Some people will see big balls of fire wrapped with a big chain tied to the solar plexus. You have been carrying this waste for a very long time.

 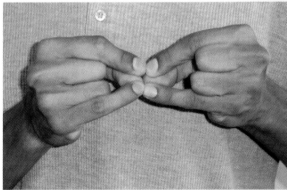

Figure 4: In the mudra for the Belief layer, the thumbs of both hands touch the index and pinky fingers. The second and third fingers are bent down to touch the palms. Both fingertips touch each other. Place both hands between the heart and the stomach area.

Layer 5: Awakening Self

The Fifth Mudra: the Awakening Self Layer

The fifth layer is the layer of the Awakened Self. It is also called the layer of understanding. Awakening is a process of understanding yourself. When you understand yourself fully, you are a master. Awakening this layer is a slow, gradual process, but it can be enhanced when you start incorporating more light into yourself.

One way is to integrate more of your soul into your body. In your mind's eye, see an ever-glowing, bright light emanating from your heart center, and with each breath, see it expanding ever more and finally encompassing your entire self. This simple step of connecting with your soul can enhance your light greatly. You can also call on angels, archangels, and your guides, teachers, and masters to integrate with their light. Ask for a synthesis with the light of the masters you work with.

This is another important mudra that helps you express the intention: "I am ready to awaken my own higher self." The tone for this fifth mudra is "hhhoooommmmmmmmm." It means, "I am awakening my divine self now."

Figure 5: On both hands, your thumbs touch the pinky fingers. The first, second, and third fingers touch each other. You will see a small hole between the thumbs and pinky fingers on each hand. Bring both hands in front of your heart.

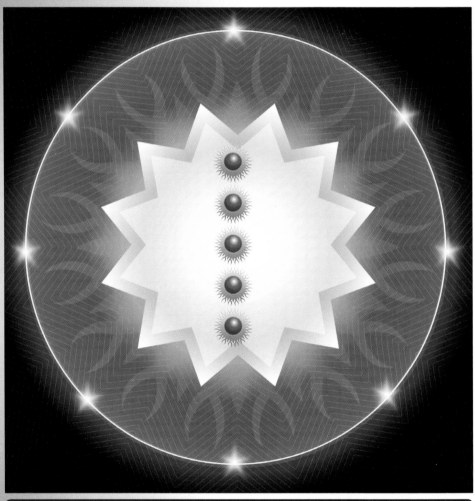

Layer 6: I Am That I Am

The Sixth Mudra: the I Am That I Am Layer

Layer six is called the I Am layer. When you work with the awakened self and understand yourself more fully, the next step is in connecting with the I Am layer, connecting with the divine soul. Your divine soul is who you truly are. Your I Am layer is connected to the I Am layer of everyone else and also to the Father/Mother God, Creator.

The more your desire to connect with your I Am presence, the faster the activation of this layer. Your desire will draw forth your soul more and more into your body. When you start expressing and experiencing your life through your soul, you will have the grand wisdom of the soul available to choose and express your life.

This is a sacred, divine layer; it incorporates Hebrew, which is a powerful, interdimensional language from other planets. Some Hebrew words are very powerful and manifest the Creator. Here is an example: *'Ehyeh 'ašer 'ehyeh* (eh he eh, a show eh he eh), "I Am That I Am."

The tone chanted for this layer is "hhhaaayyy hhhheee ooooooooooooooooooooooo." It means, "I call forth and activate the Divine God within me."

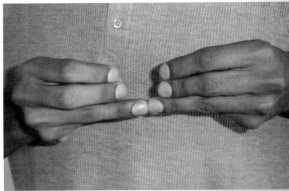

Figure 6: For both hands, your thumbs touch the first and second fingers. The fourth fingers are bent down and closed, touching the palms. The tips of the ring fingers of both hands are touching each other. Bring both hands in front of the heart area, holding them horizontally.

Layer 7: Balance

The Seventh Mudra: the Balance Layer

Balance is a consciousness in which you feel complete with yourself in your surroundings and situations. For balanced people, there is no emotional charge for situations and experiences within themselves or with others. There is a sense of complete acceptance, whatever is happening.

This tone and mudra collect pieces and parts of you from other realities and other times, bring them back, and integrate them within you. You are making yourself whole again. You are calling forth your other powerful parts to come and join you.

Balance also means the ability to become fully aware in all situations to take appropriate action. Appropriate action is the ability to create benevolent experience for all involved in that particular experience. When you are fully balanced, you will also be able to cultivate peace: in your mind, your body, your emotions, with humanity, with your culture, with Mother Earth, and with Father Sky.

The sound you make for this layer is "aaaahhhooohhhhmmmmm."

Figure 7: Close all fingers, and make two fists with no gaps between the fingers. The thumbs touch each other, right thumb on top of left thumb. Bring your right fist with all fingers closed, and place it on top of the left fist — not intertwined, just laying on top of the other fist. Stack both fists vertically in front of your heart. You will see a triangle forming, and the head of the triangle points toward your heart.

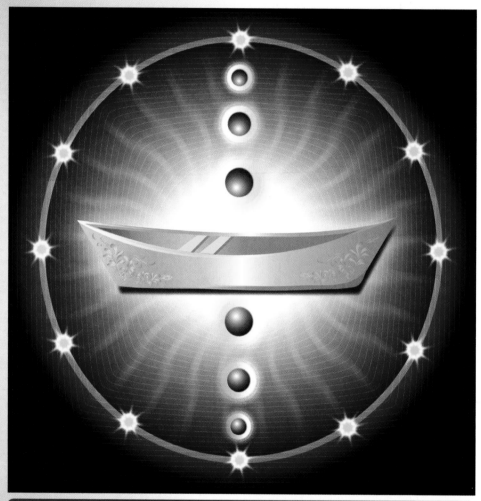

Layer 8: Truth

The Eighth Mudra: the Truth Layer

Most of humanity has great difficulty in being truthful. Unless you are completely truthful with yourself, it is difficult to be completely truthful with others. Humans are afraid to look into themselves and discover who they are. Working with the truth layer can help you discover yourself more fully and your own evolving truth. It can help you understand higher truth. Truth is always evolving and truth is large, so no one has the entire truth.

As you evolve, evolving truth appears in your life. But because of our belief systems, we often discard emerging truth and cling to old truths we have cultivated over time.

This is called the Truth layer because it expresses the truth of who we are. It is a triangle, the soul, the monad, and the I Am presence. (The monad is the soul group presence, 144 consciousnesses combined.) The mudra for this layer is given by the Creator.

The sound chanted for this mudra is from the ancient Egyptians. It is "mmmaaa hhheee oooooohhhhhhmmmmmmmmm," in a long, resonant monotone, varying the length of each phrasing.

 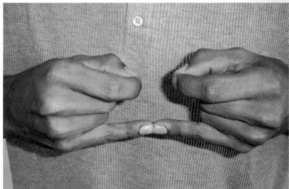

Figure 8: Both thumbs touch the first fingers. The second and third fingers bend down to touch the palms, and the tips of both pinky fingers touch each other — very simple. Bring your hands in front of the heart area, holding both hands horizontally.

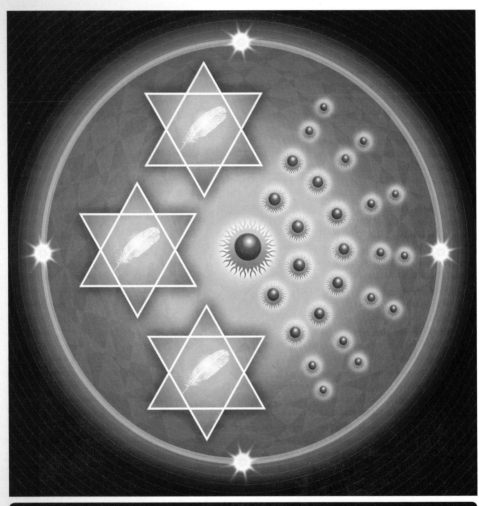

Layer 9: Opening the Grand Eye

The Ninth Mudra: Opening the Grand Eye Layer

The Grand Eye is also called the Eye of Horus, your beautiful soul eye. It allows you to see without illusion. Without the veil of illusion, you are able to perceive the reality of your life without fear and prejudice. We live so deeply within illusion that we forget that there is illusion at all.

When you are able to open up to the consciousness of this layer, you are able to see reality more clearly. All the masters who walked this planet lived their lives outside of illusion. Once you are awakened to this truth, you can live in this world joyously and with peace in your heart, for you will know that this world is a big stage where all are actors who have forgotten that they are living on a stage. You can clearly see your part as an actor in this great game and thus have the ability to choose how you want to play your part in this great game of illusion.

There are two soundings for this mudra. The first is "eeelll ssshhheeeedddd iiiiiiiiii," sung in a long monotone. It means "the name of God." These sounds will awaken this layer. Also, "hhheee mmmeee oooooohhhhhh," which means, "I am open and willing to see more with the divine eye." Many times when practicing this mudra, you will see light come in from the third eye going into each palm, making a triangle.

 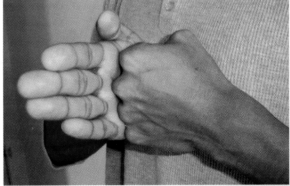

Figure 9: Close all the fingers of your left hand so that there are no gaps between them. Open the right palm so that there are no gaps between the fingers of the right hand. The knuckles of the left hand are placed in the palm of the right hand. Hold this in front of your heart area.

Layer 10: Remembrance

The Tenth Mudra: the Remembrance Layer

This layer is called the Remembrance layer, remembrance of who you are and remembrance of your life's purpose. It is a remembrance of your birth vision: You know that you know. Everything is clear. When you remember, you are also able to tap into your akash and bring forth the talents and abilities you now need to enhance your life.

You can ask your soul for its remembrances of specific emotions or talents and incorporate them into your present life experience. You can choose your emotional experience in any situation. You are no longer at the mercy of your present reality and the emotions and feelings associated with it but are in complete control of your life all the time.

The tone for this mudra is "sssooowww mmmyyy aaaaaaaa," sung in a long soulful monotone, again and again. This is an ancient tone from the Hathors. After you have practiced this tone for a while, you will see a bright light appearing in front of your forehead as if a sun appears in front of your head with light pouring down to you.

Figure 10: For the left hand, close all fingers except the thumb. The right thumb touches the left thumb. There is a gap between the fingers of the right hand; they open and spread apart. Hold both hands in front of your heart.

Layer 11: Realization

The Eleventh Mudra: the Realization Layer

This is called the Realization Layer. It also means connection with the Father-Mother Inner God-Goddess. It is through this layer that we realize that we are Creator Gods, with knowingness and complete realization of our trueness.

When this layer is activated, the entire history of our creation is known to us and we can remember and realize our essence as Adam Kadmon. This also helps us to move through many of the higher dimensions and connect with higher-dimensional masters who can further support us in our soul growth.

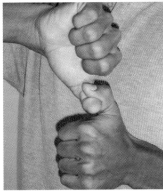

Figure 11: All the fingers except the thumb are closed in both hands. Place the right thumb under the left thumb. Hold the closed right hand over the left fist with your right thumb under your left thumb. The two fists are stacked vertically in front of your heart.

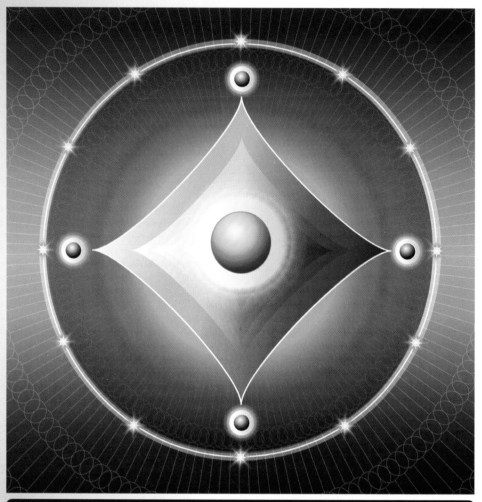

Layer 12: God

The Twelfth Mudra: the God Layer

When this layer is activated, you live your truth as a Creator God. You consciously participate in the creation of this universe. Meditate on this layer, asking that your own God Presence be fully manifested in your life as a living truth.

Hold both hands in front of the heart, not touching each other when doing this mudra. The tone for this layer is "hhhuuummm yyyooooooo."

Figure 12: For this mudra, your right thumb and the pinky finger touch each other. The right index finger is raised; the second and third fingers are closed. In your left hand, the second, third, and fourth fingers are closed. The left thumb touches the index finger, and the other fingers are closed.

Humanity is evolving to its true destiny – to be the explorers; to create; to be the expression of the Creator within you, with benevolence and magic; and to be a part of the intergalactic federation of all the planets. [King Akhenaton, chapter 2, May 16, 2013]

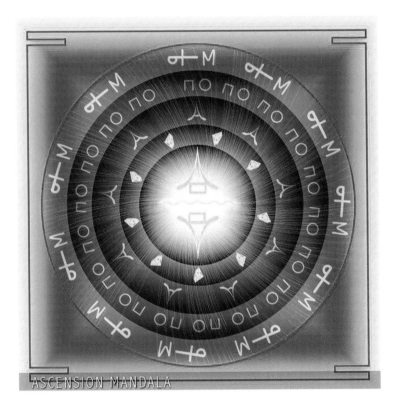

ASCENSION MANDALA

The idea of this book is that it supports people to realize that they have the capacity to reach this goal, to attain this peace, attain this freedom, and attain this joy. This is the simplest explanation of this book. It is to bring oneself into the state of consciousness where one is able to derive benefit from the techniques, and to work with them to reach a level where one is able to access higher wisdom. [Sanat Kumara, chapter 6, June 30, 2013]

Teach people it is time. We learn from people, but we must walk our own paths and discover God in our own ways, through empowerment. When we follow, on some level we are giving our power away. We receive guidance, but we do the work and find our own inner truth. The ideal book or channeling would bring every reader back to his or her own truth. Work with this and see if it supports you. [Saint Germain, chapter 9, July 25, 2013]

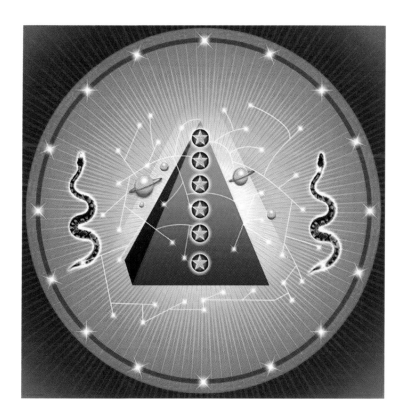

Children now being born on Earth have 30 to 40 percent of their DNA activated. Their children, the second generation, will have more than 50 to 70 percent activation, and their children, the third generation, will have 100 percent of their DNA fully activated. [King Akhenaton, chapter 2, May 16, 2013]

The new children born with the higher strands of DNA will create a new reality. They will choose wisely. They will use their hearts, the feminine part of themselves, and create only benevolent things with the higher power they carry inside. Many of you . . . are paving the way for new generations and their people. You are showing the way for great things. You are paving the way for new generations to walk on. [King Akhenaton, chapter 2, May 16, 2013]

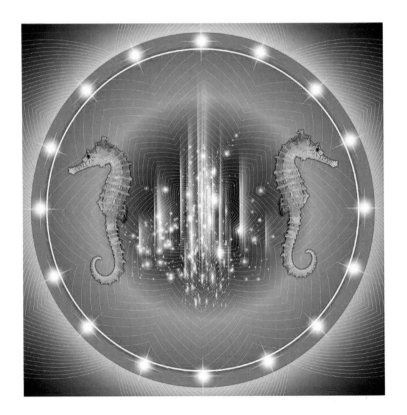

In 35 or 40 years, you will see a tremendous shift. What you and Rae are doing is paving the way for the second generation to come. You are making a road so that a new generation, our children's children, will come forth, and they will be fully awake and aligned. By the time the children being born after 2021 are 13 or 14 years old, they will have fully awakened DNA and they will know their true purpose. [Saint Germain, chapter 3, June 19, 2013]

The History of Human DNA

May 16, 2013

Masters of DNA, King Akhenaton, and Archangel Metatron

Hello, we are the collective Masters of DNA. Although human DNA was altered, from our perspective, everything was not lost. Everything was deeply hidden, and now it is time to open what was hidden inside.

We do not like to use the word "manipulation." We prefer to say "restructured" or "altered," for this was done for a purpose, and it was not altered by the Dark One to control human beings.

[Archangel Metatron: Since the planet was being prepared as an experiment, changes were made by the Council that looks after the planet so that humans would be born without a memory of who they truly are. This way, they could complete their work. This is part of what we mean by "people who changed human DNA." But DNA changing was done not to control but rather to take away memory so that

33

humans would be able to perform the tasks that they had come here to do. However, later on, nonhuman races from other planets came to plunder this planet of its mineral wealth. They knew much more about science than present human engineers, and they altered human DNA for the sake of controlling people. So there were two alterations. One was done by higher forces to take memory away. The second was done to control. But that was much later.]

From our perspective, in the course of history, certain sets of beings naturally go and new ones come on the planet. Human DNA was changed just slightly for a very important purpose: so that humans would be born onto the planet unawakened, and they would grovel in the dark, make sacrifices, and face great challenges. Thus, they would grow much faster. They could then take this awakening and understanding to other planets and other galaxies to shift the progress there.

There is not much growth in a perfect order, so the Creator devised a brilliant plan. He asked volunteers to come to the Earth plane without having access to their full conscious memories, and they would then work backward. There would be discomfort, and from this discomfort, they would grow. And they would take this growth to other planets and alleviate the discomfort there. One grows only through discomfort and challenges. This is our perspective.

There were beings who came and altered some of the genes and some of the DNA for their own good. But mainly it was done not for the purpose of controlling the entire planet but for commercial interests, for many beings from other planets came and mined Mother Earth's body for precious minerals and metals and took them away. Yes, in some ways, human beings were unaware this was happening, so they do not have their full memories.

From our perspective, everything was ordained by the Creator, and we do not believe that the Creator would allow other creator gods to manipulate DNA for the sake of control. What good would that be? This planet is isolated for a reason: It is an ongoing experiment. How will human beings wake up and claim their full consciousnesses and change so that they can take this understanding to other planets to create similar change? We understand many beings of light have brought other interpretations, but from our perspective, this is what we believe happened.

Now we will take questions from you. We have never spoken to a human being, and our communication is a little bit slow and slurred, so please forgive us. We will communicate what we are allowed to communicate at the present moment.

First, I would like to ask you to explain exactly who you are so that we can clarify that for the readers.

We are the collective essences of the Master DNA; we have been called the DNA Beings.

So you incorporate all the qualities of 12-strand DNA and all the expanded, awakened consciousness that this entails?

Exactly. This is why many human beings including Rae work continuously and consciously to integrate the twelve aspects of the one higher self, located in twelve planets. So we must bring those aspects and activate our higher chakras for activating the full 12-strand DNA.

Connecting Twelve Planets with Twelve Chakras

What are the twelve planets that you mention? Here in our solar system, we only count nine.

Can you give us a moment, dear brother? [Pause.] Sorry for the interruption. The planets are Venus, Alpha Centauri, Lyra, Arcturus, Styron, the Pleiades constellation, Maldek, Antares, Alcon, Cyrus, Andromeda, and Orion. If you were able to connect with all these planets, they contain one part of the essence. This essence could be called one mother strand of DNA self. So in your meditation time, you are connected with these elements, for they all carry a specific vibration energy and a specific quality inside of them.

So each of our twelve chakras resonates with one of these planets. Is that correct?

Exactly. Even in the materials that you sent to Rae, there is some mention of this, is there not brother?

Correct. This is amazing information. Would you be able to say which planets connect with each of our chakras, starting with the first chakra and working upward?

We would be able to give you some idea. The first chakra connects with Venus, in the order of the planets themselves, going all the way to Orion. The first chakra is Venus, and the second is Alpha Centauri. Lyra is the third, and Arcturus is the fourth. Styron is the fifth. The Pleiades constellation is the sixth, but this one plays a very significant part.

How so?

Because the Pleiades constellation contains the purest essence of the Creator, and this is completely tied into layer six of your DNA. It is the layer that is mentioned in the Bible, the I Am That I Am layer. And Maldek is the seventh layer.

Wasn't Maldek destroyed?

Energetically, it is still very much alive. Antares is the eighth chakra.

Which we call the transpersonal point.

Alcon is the ninth, Cyrus is the tenth, Andromeda is the eleventh, and Orion is the twelfth. But again, we ask you to meditate on this to see how much connection you feel, as this is from our perspective.

Changing Your Belief in Who You Are

What would you say to a person who is trying to learn, connect, and activate these twelve layers in terms of practice?

We would say that at first, you must think and believe that you are a quantum being. That's very important. If you as a human being do not believe that you are bigger than who you think you are, you will not be able to open to higher consciousness. So you must believe that you are much bigger and have a much bigger purpose in the universe. This understanding will shift humanity.

Second, during meditation, you must call forth the energy specifically associated with these planets. If you search, you will find information on these planets, their specific color vibrations, and how they can be worked with. But simply, I would say for the layperson, imagine you are sitting in a circle, and these twelve planets are around you. The twelve planets have certain color vibrations, and you can see their twelve color streams coming down into you.

It is good to call on the names of these planets, because I can call you something, or I can call you Robert, and when I call you Robert, you answer more from your specific energy signature. So when you call the name of a planet, this planet has a consciousness and will download its energies into you.

This is a very simple process. What we are trying to do is this: Many human beings, many books, and many other teachings convey the general feeling that DNA is profound, but it is not for everybody to work with. We want to simplify this by saying, "It is possible to work with DNA simply by connecting with the energies of these planets and bringing them forth, for when this happens, your higher chakras will be automatically activated."

So higher levels of consciousness will automatically follow from doing this work.

Exactly. There is also one other thing to remember: Each of the seven chakras has its own heart center. Every chakra has its own heart center and consciousness. When we talk about the first chakra, there are many layers to the first chakra of consciousness. You want to activate the quantum aspect of the first chakra.

Can you define "quantum"? Does that mean interdimensional?

Yes, exactly. For example, your heart chakra has twenty-four dimensions to it. You can even call it the heart chamber, but in the heart, there are many chambers. Each chamber takes it deeper and deeper.

It sounds as if I've just been scratching the surface!

No, no, we honor everybody who brings wisdom and information to support people. We are only presenting one thought or one point of reference; that is all. We honor all who have brought wisdom to the planet.

What else would you say to someone who is learning this for the first time in terms of the practical aspects of how much time they spend on each layer?

There is no specific time to spend on each layer. Also, they cannot say specifically, "I am going to work with layer six, or I am going to work with layer ten." All work together in harmony. All spiritual practices teach us simple things — love, joy, and balance. When you raise your consciousness (when you clear yourself and heal yourself, naturally, you will raise your consciousness), this consciousness will automatically activate these layers. You cannot call to say, "I want to activate this layer at this particular time."

I meant in terms of when people sit down and do a practice. Should a person go through all twelve and spend five minutes per layer?

We recommended that they first visualize that these twelve planets are around them, and they are beaming energy into them. They should try to find their energy signatures, the specific color vibrations associated with each of them, and their specific essences and qualities. Then work from there. In that way, they will receive much more and work for the collective consciousness of the twelve layers to be activated.

We've been given soundings, we've been given mudras, and we've been given symbols. How should we apply them?

Again, these are only supporting tools to bring you into balance. We emphasize love, peace, joy, balanced energies, clearing, healing, and releasing. These tools, mudras, symbols, or sounds are just basic guidelines to bring one into balance; that is all. From our perspective, we do not give too much importance to them because it is the raising of the consciousness that is most important, which in turn will trigger the DNA.

So the symbols and mudras are a means to an end?

Exactly. But let me tell you one thing about what the DNA generally is. DNA is basically information libraries, and you must command these libraries to open and release the information in order to access the information set. But DNA by itself cannot do much; all of these interact

...

With the person's consciousness.

Exactly. It is a box. You must command which way you want it to go, and the box will take you there. Therefore, you must activate and work with your DNA. When the information set is opened, then many things can come. What are the things that can come out? The story of you, the story of creation, and even the story of all ages. We call it information libraries.

A teacher once said we have the universe within us. I think this is a key to or at least part of the reason why each of us has the universe within.

Once you remember who you are, you know the completeness of who you are, the history of yourselves, the history of the planet, and the history of the universe itself.

Stating and Following Intentions

Now I want to ask you some questions about how you would advise people who want to undertake this work in terms of the practicality of their lives, what they should do and what they should avoid in terms of things like alcohol, drugs, sex, and certain foods. Are any of these deleterious to their efforts?

When you are trying to re-create yourself, every experience you create must be in harmony with its true purpose and intention. Whether it is any activity, it does not matter. What matters is the intention you are trying to create. There is no specific reality that you must not eat "this" or you must not indulge in "that" or you must not do "this." You might also wonder, "For each individual on his or her path, does this support the creation of what he or she is trying to achieve?"

Simply state your highest intention. The universe hears it, and your desire to know more of yourself will set the right tone for the activation of the DNA. Truly releasing and connecting with more light will raise the consciousness and start the process. So when you have the wisdom, you communicate with your cells, for DNA is in every cell of your body.

Does any of this work have to do with establishing a connection with the consciousness of Earth?

It's only natural that once you start activating this, you are connected to All That Is, including Mother Earth and the consciousness on a higher level of the Creator.

What else would you have me know or convey to others?

Believe that you are a grand being with many higher potentials and possibilities. The present you that is here in a physical body is only one small portion of who you are, and you have a grander purpose for being here. You are connected with the entire universe itself. This belief in yourself will instantly start the process. Most human beings even now do not believe they are much bigger. Eighty percent of humanity might believe in some form of life after death, but they still do not believe they are much bigger than their physical presence of Earth. Do you believe you are bigger than yourself?

I believe there are parts of me that are, but I'm not really in touch with them very effectively.

This is the understanding we wish to bring forth. Once you believe this, you can work toward finding out more about yourself. If you do not know about your higher self, there is no thought to connect with it. It is like anything in life: If there is a dream, you can work toward it. If you believe you have a higher potential and you can achieve it, then you can work to connect with the higher aspects of yourself.

December 21, 2012

Can you explain what happened on December 21, 2012, to initiate this process?

The time was right. The experiment in which people came in with a limited understanding of themselves and who they are is slowly finishing. More and more people are awakening to their true natures. More human beings will awaken. And everything was designed perfectly for this to happen. First, there was the magnetics, and now the crystalline consciousness. First, the magnetics were shifted and altered, and now there is this new opening of crystalline consciousness.

With the Harmonic Convergence of 1987 and onward, people chose to have a new reality. Many new teachings and understandings came forth. In the same way, when human beings choose a higher reality — and they believe in it — they will go for that, and they will create another new shift. This is how the universe works. The danger we see is that human beings have been too focused on December 21, 2012. Yes, it was a marker point, but we do not want people to rest there. There is more, much more. There are many more marker days than December 21, 2012. Otherwise, they would stay in that space, but if they know that there are other days, other energies, and other dates coming, they can work toward them and develop their connections to their higher selves.

Expanding Your Awareness of Yourselves

Do you have any advice for us about the presentation of this work? Should it just be basically the mudras, the soundings, and the symbols? How would you teach this to someone?

Teach people about these understandings — that they have much more to themselves, to their essence, encoded into their DNA, and this can be activated by raising their consciousnesses. From our perspective, that is the basic key, to say again and again, to let people know about the grandness inside of them. To give you an example, think of a great redwood tree (or any big tree) and how it was first a seed. Think of how the seed had the capacity to grow into a huge tree living hundreds of years. The seed also had a capacity not to grow and to die in a few years.

The same is true for humanity. If humans can shift their patterns of thinking, more and more people will awaken and activate their DNA and let people know about the much bigger, higher aspects of themselves that they can access. It is not magic. It has been done by other teachers. It has been done by many masters. The world has seen many masters. These masters believe that there is something higher, and they work toward it. These masters were just showing an example of what you can do. And because of the shift in the magnetics in the ground, it is much easier. The veil has been removed, and the experiment is now coming to a close.

What do you mean by coming to a close?

The experiment in which human beings came here with limited knowledge and understanding of their growth is finishing now because the new children being born are coming with higher vibration patterns and higher DNA activation already.

So some of the children being born on the planet now already have many more strands of DNA activated, is that what you're saying?

The children being born now have 30 to 40 percent of their DNA activated. Their children, the second generation, will have more than 50 to 70 percent activation, and their children, the third generation, will have 100 percent of their DNA fully activated.

Would you be able to speak for a little bit about what happened in ancient Egypt and how these practices were performed there?

Well, let's communicate with some of those masters.

✳   ✳   ✳

Raising Consciousness Responsibly

This is King Akhenaton, my precious brother. We, the masters of ancient Egypt, knew very well that DNA existed inside every human body and was later forgotten. All our practices were designed to activate the dormant DNA. All the rituals and the ceremonies and the initiations of the temples and the mystery schools were for this reason only: to activate the DNA and expose the higher chakras.

Thank you. That's beautiful. Presumably, that information got lost or was distorted by some of the priesthood.

Many times, it was kept hidden because, as you know, completely awakened DNA carries a much higher vibration, and in the process of manifestation, creation becomes instant. If you were not aware of the consequences of your creation, then there could have been situations in which humanity would have used this information to cause great havoc and destruction of the planet. The purpose of human life on the planet is only one thing, dear brother: to completely understand all the nuances and aspects of all of creation and its consequences, for you will take this understanding to other planets and stimulate growth.

Was this DNA activation understood in other cultures besides ancient Egypt?

Of course — India, Tibet — many cultures and all shamans knew about this. It was kept secret because they did not want this high-vibration energy to fall into the wrong hands. Let me ask you something: If tomorrow an average person is given one million dollars, do you think that person will use it wisely?

Very unlikely.

If you look at many young people who have received considerable financial support, more often than not, they destroy their lives or completely waste their energy. It requires a certain maturity to have the wisdom to have so much money in their lives. The same thing is true with DNA. When you work with all the layers of DNA, you are holding tremendous creative power in your hands. Just imagine what a random thought could create when all your strands of DNA are active.

It could create havoc, absolutely!

Exactly! So this was hidden and kept secret. That is why many of the initiates were tested again and again and again.

So why is it any different now? Why won't humanity create havoc with this expanded consciousness?

Because people understand that they have destroyed their beloved planet many times. At first, this was forgotten, but they have raised their vibrations collectively and now understand, and they do not want this to happen.

So is there danger that these faculties of consciousness could be misused by some people?

Of course, even now. That's why it took many years and many lifetimes to come to a stage in your higher consciousness in which you would never misuse this power, never. You would only use this power to create benevolence and love.

Just imagine that you have the capacity — once the 12-strand DNA is activated — to be in two places or three places at one time, to bilocate. Can you imagine what some people would do? They could be in somebody's bedroom or create many things — the ability to manifest the thoughts of other people, to control people. So of course it must be kept secret; it must be hidden, because human beings must truly understand the consequences of every action. You're playing with fire, dear brother.

But we're making it public now.

Because we believe that human beings have already reached a level of consciousness that they will not misuse it. This information will not be touched at all by people with lower consciousnesses.

They will not be drawn to it?

No, not at all.

What can you say about the future of humanity? What do you see in 100 years or 1,000 years with these changes that we're going to release? What's the plan for that?

We believe there is hope for humanity.

Where do you see us going?

To your true destiny — to be the explorers, to create, to be the expressions of the Creator within you with benevolence and magic, and to be a part of the intergalactic federation of all the planets. This is a very high possibility.

Still, a possible doubt exists whether humanity can shift again. You see, if you look at the news presently, you will see things differently. It seems to be going the opposite way. But we feel and we believe that the collective consciousness can again shift this reality. Humanity already shifted between 1987 and 2012. The next important times are 2020, 2032, and 2044. These will give us the determining factor of how humanity has truly moved into a new era.

We believe that the children born with the higher strands of DNA will create a new reality. They will choose wisely. They will use their hearts, the feminine part of themselves, and create only benevolent things with the higher power they carry inside. This is our true hope. What we believe is that many of you, Rae and everybody else, are paving the way for new generations and their people. You are showing the way for great things. You are paving the way for new generations to walk on.

That's beautiful. It is certainly my belief too that humanity is headed in a good direction. What we witness today in terms of the chaos on the planet are the death throes of the old order, which need to come down before something new is established.

But you know human beings have the capacity to shift this, to create benevolence. So we believe that they will make wise choices. Now Archangel Metatron will speak with you.

※　　※　　※

Using Sound to Raise Consciousness

This is Metatron. I personally raised some new tones last week with Rae. It was done by Babaji and also the goddess beings. The sound is "oh him," and the goddesses' sound is "ah him" so that when you sound "oh him" and "ah him," you are calling forth the balancing of the male/female energies within yourself, God/Goddess. [Archangel Metatron tones each sound three times.]

In all ancient schools — in India, Tibet, Israel, Egypt, Mongolia — sound was used principally as a frequency-raising vibrational tool. Sound resonates very much with the consciousness inside of the body. Cells resonate to sound, and cells contain the DNA, so DNA resonates with certain sound frequencies. So you must always use sound.

Behold the Creator in all, and you will naturally awaken to the highest strands of DNA consciousness. When you are able to see God in everything — the flower, the dog, the total, the human being — naturally you will awaken to God consciousness, which is the full activation of the DNA layers.

Some ways to use sound are the metal singing bowl as well as the sound of falling or gently flowing water. How do you feel when you hear this sound or when you are near a brook or some other gently flowing water? You feel good. Why do you relax? It is your cells; the sound affects the cells in your body. So you may want to include some water rituals to raise your consciousness, for water has the capacity to transform and truly activate higher strands of DNA.

I will do that.

Chapter 3

The Awakening of Crystalline Consciousness

June 19, 2013

Saint Germain

This is Saint Germain. When you wake up in the morning, the way to start the day is to bless the day and say, "Today I cocreate the greatest day of my life. I bless this moment. I bless this day." This simple practice can really enhance your life, empower you, and make everything easier.

It is a good idea to start the day with an intention. When you are in harmony, you are set to cocreate whatever will happen that day. You are in the flow of things, the universe will respond to you, and things will fall into place because you are requesting assistance. When you request assistance, assistance is always given. When you were traveling in Israel and setting intentions regularly, everything fell into place.

With an intention, you give intent to cocreate what you are supposed to do today in the most benevolent way

47

that you can, in the flow of things, where you are supported by the universe and the guides who support you.

Crystalline and Magnetic Consciousness

What is crystalline consciousness as opposed to magnetic consciousness in the context of humans starting to know their origins?

This planet was set up to raise vibrations so that human beings could come here without understanding the full idea of who they are. They would grow and learn in the dark. There were many factors involved for this to happen, and one was the magnetics laid in the ground. When there are strong magnetics, you have the tendency to stay rooted in one idea or one place and not move forward. This was done intentionally.

Recently, the magnetics of Earth changed. Those piloting vessels know this. They have had to adjust their maps; you will see new lines reflecting the changed magnetics. This is one of the reasons for animals beaching or going off course. They were following a particular magnetic path for their migration. The magnetics changed because human consciousness changed. It was uplifted.

Beneath the magnetic grid is the crystalline consciousness grid. It was put in place by archetypal dragons long ago. This awakening of crystalline consciousness could only happen once the magnetics were removed. This would only happen if human beings were raised in consciousness. This shifted the paradigm of ending the world by 1999 almost until 2012. Humans shifted the paradigm so that a new timeline was opened — the timeline of crystalline consciousness. Now we are in crystalline consciousness. This energy is inside every human being, and it is not only an awakening of crystalline consciousness but also known as the coming of the second Christ.

What does it truly mean when you become aware of your sacred divinity and accept that you are God inside? This acceptance — combined with the acceptance that you are in communion with the All — will change the cellular structure in the physical body to crystalline consciousness. The body must attain at least 33 percent of the cells having crystalline consciousness before it can ascend. People who attained more than 90 percent of their cells in crystalline consciousness when they ascended are the teachers and masters. Their photographs show auras around their throats because their cellular structure has fully developed crystalline consciousness.

In 300 years, the entire population of Earth will have changed its cells to crystalline structure. So the true meaning of crystalline consciousness is the awakening of the Christ consciousness, the awakening that you are in communion with the All, you are part of the All, and you are divine. You are God.

That is a wonderful answer, and it is very inspiring. Thank you very much. It's beautiful.

Shifting Duality

What is happening to duality on the planet in terms of the forces of negativity that have influenced humankind for so many eons?

Duality now is slowly being shifted. Slowly, people are awakening and saying, "There is much more to my life than mere existence, making money, or making a living." This is not happening to everyone. It is happening to a few people. The energy of the awakening ones is influencing the unawakened ones.

The unawakened ones are still sleeping. They want to sleep. But when some awakened person shines a bright light, this is really distracting for the unawakened people. Suppose somebody turns on a bright bulb in a room where someone is sleeping. Would the sleeping person like it? That person would probably get really angry.

This is what is happening at this time: More and more light is being shown in all the dark corners. You see this in America, how the American government has secretly been taping people's conversations. Somebody has shone a light, and the ugliness comes out: "We need to kill the guy who turned the light on." So this is one of the major things that is happening now. You will see more and more people awakening and shining their lights.

Duality is slowly coming to not a close, but people are coming to an understanding of the nature of duality and why duality was created. This is a huge shift.

What is the purpose of duality and the kind of action and drama we play on the world stage? The understanding that we designed duality to teach lessons is a huge shift, a quantum leap in the consciousness of the entire planet.

We are not ready for this understanding yet. This will happen in about forty years, or two generations. In thirty-five to forty years, you will see a tremendous shift. What you and Rae are doing is paving the way for the second generation to come. You are making a road so that a new generation, our children's children, will come forth, and they will be fully awakened and aligned. By the time the children being born after 2021 are thirteen or fourteen years old, they will have fully awakened DNA, and they will know their true purpose.

DNA of Ordinary People versus an Ascended Master

What is the difference between the DNA of an ascended master and an ordinary person?

I would say that there is not much difference. They contain the same essence. But the DNA of an ascended master has more than twelve layers. The masters have many other dimensions to their DNA. For example, a grand master has all 144 strands of activated DNA. An ordinary human, even at the ascension level, would have activated only the twelve layers, so even if you are able to activate all 144 layers of DNA for even just short periods of time, ordinary humans must work to maintain and stabilize this energy.

Perhaps you will be able to activate this consciousness sporadically for certain periods of time, but it must be maintained and checked at that level so that a master can grow. Masters are able to hold the vibration and keep it maintained so that it becomes part of them. People go through layers of the ascension reality. You do not ascend only once. Ascension is a process. You go through many ascension layers.

What happens is we go up many times. You [Robert] were in Israel a few weeks ago, and you raised your vibration through many activations and channelings or just by being in the energy of that country. But were you able to maintain the same vibration when you returned to New York? Maybe not. It is the same with ascension.

You have energy shooting down through your spinal column into your crown chakra, enlightening you at certain places, at certain times, or during your deep meditations, but you were not able to maintain this. Ascended masters are able to maintain. So that is the difference between a master and a person who is on the path. A master can maintain.

Look at the Dalai Lama. Do you think the Dalai Lama does not have challenges or problems? Of course he does, but he is able to maintain his composure. That is the difference between an ordinary human being and a master. A master is able to maintain. People say, "I have kundalini rising," and we say, "Very good, but are you able to maintain it and keep it and then grow from there?" I would say there are not very many differences, other than masters are able to maintain high vibrational energy, integrate it fully into their beings, and then take it to another level — for masters are also growing.

You mentioned 144 layers, which is twelve times twelve. In other words, the potential of humans is not just twelve strands but to increase that exponentially?

Exactly. When you look at the life of Anna [the grandmother of Jesus], she lived for hundreds of years, and she activated not just twelve layers but also the other higher layers. It is possible for human beings to do this at this time, for the time is here, and people must start believing they can do it. This is one of the main things. If the whole world believed that you do not have to die, then naturally you would see people dying less and less. People's beliefs are so important. Of course, people will still die, but they will die consciously, choosing when they want to go, and they will have longer lives.

So it's a matter of changing the belief layer in order to do that?

Exactly, *believing* that they can do it. Masters are very sure and do not waver in their faith that they have command. This is how Sai Baba and Jesus did miracles. Do you think that when they called forth, they doubted that they were going to manifest? They were 100 percent sure that they were going to manifest at that moment. The same thing is true when masters command their bodies; they know that when they command their bodies, they change the cellular structures of their bodies.

When you look at yourself now, the power of words has become stronger in your own life, and the time to manifest your given intention is getting shorter and shorter. But masters make one statement and believe in that truth completely, so their DNA accepts it completely. But DNA is only a toolkit, an information kit, and it is your consciousness, your command, that activates this toolkit. It is your belief, your will, your words, and your faith.

DNA of Animals and Humans

In the Kryon book on 12-strand DNA,[1] I read that non-human DNA does not have the Creator inside it and that, presumably, the essence of the Creator is in human DNA. I am interested in what you have to say about plant and animal DNA versus human DNA.

From our perspective, all living creatures have DNA, and they are all part of the Creator Itself. Everything and all DNA are interlinked together with human beings, and even animals have great wisdom and great consciousness development. Can it be said that the dolphin does not have great consciousness? Or trees? They all have consciousness; they all have DNA.

They are all interconnected with each other. Why do you think whales sing? They sing so all creatures, whether animals or plants (including humans) that have water content in their bodies, get their DNA activated by hearing their sounds.

Some animals have different layers of DNA. For example, Mother Earth has more than 12,000 layers of DNA. So there are varieties of DNA; thus, different varieties of DNA have different kinds of consciousness. Turtles have 7 DNA layers while humans have 12 layers to work with, but the turtle's 7 layers have a different type of consciousness; the lion may have 14 or 15 layers.

Connecting with Creation through Your DNA

Can we connect with animals through our DNA?

Of course, not just with animals but with all of creation. When you start working and activating DNA, you are in communion with All. You will see that there is no difference between you and animals, for the consciousness is the same but at a different level of vibration. This shows that you are becoming enlightened, that you are one with All, and there is no difference between you and a dog.

So how can animals help us raise our DNA?

Each animal carries a certain consciousness and vibration, and each animal is a support guide for every person. Native Americans knew this. When you connect with animals, ask for the transference of their consciousnesses into your DNA, into your energy field, and

---

1.   Lee Carroll, *Kryon Book 12: The Twelve Layers of DNA*, (Sedona, Arizona: Platinum Publishing House, 2010).

this will raise your vibration and your consciousness. Your DNA will be activated.

Perhaps you would like to connect with the lion, for lions have great courage and great responsibility. The lion is a wise leader. If you are missing those qualities or would like them to be enhanced, this will raise your vibration right away, and you will become more balanced and responsible human beings. Lions are balanced, responsible animals. They do not kill for fun; they kill when there is a need, and they respect other animals. That is the kind of quality you can gain by connecting with animals.

Suppose you connect with a cow. A cow is a total master. Someone who has difficulty with giving or is holding on to things would benefit by connecting with a cow. Cows are completely giving, and they can help someone open up completely. A cow says, "Come and take it. I don't care, for I know that I am an eternal being." A cow is a true master.

Take the bald eagle: Why do you think America and other cultures revere bald eagles? They have many specific qualities, not only nobility. They are the king of birds, and they are also very focused and intent. They know the exact timing of everything. In anything, there is always perfect, divine timing. Even the right timing within consciousness itself is divine timing. It will not happen before; it will not happen after. It happens at that moment in time. So everything is divine timing.

The eagle will help you to find the perfect time in your life to exit from any particular project, for the eagle is able to see 7 kilometers from the sky, but it doesn't fly straight to pick up its prey. It waits for the perfect opportunity, and in one swoop, it picks up the prey and is gone.

When you integrate this energy into the part of your life that needs enhancement, by using intention, your consciousness and your vibration go up automatically. Everything helps to enhance your vibration. Animals help to enhance your vibration and cause your DNA to activate.

Explaining 12-Strand DNA to a Geneticist

How would you explain the 12-strand DNA system to a geneticist who works with DNA on a scientific, rational, physical basis and only knows it as a double helix?

This has been the crux of the problem for the past 400 or 500 years in which people of spirit have tried to convince the scientific [or religious] community, and many experienced condemnation. What happened to

Copernicus or Galileo? Nothing much has changed. Now, if you say something like this, it is likely that either you will be called nuts or someone will put you in a lunatic ward.

It is very hard for scientists to comprehend the energetic and consciousness aspects of DNA. But scientists have started discovering that there is a difference in children: They think differently. This is slowly starting to be noticed by educators who see the difference in newer children. The New Children are very different from the previous generations. Educators will start to figure this out. Some teachers think this is attention deficit disorder (ADD) and recommend medicine. But the wise teachers know there is something different about the New Children being born, even though they cannot put a finger on it.

It will be the same with the scientists who start to realize that the New Children have something much higher when they are born, and they will start examining this. They will discover that one must go back to the time when these children were born and how they are being born into this new reality. These children understand reality much differently from the three-dimensional world. They will discover this first in England.

Scientists need to be able to see it in their laboratories in order to believe it. But you're saying they'll just get it because of the New Children coming in?

Not only that, but when the right time comes, the inspiration will be picked up by the people who are ready to receive it. When people are not ready for a quantum jump, that information is not given to humanity. But when you raise your vibration, more spiritual gifts are given.

For example, the great scientist Tesla brought in much information about free energy, and he showed people how they could get free energy permanently through the magnetics in the ground. But he was not able to capitalize on it. Why? He was stopped by the spiritual hierarchy, because these inventions would have been used as weapons by the military. Humanity was not ready to use this for good purposes, so it was withheld.

Presumably, are we getting ready to be able to have free energy now?

Within four to five years. You will see more and more new information coming about this. When consciousness gets higher, you will see more and more techniques and technology being downloaded because more human beings are consciously ready to accept it.

Here is a small, practical application. In the past, bridge builders needed many pillars for support. In India, Spain, and Europe, pillars are not needed any longer. Bridges are supported with tension wires. Why has this happened in the past ten or twenty years? Why didn't this happen in 1940 or 1950?

Because we weren't ready for it?

Exactly. It is the same thing. So when human beings are ready, more and more technology can be downloaded. But we must be sure the technology does not fall into the hands of those who would build weapons of mass destruction.

Will science ever be able to detect and measure the energetic or consciousness aspects of DNA?

Not for about forty or fifty years, but science will eventually start to accept that there is much more to human beings than what they are seeing in the physical body. They will not call it interdimensional, but they will say there is much more to a human being than what can be detected in the physical body. That itself will be a quantum jump. They may not call it interdimensional, but they will say there is something much bigger to human beings than just their physical bodies.

Effects of Cosmic Energy and Staying Connected with It

Can you discuss the effects of cosmic energy on human DNA during the past ten or twenty years and further into the future as well?

Cosmic energy contains higher vibrations. When you integrate higher vibrations through inner matrixes with the help of the masters and guides, naturally your consciousness is raised.

So is Earth being bombarded with energy that is lifting those who are able to receive it and integrate it?

Those who are able to understand that this is happening and are willing to work with it and accept it. It is not everybody who has been receiving this energy. But how many people know that this is happening, and how many people are willing to work with it?

Last year, we had the transit of Venus. It was a very significant event because we had Venus transits eight years apart. This usually happens every 130 years. This is a very significant event. If you look at the whole population, how many knew of the Venus transit?

Cosmic consciousness is always available and is now being downloaded, but how many people are willing to work with it, even if they knew of it? Cosmic energy is available, but one must work with it constantly and continuously. This is what Master Jesus did. He prayed every day and was in direct communication with the Creator and in constant communication with his higher self. Although he was very busy with physical responsibilities, he was continuously in touch inwardly as well. That is a master, dear one, and you must do the same thing — constantly stay connected and work with the energy you receive. Consciously *choose* to stay connected. Can you do that?

I'm going to try.

DNA as an Infinity Loop and the Flower of Life

Our common conception of DNA is the double helix, which is like a ladder. But some research has shown that it is not a ladder but rather a loop, and induction or energy generation happens among these intertwined loops. Is there validity to that?

That is the truth. Actually, the DNA is changing, and all DNA is becoming loops now, like the infinity sign.

So it used to be like a ladder with two ends, but now it's connected and changing into loops?

It was never completely like a ladder, but it was intertwined. We understand what you are asking, but now it is truly changing into loops. Eventually, it will change into a Flower of Life with the loops going around it.

That will happen as additional strands become activated?

Yes. When you raise your consciousness higher, you command your DNA to be activated. DNA is information, and you need to command it. It is time for people to accept that they are twelve-strand beings. If people do not believe they are quantum beings, then nothing will stick, no matter what teachings we are giving them.

They will still see themselves as strictly physical beings. But once people believe they are much bigger, there will be a huge shift. Right now, in your daily life, do you believe you are a quantum being or just

Robert? On a conscious level, when you are driving to work, are you coming from quantum consciousness, or are you only regular Robert?

I would say I am coming all from me, from Robert.

Exactly. In everything you do, try to see yourself coming from all aspects of yourself — a quantum, or multidimensional, being. Slowly integrate this perspective until it becomes natural for you. Next time we talk, try to let the questions come from your twelfth-dimensional self and not your Robert personality. I guarantee the questions will be much different.

Meditation Techniques

Could you give us some meditation techniques we can practice?

One simple thing you can do is visualize that you are inside a pyramid, and there is an upside-down pyramid on top of the pyramid you are sitting in. Your 12-strand DNA — or your mighty I Am presence — is on the top of the upside-down pyramid. Breathe that presence into your being, and integrate it into yourself slowly, slowly. We suggest that you try this, for it can raise your vibration.

Another technique is to imagine there is a circle of light in your heart, and 12-strand DNA is coursing through your throat and your body like an infinity sign. Imagine you are the Flower of Life with twelve infinity loops crisscrossing.

The center of the crisscrossing is in your heart?

No, there is no heart in this one. It is your entire being; you are the Flower of Life. You are at the center of a circle, and the twelve infinity loops are going around you. You are not in a humanoid body. You are an energy body, and these twelve loops are going around you through your energy body. You will begin to integrate this energy and meld it, and eventually, you will become the Flower of Life.

So the idea is to meditate on being in the center of these twelve infinity loops?

Exactly, and if you want to add more spice, imagine these strands in twelve soft colors — the seven chakra colors [red, orange, yellow, spring green, robin's-egg blue, indigo, and violet], plus gold (8), platinum (9), turquoise (10), soft pink (11), and magenta (12).

There is no one right technique for everyone. You must believe that you are a quantum being — that you can raise your vibration — to activate your 12-strand DNA. Even if you do not work with DNA, you must have the idea that there is something you can do.

Very few people talk about DNA in the New Age community. Our task is to bring the idea of DNA to a much larger audience, because if you don't think that something can happen, it probably won't.

Effects of Catastrophic Death on DNA

It seems to me that the United States has accumulated a lot of karma.

Many countries have accumulated karma. Countries can also change karma and heal it by doing good deeds. When you do good deeds, you heal a lot of karma. Before 9/11, the United States had a much bigger heart. The government let millions of people immigrate. When a country opens its borders and brings in people from all parts of the world, its heart center is fully open. Americans had big hearts, and they generously gave people access to their country. Whenever there was a natural disaster anywhere in the world, Americans were always there first, emptying their pockets in support. But now they don't do that. When they closed their borders, they closed their hearts.

Why do you think Americans are so rough and aggressive? Canadians are much softer. Canadians are more connected with nature; their land is purer and so are the people. And so many Americans have guns.

So there is much work to be done.

But there will be new teachers and new masters coming who will be able to work with healing and restoring these past lives, especially restoring the spiritual teachings that were lost through torture and trauma. That will be one of the greatest gifts we can give to humans. This is a very big subject and needs to be worked on at a different level, but it is possible to do this now.

We are always at your service. This is Saint Germain, your friend.

Chapter 4

Working with Energy to Raise DNA Levels

June 24, 2013

Archangel Metatron, Saint Germain, the Masters of DNA, and Yeshua's Grandmother, Anna

Good morning, this is Archangel Metatron with Master Saint Germain. Greetings and love to you! In your own ways, you are moving rapidly in this new timeline. One of the many gifts you will have will be bypassing many timelines and going into dimensional travel and dimensional experience. This is a gift from your own souls, for you are ready. You will be able to travel to other dimensional realities. You may want to call it some form of travel, astral travel or something else, but we would call it "beyond."

Creating Energy Reservoirs

One of the things we ask you to consider is the possibility of depositing good energies in a part of your house when you are feeling good. When you do not feel good, you can go to where you deposited your good energy, and you will immediately feel uplifted. This is called making an energy reservoir.

[Archangel Metatron: You feel very good some days. You are in the flow of things. Everything is perfect. You feel good. You have a lot of energy. Go to a corner in a room you choose in your home, sit down, meditate, and anchor this excess energy in this corner. You could also use an object: a crystal or a stone.

Humans are not in the same flow every day, the same energy and enthusiasm. On low-energy days, you can go to this spot and breathe in the energy you left before. It is like going to the bank and picking up money you had deposited. Just breathe it in.

Alternately, you can program that energy into a crystal. Hold the crystal in different parts of your body, especially the chakra column. Breathe it in, and you will fill up with the energy you need that day. This is a very good exercise to do every day. We also suggest sending some excess energy to Mother Earth.]

Suppose you are having a very good day. Energy is flowing through you. You have excessive energy and feel very connected. Deposit this excess energy in a particular area of your house. Later, you may not feel very good. You may not be in the best mood. You may not have clarity of mind. Go to where you deposited your good energy, and in less than an hour, you will pick up your good energy and start to feel better.

So start creating a reservoir of energy in your house. Similarly, you can deposit your good energy in a planetary reservoir and draw from that when you need it. You are creating a battery where you can deposit energy, and then you can pick it up when you need it. This is a gift. We would like you to start examining this and work with it. This is a new tool that is being offered to humanity at this time.

It's like having extra money at the end of the month, and you put it in a bank for a rainy day. If you have extra energy, put it in a reservoir in your house, and when you are feeling down, you can withdraw this extra energy. We would like you to start doing this, for it can support you in many ways. We cannot be in the flow of life every day until we reach a level at which we are consciously choosing to be in the flow of life. So save this energy for a rainy day.

The planet also has extra energy stored. The Pleiadians have extra energy stored. Every civilization has stored extra energy, and we can go back to the energy storage in a different dimensional reality and collect this extra energy. The Essene communities stored energy. Although they are not on the planet at this time, their stored energy is still available in a time lock you can access. You can store this energy in your house, but we ask you to also store about 5 percent in what we call collective banking so that the energy is available to others.

[Archangel Metatron: When a group of people meet and there is harmony among them, they can create a pillar of light, a triangle of light, or even cities of light through their intention. They can collectively put this energy somewhere as a collective bank of energy. And when someone goes to that place, they will feel the good energy.]

Can it also be stored in a crystal?

You do not need to do that. Crystals are just tools, a means to an end. We are now in a higher dimension, and these energies can be stored just through your intention.

✳   ✳   ✳

Interdimensional Aspects of DNA

My dear family, we are the beings connected with the essence of DNA. We have spoken before. DNA is much more than you can comprehend. The interpretations given by the teachers and the masters throughout the centuries do not fully explain what DNA is. It is beyond human understanding at this time. DNA is your full store of energy for this dimensional reality and for other dimensions as well.

Even if the activation of DNA is complete on the third dimension, there are many other dimensional realities of DNA. Depending on your intention to move past the 12 strands, this can take you into the higher-dimensional realities of DNA. So from our point of view, DNA is not just 12 strands, not 144, but much, much more. How about 144,000 strands of DNA? It is so, dear ones.

You do not have to think about this or try to figure out what it means. We would like you to stretch your imaginations and say, "There is much more to me than I can figure out." Only when you stretch your mind can you grow.

Ways to Raise Your Vibration

There are some specific crystals that can be used to support raising your vibration to activate your extra levels of DNA. You will have to find these out on your own, but one of the crystals you will be able to work with is moldavite. That can help to raise your consciousness and your DNA. There are also other crystals that can support you as well. Experiment to see which work for you.

We would also like to bring your attention to the support system you were born with. Everyone is born with a support system. One aspect is a dragon. Everyone is assigned a dragon, a special being of light to support you in raising your DNA. There are specific dragons — one is a Rose Dragon and another is an Indigo Dragon.

You also have the support of a star, for each of you is assigned an individual star when you are born. Find out which star was assigned to you, and draw forth its vibration.

Each of you is also assigned a gigantic, beautiful tree. Find out which tree you are aligned with and draw forth its essence to activate your DNA. Also, look for a color, an animal, and a sound. Look into these, for each of these is available to activate your DNA. Call for your support system, and you will see how you will have different ideas, different thought processes. From these thought processes, your DNA energy consciousness will naturally start moving.

There are also specific days that can support the activation of higher consciousness, and one of these is the day you were born. Your birthday is a very special day, for you have an opportunity to connect with your entire source energy that you brought forth on that day. Like a tiny seed that contains the essence of the highest potential for growth of a tree, when you were born, you also contained your highest potential. Your highest potential will activate your twelve strands of DNA and help you become enlightened beings. So go into your meditative state and tap into these aspects.

We have mentioned that when you were born, you brought your full essence as a spirit child. You are spirit now, but you came with your full consciousness and full awareness, and you can tap into this awareness even now through your meditative state.

Full Soul Integration: Connecting with Your Past and Your Future
We ask you to start traveling to the past and to the future — to the past when you were born, when you were 100 percent spirit and completely aware of the spirit inside you. You still have spirit inside you, but you are usually not aware of it and do not know how to access your spirit

self. But when you were a child, especially when you were born, you were aware of this spirit essence. A child is very aware and knows that spirit can create magic if it wants. So go to the past in your meditation state and also into the future.

[Archangel Metatron: When you are in your heart space, ask, "What am I ready to release now?" It may be a thought, a belief, sadness, or a hurt. Then ask, "What happened to create this distortion in my DNA?" Ask to be shown when this misalignment happened. You can go back in time to find a lifetime when you had the positive quality you are now seeking. Your soul knows exactly what talents you are seeking.

You can also go forward in time. Almost every human on Earth will be an ascended master in 300 to 500 years. Since there is no time, it has already happened. In one reality, you are an ascended master. Breathe from your heart while visualizing this reality. Perhaps you want something to happen; you want to write a book. Imagine that it is already written. Every day, it will get clearer.

Send a beam of light from your heart into that reality and — like a hook hooking into that reality — breathe it back into yourself. You are drawing forth a future reality into yourself through breathing. If you do this, within three or four months, you will see that reality that, without that support, could not have happened for another five years. This is called building a bridge. It is also called mining the akash — going back, but also going into a future timeline. Do this exercise, dear ones. It is very beneficial.]

In the future, you are an ascended master. You are already enlightened, and you have already activated your full strands of DNA. On the Earth plane, you can activate more than 5,000 layers of DNA. Stretch your minds. Intend that you want to access this.

This was demonstrated by Moses. Moses did not know that he had the capacity to transform. But his soul urged him, so he left everything and wandered through the desert. He started seeking, and he realized his true potential and was able to claim it.

In the same way, dear brothers, you can go far into the future when you will be in complete alignment with the Creator. All your strands of DNA are then activated; breathe into that, and bring them forth. Draw forth the future reality into yourself using a breathing technique.

We also ask you to go to past timelines when you were enlightened, walking as masters and great teachers. So go back to those times when you had the highest wisdom and the highest consciousness. We cannot tell you how to do it. We can only tell you to access it through your meditation and contemplation state. Send energy from your heart to that part of you.

Let me give you an example. Imagine that you have 144,000 parts of energy all over this galaxy, this star system, other dimensional realities, this universe, and some other universes. So in meditation time, call for these 144,000 energies to come back into you.

You can call this "full soul integration." For what is DNA activation? It is only the integration of your full consciousness or energy back to you with the remembrance and the ability to hold it. Bring forth the 144,000 parts of your energy every day, work with them, and I tell you, dear ones, you will raise many, many levels of DNA strands. It may take some time, but as Metatron always said, spiritual work is only for the person who is ready to take action and never rests, who has the intention to connect with the highest source and never gives up. He or she may take a break but never gives up.

We are the essence, or the DNA Beings. Now we will take questions.

Working with Your Auric Field

Is there a correlation between the frequency of our auras and DNA?

Of course. As you must remember, your aura is not just your energy field of this lifetime. It contains your akashic record — every experience and every thought you have ever had is recorded in your akashic record. The akash is part of the auric field. So when you activate and cleanse your aura every day, you are slowly activating your DNA.

If you work on your aura on a daily basis, 50 percent of your work is finished. Your aura is another piece of your evolution. It contains the entire history of who you are. When you activate your DNA strands, you will know exactly who you are and integrate that into your auric field.

Pulsing

I teach a simple vibration in the sound of the letter M — *as in Metatron, as in Moses, as in Michael* — M *as in the final M of shalom or Om. That* M *sound increases the frequency of your own aura.*

What you are trying to say is that it is not just the sound but also the extra pulsing. The aura should be pulsed with the light and sound.

This will raise your consciousness higher to activate your DNA. Most human beings are not able to pulse more than 200 or 300 pulses per minute. Work on increasing the pulsing rate every day; bring the rate up to 800 to 1,000 pulses per minute. For ascension, pulsing must be up to 3,000 to 5,000 pulses per minute. You are working to transform a steam engine into a diesel engine. That is part of what is next.

You must work every day with pulsing energy. DNA activation is a rapid science. Every day, you must give intention to pulse your auric energy faster, pulsing with light, and pulse it to the highest maximum you are able to hold at this time. Every day, increase it. For example, say today you pulse at 150 pulses per minute. Set your intention to pulse at 200 pulses per minute, and work on that all week. Next week, practice 250, then 270, then 300, and you will get your auric energy up very high. You will raise your vibration very high, and this in turn will activate your DNA even more. Working with your auric field is one of the main keys to activating the DNA.

How do we work on pulsing our energy at 200 or 250 cycles per minute?
Imagine that your aura is filled with pulsing light, like a strobe light. If you go to a disco, a strobe light is pulsing when you are out on the dance floor. Imagine that your body and your auric field are pulsing with light. Let it pulse faster and faster. You might feel discomfort, a headache, or spaced out, but you should continue. Do it as fast as you can, and increase the pulse rate. Give intention; consciously work on increasing the pulse rate. When you command your body, it will start the work of pulsing. Once you give the command, the process begins naturally.

This can increase your consciousness rapidly. Activation of DNA is not just flipping a switch. It is raising your vibration, which automatically activates your DNA. This truly means giving more of your soul energy into your physical reality. That is done through pulsing.

DNA essence clarifies not just one sound but many sounds, intentions, vibrations, and the support system from guides and angels. The cumulative effect is what raises the DNA. Try connecting with your guides — who have higher vibrational energy. When you connect with them on a daily basis, you are raising your consciousness and raising your vibration.

For true ascension to happen, there must be alchemical transformation. It is like leaving a layer of your physical body. Let me give you an example. Before a rocket is launched, there is a lot of energy in the rocket, and after the blast, it goes into the atmosphere and then releases a part of the rocket. This is what must happen with you. You must gather all the energy and then release a part of you so that you can move forward, stripped down, to a higher vibrational existence. It is an alchemical transformation — such as turning lead into gold.

Archangel Uriel taught about raising the golden and black serpents inside of you. The golden serpent represents the part of you that is enlightened. The black serpent is the part of you that is still in darkness. When these two come together, an alchemical transformation happens, and a new reality is created.

More Connections with Your Support System

We are trying to give you suggestions for how you can raise your vibration every day: using the pulsing method, connecting with star energy, connecting with dragon energy, connecting with tree energy, and using your entire support system. Your support system is not just your guides. Each of you has a support system from the day you are born with a star, a dragon, a plant, a tree, a color, an animal, and a smell.

Connect with the fairies; connect with the elemental beings, because they are the ones who make magic happen for you. To connect with magic on a daily basis, you must connect with elemental beings, because they are the ones who transform magic. And they are in support of you. Call on these beings. Call on the rainbow dragon; call on the rose dragon, for these are your support systems.

They will assist you if you request. A request must be made to them. They are like angels. They are here to support you, but you must knock on the door. They will not open it on their own. After December 21, 2012, every human being was assigned three to five personal angels, and their only work is to support you to raise your vibration to move easily into fifth-dimensional reality. But how many people work with angels at this time? Very few. They think of angels with wings to support them making money, but they are here to raise your vibration so that you can access higher levels of DNA and move into higher levels of reality.

When you work with layers of DNA, never work with one layer at a time. Work on all layers at once. DNA is a quantum soup. And you cannot say which layers should be activated. This is done by your soul when you raise your vibration. Some people say, "I want to work with layer six, the I Am That I Am." But it does not work like that.

It's like quantum spontaneous combustion!

Exactly! Let's talk again about a rocket. Everything must work together to make the combustion for the rocket to contain such strong force. Many people make the mistake of working on just one layer, especially layer number six, so that they can be like God. One layer supports the other, and all layers support the totality.

Maintaining a High Vibration

In our last session, Saint Germain spoke about how it is all in the maintaining. Please share more about techniques to maintain. Masters maintain. We can achieve momentary or short periods of higher vibration at one time, but masters maintain.

This is a multilayered question. Human beings came to this planet to work out their lessons. If they were able to maintain higher levels for long periods of time, they would not still be here. They would have moved on. We allow souls to make mistakes because it is through mistakes that they learn. They slowly realize that their mistakes do not support their energy fields and do not raise their vibration, so they naturally move on. If there were no lessons to be learned, no humans would be left on the planet. Masters have completed all their lessons.

How can you raise your vibration, keep it high, and work to raise it further again? Any time we do not see beauty of life or divinity in others, our vibrations lower. When we hear any fear-based information, we are affected collectively.

Let me give you an example. Many people say, "I wish I could live on air alone, on prana. I don't want to eat! But I cannot do it!" Yogis are able to do it, and great spiritual masters do it. What is the secret of not eating food and still surviving and maintaining a good energy field? The answer is maintaining DNA — maintaining high-vibrational thoughts. When you do not have thoughts of lack in your life, you do not need to eat. You may eat for the joy of eating, but you will not need to.

Similarly, you can maintain your DNA by staying in a joyous state, no matter what is happening in your life externally. The Dalai Lama, the late Mother Theresa, and the great teachers of the world are able to maintain their high vibrations for long periods of time because they are able to see only the highest divine.

As Archangel Metatron asks, "How do you feel when you hear a bird singing?" It brings joy to your heart; it brings love to you. See a flower blooming. It brings a feeling of beauty and love, and it maintains your highest vibrations. The moment something negative comes into your mind, your vibration drops immediately. You must train your mind to consciously choose and engage only thoughts with the highest vibrational energy to bring you the energies of beauty and joy.

Living in Full Essence

Along with the described suggestions, also maintain proper breathing. Most humans do not breathe properly. I ask you right now to place your right forearm underneath your nose and breathe. Do you breathe through both nostrils? If you can breathe properly, you will maintain the beauty of life with appreciation and love.

What is proper breathing? You breathe through both nostrils and release it through both nostrils. Eighty percent of the population breathes only through one nostril and releases their breath through a different nostril. But proper breathing is breathing in through both nostrils and releasing through both nostrils. The only people who do this are young children less than three years old, because they are able to maintain high vibration and remember who they are!

Is it that simple? Is there a certain technique, like the pulses, a certain number of breaths?

In the yogic tradition, there are many different ways of breathing, but if you start breathing like this tomorrow, say, for ten minutes a day, you will see differences in your life. Your mind will become very clear. There will be clarity, and your vitality will increase. Go inside and consciously direct your breath to different areas of your body — your pineal gland, your pituitary gland, your crown chakra, or your thymus area.

Everything is possible, but first you must have a basic foundation of how to breathe deeply and properly. You can breathe through one nostril and count to ten, then release through the other nostril, but first master this simple technique. From there, you can direct the breath through many parts of your body.

These two simple techniques will raise your vibration because you will be in a state of bliss; bliss means joy at every moment. The idea is to breathe correctly to maximize your essence.

What is the potential for humanity? The full potential is for people to live in the full essence of their beings, the full strands of their DNA activated, and the Flower of Life activated inside. Remember one thing: Your kidneys contain the Flower of Life, your heart contains the Flower of Life, and your hands contain the Flower of Life.

Your chakras are also called the seal. What is the seal of ascension? People ask how they can break open the seal of ascension. They are their chakras. There are many ways to describe chakras. One way to describe chakras is as energetic seals.

Inside each chakra are the petals of a lotus; underneath, there are different colors of the Flower of Life. Imagine that your body is filled with millions of Flowers of Life. Your palms are spinning with the Flower of Life. So is your forehead, throat, thymus, solar plexus, second chakra, first chakra, shoulders, the soles of your feet, the back of your body, and underneath your kneecaps — everywhere.

Using Sex to Raise Your Vibration

What is the role of sex in either raising or lowering a person's vibration?

What is sex? It is the best gift the Creator has given, the best fun you can have with your body, and it is free! So have more sex! With people in union, if it is holy and sexually divine, there is an explosion of energy. And most of the energy can be controlled and directed. It is called working with orgone energy. What did the great teacher Wilhelm Reich[1] teach? This poor man was from a different planet — people thought he was mad. He taught about orgone energy, he was jailed in America, and he died in jail. He was far ahead of other people. He spoke of an explosion of energy, of two forces coming together and making a third energy, a blast off.

[Archangel Metatron: Orgone energy is the greatest power inside a human being. It is your sexual energy. This is your most powerful

---

1.   Wilhelm Reich (March 24, 1897 – November 3, 1957) was an Austrian psychoanalyst and known as one of the most radical figures in the history of psychiatry. Reich discovered a cosmic energy for which he coined the term "orgone" — derived from "orgasm" and "organism" — an energy he said others referred to as God. Reiche started building orgone accumulators in 1940 (machines people sat inside to harness the reputed health benefits), leading to newspaper stories about sex boxes that cured cancer (http://en.wikipedia.org/wiki/Wilhelm_Reich).

energy. It is what creates the ascension process. It is what contains the essence of life itself. Life is created, and it is through this creation process that you awaken the golden serpent inside of you. Orgone is the highest power you can have inside of you. It is a combination of love and the inherent power of creation within you. Sexuality is creation — if you use it wisely. One day, the importance of orgone energy will be taught in schools: how it can be channeled and how it can be used to create a beautiful, balanced, and sacred life. The American writer Wilhelm Reich taught about orgone energy, and he was put in jail. What he said was so true.]

Have sex as much as you want, but make sure it is sacred sex — an honoring of another person. Honor the God; honor the Goddess. When you make love, can you see the other person as a god or a goddess, the emerging of the God/Goddess energy? This is what tantric sex is. Intercourse is only the last part of tantric sex. It is playing between two people, perhaps naked, but playing with devotion and sacredness, honoring the god within both of them, and playing with their bodies.

There is no vulgarity. But as soon as you bring vulgarity or lust or any other form that is not sacred — of the divine order — then the sex becomes only an act. Enjoy sex. If God did not want you to have sex, then why did God give this instrument to you? It is the best fun you can have. All religions have taught that sex is bad: "Money is bad; sex is bad." Money is good, and sex is good. Enjoy everything. Sex is the best fun you can have with the human body. So bring sex into God.

Isn't that what kundalini is? Bringing consciousness and intention? If you talk about that magic moment ... ?

Exactly! And that magic moment is the transformation moment. Why do you think people want to have more and more sex? Because in the magic moment, people feel complete. You feel centered and whole. People want to have more and more sex because they want to capture that moment. This is the coming together of yin and yang, God and Goddess joining together to create an amazing force. Sex can be addicting because people want to capture the moment of complete union; there is no separation at this time. Does this answer your question?

So in other words, just go and do it!

No, do not just go and do it. Do it with the utmost reverence, sacredness, and holiness; see the other person as a Goddess or a God. Sex must be honored. It is the sacred, divine joining of two forces coming together to create a beautiful, amazing alchemical energy. What is the intention behind this union? Intention is most important. It is the key to raising one's vibration. What if you want to build a school? What is the intention behind your desire to build the school? Is it for a tax write-off, or is it coming from your heart? Intention becomes everything in the new consciousness, for when you make an intention, you are making a statement to the universe, to God. When you pray, you are making an intention.

Connecting with Animals and Other Life Forms

This is a follow-up question from our last session with Saint Germain on connecting with animals to enhance consciousness. The first question is: How do we connect with animals to enhance consciousness? The second is: How do we reach an understanding of what qualities different animals carry so that people can understand how the animal kingdom works and how they connect to enhance their own consciousnesses?

When you look at an animal and you see it through the eyes of God, what do you see? Take a turtle, for example. Do you see a great creature with a big bump on its body, or do you see a beautiful being crawling on Mother Earth's body, connected to Mother Earth? Turtles have beauty, they have intelligence, and they support humanity. If animals were not available on the planet, people would not live past thirty-five years of age! Animals hold energy for humanity. Honor these amazing beings of light. They support humanity, so seek to see the beauty of each animal that you connect with.

When you see a dolphin, does it not evoke joy, a blissful moment for you when you see it gliding through the water? Does it not make you smile? Connect with their consciousnesses, for dolphins have the capacity to bring you the innocence and purity of children. Connect with whales, connect with butterflies, and connect with bees, for bees in their little heads carry the evolution of humanity, where we are going. If bees were not there, humanity would forget its path, for bees carry that direction. Connect with bees, and you will know where you are going and how to get there. They are like guideposts saying, "You are here now, and you can go another 100 kilometers. This is part of your soul's path." Bees can take you far.

If bees were not here, most of humanity would be stuck. Invite them back into your reality, for they have been mistreated so badly that they have left Earth's plane. Call on animals that can support you, especially those you like. Talk to them; communicate with them from your heart.

Take a cat. Cats are interdimensional beings. They are always communicating with higher beings, especially on the cat planet. When a cat sits and purrs, it is connecting with its master, its guide from its planet. Even when cats go out at night, they often gather outside and talk in council, sitting around and talking about their problems and where they are going. They are connecting with their cat planet. They have come as our teachers.

When you look into the eyes of a dog, what do you see? You see purity, innocence, deep friendship, and loyalty. That is what dogs can teach you: unconditional love.

Each animal carries a certain vibrational quality. What does a cow teach you? A cow says, "Take me; milk me." And when their milking time is over, cows give us their meat. A cow always gives and gives. Cows know they are eternal beings and can never be killed. They can be killed physically, but they cannot be destroyed. Cows are true masters. Why do you think ancient yogis honored cows? Because they know cows are spiritual masters walking the planet, showing people nonattachment to physical things.

When Jesus walked the planet, do you think he had the power to throw off his guards when he was arrested? Being a true master, he *allowed*. The same could be true with you. When you connect with a cow, the eternal, natural part of you can come forward.

Elephants carry wisdom and strength. They carry group consciousness for people who have difficulty being in groups. They can teach you how to be part of a group or a community. When you connect with any animal, connect with its highest loving energy.

Animals live in a third-dimensional reality, and they have been treated very badly. Many animals do not trust human beings, for we have not been good to them. Connect with the beings you feel connection and resonance with, and talk to them in your meditation time. You can access their energy, but always ask that you connect only with their highest positive aspect. Their genes have changed due to their conditions on the planet, and they cannot trust humans, so always call for their highest aspect.

[Archangel Metatron: Connecting with animals is very simple. Everything is energy — you, an animal, the trees, and the stones

— everything is energy. The only difference is that they are vibrating at a different level. That is all. The current that runs through everything is a light force, a light force that is supported by breathing. Do you know that mountains breathe? Rivers breathe. Trees breathe. Even the masters on the other side breathe, just in a different way. So breathing connects you to All That Is, including to Source. Why do you think breathing is emphasized in all ancient spiritual practices? It is the key to liberation.

If you want to connect with an animal, send your breath from your heart. Build a bridge. Send a breath from your heart to the essence of the animal and see a beautiful energy coming back as an infinity sign. In Rae's channeling workshops, he teaches how to connect with stones, wood, plants, water, gold, music, animals, and masters, just by the simple technique of breathing. Send your breath from your heart and see beautiful energy from the animal, the tree, or the stone coming back into your heart. Do it for a few minutes to lift your energetic connection.

How do you connect with the Creator? One way is through breathing. Breathing is the key. Breathing can liberate you.

Spring is coming, and there are many creatures outside, like grasshoppers, dragonflies, and ladybugs. Spot a grasshopper, and say hello. Send a beam of light from your heart into the grasshopper, and I guarantee you that he will stay there. Then you send a beam of light from your heart into him, and say, "I would like to communicate with you." You don't have to say any words. Send love and light from your heart and keep breathing into him, and you will see light coming back from him into you, unless he is very busy.

He will almost certainly wait there for you to have a conversation. They enjoy communicating with you as long as they feel safe. Once this trust is built, they will share their wisdom. This is what happened when the teachings of ancient martial arts were brought into the world. Many martial arts movements originated in Taiwan and China and were taught by grasshoppers and other animals. Grasshoppers taught how to make a move, how to attack, and how to defend.]

The same is true with flowers. Call for the highest aspect of the flower kingdom to impart its wisdom to you. Breathe into the flower. Tomorrow, I ask you to go into your own garden and spend thirty minutes looking at a flower, just breathing into the flower, completely breathing with 100 percent of your focus. Breathe from your heart into the flower, and breathe the flower into your heart. Within thirty minutes, you and the flower will become one. You will smell that flower not only with your nose but also through your entire body. You and the flower will become one. It will take you to a heightened state of consciousness.

Metatron recently said that the sequoia tree has the capacity to transport people to gods and interdimensional beings. Sequoias produce the highest levels of oxygen. When you spend time in the vicinity of these trees, they will transport you to higher-dimensional realities within minutes.

Everything is community, not just individualization. All will support you in raising your vibration. Maintaining a pure auric field and pure thought forms is also very critical.

Before you go to the next question, I want to say this: Sometimes there is no direct answer to a question. It could be an explore-it-yourself question.

Your Star Heritage

How does one's star heritage affect the DNA?

That is a very good question. Stars have a very big influence on us. For many people, there was time during a particular incarnation when they went to other planets, other star systems, to work out pure energy and learn lessons. Stars also bring in star karma, so we have many connections to stars. Why do you think people are so fascinated with looking at stars? People look at the stars, but they never explore star energy. Everyone on this planet came from the stars. Did you know that?

Can you stretch your mind to see yourself as a starbeing coming from a star? Stretch your mind to think of the possibility that you are a starbeing, and you inherited a star. What image does it conjure in your mind?

The first image that comes is a sense of purity and coming from Source.

Yes, so this is your true essence from the star, and this is the energy that you brought from your star. You can now ask, "What star do I connect with, and what is my heritage from that star?" Again, you must ask from your soul, and ask your soul to open up that part of you that is connected with that star.

I seem to connect with the energy of the Central Sun.

It is layered in your DNA. The ninth layer is directly connected to your star heritage, so you must work with the ninth strand of your DNA to connect with your star heritage. We ask you to connect with your star because your eighth and ninth strands are connected with your ancient heritage. When you remember your star heritage, you are connecting with your true heritage.

The Pleiadians gave their DNA to the present generation, but many people have had many star connections and were raised in many other star systems, so you must establish that connection. It is like a big umbrella. Under the umbrella, there are many spokes, and one of the spokes connects to one of the star systems. You must connect the energy of that star system with the central core of your Pleiadian energy. Imagine that the top of the umbrella is the Pleiadian DNA, but there are twelve spokes in the umbrella, and these, collectively, are your star energy support system. Do you have any other questions?

Cleansing Your Auric Field

How can we connect with the different levels of planetary, solar, galactic, cosmic, universal, and multiuniversal consciousness? What is their relationship to DNA?

This is a very simple question. All these layers carry different vibrational energies. One is no better than another, but each has a different essence. The essence of the galactic energy is different from the solar, the cosmic, and the multiuniversal; everyone is different. When you start connecting to the energies of these different dimensions, you will naturally raise your vibration.

So when we meditate, we would ask to be connected with each of these levels?

Exactly. For example, the planetary masters are now Lord Buddha and Sanat Kumara; you can work with them. Then there are galactic masters Melchior, Solar Mother, and Solar Angels. Lord Melchizedek and Lord Mahatma are the cosmic masters. The multiuniversal master is Archangel Metatron. When you start connecting with these beings of light, you naturally raise your vibration. You must work with these masters on a daily basis.

Metatron has emphasized many times to Rae that one way to raise your vibration all the time is to constantly and continuously cleanse and purify your energy field on a daily basis.

How can we do that?

Work with whatever you need to cleanse whatever you have picked up, using gold light or violet light, cleansing your spiritual energy. You can work with Lady Nada; Lady Nada works specifically to cleanse your spiritual energy. You can work with Lady Quan Yin, a teacher of the ninth ray. She is the teacher of balance. Lord and Lady Andromeda work on the tenth ray. And you can also call on Archangel Metatron or Saint Germain to cleanse your soul energy field. Your soul energy must be cleansed and purified on a regular basis.

✳   ✳   ✳

Ascension

I am Archangel Metatron, the gatekeeper, or the guardian, for the portal of ascension for this planet in Arcturus. You can ask me to anchor the higher-vibrational energy of the Creator. For example, the first day you could ask, "Please anchor the energy of the Creator." The next day, you could ask, "Please anchor a higher vibrational energy than yesterday," and you can continue this process day after day. You can call on me to place my hands on your shoulders, on your forehead, or on your heart center and ask me to transmit higher-vibrational energy, my energy, to you.

I am the guardian and the gatekeeper for the portal of ascension for this planet. Why do you think I have been designated for this? I was Enoch, and I have experience being a human and also an angel. So I can relate to humanity, for all of you are angels in disguise.

You said there was a correlation between the aura and the DNA. So, in other words, the DNA is consistent through incarnations?

Yes, it is consistent through incarnations. Our genes may change, but our DNA is consistent.

So, actually, would you call the DNA your soul's ID?

Exactly! You got it exactly right! You put it beautifully. Now I ask you to be still, and I will place my hands on your crown chakras, emitting energy. You can call on me every night and ask me to transmit higher vibrations of the Creator's energy to cleanse and purify your soul energy so that your senses, your emotions, and your minds are cleansed and purified.

[Archangel Metatron intones a beautiful *Om* three times.]

Blessed beings of light, you have had an activation from the energy of the Star of David. Blessings to you. I am Archangel Metatron. We bid you goodbye at this time.

✳   ✳   ✳

Expanding Our Horizons and Living in Service

My dear family, this is Anna. Many of you have heard about me; some of you have read about me and said, "I wish I could be like her. She lived 600 years!" But what I was trying to bring through the book [*Anna, Grandmother of Jesus* by Claire Heartsong] is that all of you have this possibility. The intention of putting this in a book is to give a marker to people of what is possible for every human being. It is your birthright.

As Archangel Metatron said, we want you to expand, to have the highest possible aspirations. For most people, what is their highest possible thought? "I want to make a lot of money, then I will be happy," or "I want to know this." They never really get to their highest possibilities. Choose to create a reality where all of you live 150 years. That is one of the highest thoughts you can have at this time: to rejuvenate yourselves at a much faster pace than before, believe in it, and work toward it. For others, it could be eating only when you want to eat, teleportation, or bilocation. How about leaving your essence right now and traveling to South Africa, consciously reassembling a part of you so that you are in both places? This is possible right now. It is possible in this new reality.

These are the quantum thoughts we want you to hold. These things are possible for all humans, especially lightworkers, for they are prepared. These are the gifts you must claim now. For the next few days, we want you to imagine the highest possible outcome for your present life — what you can become. If you do not know what is possible, how can you even think of it? This is very important.

[Archangel Metatron: There is no best time, but it is always good for a novice to do this before going to sleep. You are provided with a personal angel. Call your personal angel forth to channel the energy of magnification. Do not have an agenda for why you need this energy. Ask for the energy of magnification and for the energy of expansion in its entirety, for as much as you can hold in your body.

Secondly, talk to your elementals and ask them that your body be expanded to hold the higher energy coming through angelic beings. You can also ask the angels to support you in expanding your nonphysical bodies so that they are able to hold this higher energy. These are very good techniques for everyone to do. You will see a great expansion, an opening of your mind, and greater wisdom coming into you because you are not stating why you need this. You are only asking for expansive energy. When you have more energy, you can do many more things.]

When you ask for expansion energy every day and hold the energy that you will expand energetically, many new tools will be given from the ancient mystery schools to aid your rejuvenation, bilocation, and teleportation processes.

[Archangel Metatron: There were many mystery schools all over the planet. They were in Greece, Israel, Egypt, India, Tibet, France, Ireland, and Mongolia. Each differed, but the essential teaching was transformation of lead into gold. This is a metaphor for transforming darkness into light. There were some common practices used by almost all the mystery schools. Some are still being practiced today — sacred geometry, sound, water, and numbers. Today, you are your own mystery school. There is so much more to know about yourself. You are a mystery being. So unwind that mystery and you will change lead to gold inside of yourself.

Some examples of the new tools are how to consciously work with your body to lengthen your life span. Another is to be aware of the exit points you have in your present life contract so that you can change them through intention and meditation. Third is the ability to open new blueprints and new contracts in your life. Fourth, and most important, is the ability to change and rewrite your own akashic records.]

How about having the thought that you can see far into the future, two or three years from now, to see a person or a group who wants to disrupt the world through mischievous deeds? You can go there and heal the energy, for they have set this energy already, and this energy can be intercepted inside and worked with to be transformed.

For example, on June 13, 2013, there may be violence in Egypt in which two groups are planning to have a mass rally. How about going to this place to transform the energy so that there is a dialogue without violence? Perhaps somebody is trying to make a bomb or a boy is being bullied in school. You can go and say, "How about transforming this?" You can do this now.

Hurricane season is coming to America. There could be hurricanes that would disrupt the lives of many people. You can look at the approximate time it would come, which coastline it might hit, and what you could do as a lightworker to change this. This is the potential at this time. These are the possibilities all of you carry. Dream big — the biggest dreams.

You must also dream big about the potential to heal the planet, Mother Earth. We need you here at this time! We do not want you to leave. You have worked so very hard. You have raised your vibration through many lives. Why would you leave now? We want you to stay here to be the anchor and the light for the next generations. Many of you will say, '"It has been very hard, and I am out of this place!" Dear ones, we need all the souls like you with their bright lights to be the anchoring light on this planet. So dream big for the biggest possibilities that you can have. This is Anna.

Chapter 5

Ways to Raise Your Vibration

June 28, 2013

Yeshua

This is Yeshua, or Sananda.

Can you talk to us about DNA and numerology?

This is a very interesting and deep question. Numerology is very directly connected to DNA. Why do you think people like numbers? Many people, whether Christian, Hindu, Muslim, Jewish, or Catholic, are fascinated by numbers. This is called numerology. Numbers fascinate people because numbers speak to the heart. Numbers speak to the DNA. Each layer of DNA has its specific vibration that matches the numerology, and numerology is directly connected to the configuration of the stars when you were born. Your connection with the stars, your numbers, and your DNA are all correlated.

Of course, it is a vast subject, but we ask you to look into how numbers affect you. For example, you all have a birth number. Your birth number depends on the life lesson you have come here to learn and master so that you can grow. But you can enhance your birth number; you can add a number to it.

[Archangel Metatron: By adding a letter to your name, you will be able to immediately alter a certain vibration and create a new vibration. This can bring you much closer to the truth you are trying to create. This is a very powerful tool. It was used in all the mystery schools. When you entered a mystery school, you were given a new name and were initiated into this name. You became somebody new with a new, higher vibration.

Ask in your meditation for the highest letter you can use to support yourself in the new reality you are trying to create, for from now on, you are your own master. The first letter that comes to mind will be that letter. If you still doubt, write the letter down, and pass your hand over it to see whether you feel any energetic vibration. Then you can visualize a beautiful tube of gold light from the Creator energizing your new name. This is a good exercise. You will see great benefits.

You can also choose a letter for a particular purpose. Once you accomplish that purpose, you can choose something else. Have fun with it. It can only support you.

You do not have to change your name. Just imagine this letter in the front of your name in your meditation for the next twenty-one days, until your energy body gets the message. This is a very good technique to use. It was used in ancient times.]

This is like enhancing your name. You can add certain letters to change your name. In the same way, although you were born with a certain birth number, this number can be enhanced by adding a number to it during your meditation through your intention. In that way, the numbers can be more powerful and will automatically have an impact on your DNA. This is a gift you have. And this is one of the techniques used by my grandmother Anna.

You can calculate your birth number using the "Birth Path Numerology Formula" from www.healing.about.com. The example given below is for the birthdate of November 26, 1973:

Month: 11

Day: 26 (2 + 6 = 8) 8 = Primary Birth Path Number

Year: 1973 (1 + 9 + 7 + 3 = 20; then 2 + 0 = 2)

Month + Day + Year (11 + 8 + 2 = 21; 2+1 = 3) 3 = Secondary Birth Path

Note: Master numbers 11 and 22 stand alone and are not added together. Simple numbers are 1 through 9. Master numbers are 11 (11 not 2) and 22 (22 not 4).

Number	Type	Traits
1	Achiever	born leader, ambitious, do-it-yourselfer
2	Idealist	loving, peacemaker, optimistic
3	Artist	creative, imaginative, joyful
4	Pragmatist	organized, hardworking, practical minded
5	Opportunist	likes to socialize, big spender, chance taker
6	Caregiver	dependable, compassionate, nurturer
7	Seeker	spiritual, questioning, eccentric
8	Affluent	wealthy, accomplished, educated
9	Philosopher	analytical, inspirational, intuitive
11	Visionary	enlightened, thinks outside of the box, futuristic minded
22	Global Thinker	goal oriented, business minded, international interests

Let us say that you come up with the number 7. Seven is your spiritual number, 3 is a catalyst number, 8 is a completion number, 9 is the number for a teacher, 11 is for a master teacher, and 22 is for a world teacher, that sort of thing.

Let us say someone has come to the number 5. This person has a very specific vibration related to the number 5. What is the life lesson there? Five can be achieved, and the efficiency of the number 5 can be improved on by bringing some other number to it. With this, his life can be changed and improved. It is not as if he can change 100 percent, but let us say he has a bad habit. By changing this number, he will be able to see clearly where this habit is inhibiting him so that he can take steps to change.

Take the number three, the number of the catalyst. People with the birth number 3 are catalysts for change. But perhaps this number causes people to change too much. By adding a number to that, they will see how they are playing a part in changing their lives and changing the lives of everybody else they touch.

So with that practice, they would certainly alter their DNA?
It has the potential to affect the DNA too.

DNA and Earth Codes

As you know, Earth is now shifting. So, naturally, DNA is shifting, just as God is shifting. God is not static. When you change, God changes too. The same thing happens with Mother Earth. There is a new consciousness on the ground with Mother Earth's changes. You must upgrade your personal genetics to come into alignment with Mother Earth's new consciousness. So when you work to activate DNA, ask that your work be in complete alignment with the new consciousness of Mother Earth.

But DNA has many, many layers. When you activate the first strands of DNA, it may take many years. People say, "I have activated my DNA." They want ascension in terms of many, many layers: 120 layers. Many of you have already activated many more layers than you realize. Now you must make sure this activation is in complete alignment with Mother Earth and that it is in complete harmony with Mother Earth's newly opened DNA.

How would you define Earth codes? Is this the DNA to open the new consciousness of Earth?
Yes, because Earth codes are time capsules. People who supported the manifestation of the New Earth put these codes in place long ago. These codes would become activated if and when human consciousness was raised to a certain level. It is a mechanical or biomechanical process; if this happens, then that can happen. Now this is happening. It is happening because the consciousness of humanity has risen.

Is this something like what James Tyberonn has been doing in Arkansas with crystalline structures underground?
Many beings are now being called to activate these codes, but there are also specific places on the planet that are being activated without anyone's support. They are naturally being activated because of the consciousness in the ground. Many sacred power places will lose their

power in a relative sense. Perhaps not "lose" their power, but a new activated Earth core will create more powerful sacred energies on the ground than some of the present sacred energies available on the planet.

What else should we know about DNA and Earth codes?

Let me give an example of Rae. He has been to Israel a few times, but this last time he felt much more. He shifted, and he was able to be in alignment with Mother Earth's consciousness, not fully but still at a considerable level. He was able to feel much more this time than any other time, and he kept saying that this time he felt much more connection, and he felt so much more from certain places. These places have always been there. There were fewer people in the past, and now there are more people. So this place existed for thousands of years, but he was not able to feel it until he raised his vibration to be in alignment with this place.

This is what is now happening. With the new Earth codes activating, many people are called to new places. And when they go to these places, they feel uplifted in consciousness. Once uplifted in consciousness, naturally, their DNA is activated.

You must remember, activation does not happen instantly. It happens in layers, very subtly. Let us say that your intuition increases and your inspiration increases, and you know much more as part of DNA activation itself. Many people say DNA activation is magic and ultimate. Yes, it is magic and ultimate, but it is a gradual process. When you start regenerating your body, what are you doing? You are activating your DNA. I am trying to put it in nontechnical language, in a simple way, so that people can understand everything.

So the next time you go to any special place, it is good to intend to activate higher strands of the DNA. Many people do not ask for this. But you can consciously ask, and in consciousness, you are attuning to this place, and this helps you raise your own vibration level, which in turn can help you to open to your own DNA consciousness.

DNA and Inner Earth Cities

There are many Inner Earth cities on the Earth plane that are slowly coming into the forefront, and people may not be aware of this. Different people are becoming aware of this, and this means there is a shift in human consciousness. People will start to know that they are not alone, and they will realize that they can also achieve this status or somewhat emulate these Inner Earth residents. When beauty is there, then you try to emulate it.

These beings of light of the inner cities carry higher-vibrational energy already because they went through similar processes like those that all of you have. They raised their vibration and transcended this reality into a higher reality. They are able to maintain and hold on to that.

You see, it is like this: You go near a heater, and what happens? You get heat. These people are already activated. They are on a higher level of consciousness, and when you are with them and in their presence, naturally you are affected by their consciousnesses. If you are in a very good mood, feeling joyful and happy, people come to you and want to be near you. They feel joy in your presence. Similarly, when you are in the presence of these Inner Earth people, you feel love, benevolence, and grace. You feel uplifted, because they are emitting a higher level of energy. And you will see more and more Inner Earth beings coming out to communicate and interact with the surface dwellers.

Recently, Rae took a group of people to Mount Fuji to connect with the people of an underground city called Mu. It took four years for him to be able to do this. This is a city under Mount Fuji, but it took four years for the teachers of Mu to allow for the passage of their people. The people who went inside during their meditations all felt uplifted when they came back, not afflicted. This is part of raising your vibration and consciousness. This means you have more light inside. So working with Inner Earth humans can support raising your light.

Just to clarify, so the inhabitants of Inner Earth are living on a higher dimension, and it is a nonphysical dimension?

Of course. They are living in a higher dimension. Most are on the fifth dimension, and Mu is on the seventh.

So we couldn't tunnel into their cities on a physical level?

No, of course not. But Admiral Byrd[1] traveled to an Inner Earth city, and he was called crazy.

---

1. Rear Admiral Richard Evelyn Byrd Jr., USN (25 October 1888–11 March 1957) was an American naval officer who specialized in feats of exploration. It is believed that Byrd flew over the North Pole and into the hollow earth in February 1947. F. Amadeo Giannini wrote about Byrd's experience in his book *The Worlds beyond the Poles*. Giannini wrote that Byrd encountered a humanoid being from another world who warned humanity to pursue peace and not war (http://en.wikipedia.org/wiki/Richard_E._Byrd).

[Archangel Metatron: It was in Admiral Byrd's life contract to bring forth information about the Inner Earth, and he did. He was ridiculed, but this was part of his life contract, and he fulfilled it perfectly well. By the way, he is now back on Earth.]

Good. Because I know Admiral Byrd was thought to be crazy when he related his experiences.

All truth at first is called crazy or laughable.

Collective Toning and Power Places on Earth

One of the ways of raising your vibration is being in a sacred place. A sacred place can raise your vibration. You can all do toning collectively with others. This will raise the collective vibration. It will help to contact the Inner Earth beings — much more easily than one person working on the fingers [mudras] individually.

As you know, when more than one is gathered in my name, this generates tremendous power. If a hundred people gather to pray, is this not more powerful than an individual prayer? In the same way, because most of us say that the time capsule can be opened, it must be opened at this time. It can only be opened when collectively you raise your vibrations.

A group of people having a happy time will be able to manifest this. During December of last year in Hawaii, Dr. Todd Ovokaitys and the Lemurian Choir were collectively singing tones to bring in and connect to the higher vibration being downloaded onto the planet. So, again, this is to support raising your vibration.

Could you speak about DNA and power places on Earth?

As you mentioned, power spots have been used since ancient times. A new time capsule will be opened, and in the coming months and years, it will release more pure crystalline energy of a much higher vibration. When you go to Israel, many people say it is holy or sacred, which is true. But when you went to the Church of the Holy Sepulchre on the Via Dolorosa, did you feel holiness there?

No, not really.

This is because of the people there, hundreds of thousands of people, with their energy and their anguish. They are coming to say, "Holiness, take my anger. Take my anguish. Save me."

But there is a new core, a new energy that has been activated by a time capsule. It will be pure crystalline, pristine energy — never touched. It has a purity of its own. It is like a new baby. All of humanity falls in love with a new baby because a baby is not contaminated and is of the purest essence, especially if the baby is very small. Everybody loves a baby; I should say that most of humanity loves a baby because of the purity in its essence. In the same way, this new crystalline energy will carry a pristine energy, and this will become more powerful. When you are able to contact these energies, immediately they will be able to raise your vibration. They say when you go to certain places, you feel good.

A simple way to raise your vibration every day is to see beauty always, to see beauty everywhere. If you stop seeing beauty, immediately there is a shift in your perception of reality — in your mind, in your thoughts, in your emotions. If you cannot choose beauty, then try to see beauty in nature around you: the green leaves, the water, and the trees. Slowly, you will start feeling a perception of that truth. And this will support the raising of your vibration. When you have this, naturally, love is the outcome.

DNA and the New Children

It was mentioned in the last session that children are the New Earth. They carry a higher vibration, and their DNA is much more evolved and activated. But these children must be guided to move into their realities so that they can change the world.

Let me give you an example of the present system in your country. Everyone talks about [Edward] Snowden, how he betrayed the country. But he is a New Child with a higher vibration, living in his truth, and he cannot allow a big, intimidating country like yours to bully other people. For him, this is not what God intended. He wants to expose the criminality of the government. He carries higher-vibrational energy.

That was my concern too: that people would be alienated. I know Admiral Byrd was thought to be crazy when he related his experiences.

All truth at first is called crazy or laughable.

[Archangel Metatron: Snowden was a great scientist from Atlantis. Why did he reveal the activities of the NSA? He and others vowed that science would not be misused to deceive humanity, as it had in the past. Celebrate this young man for his courage.]

These New Children will not follow the old methods of control. But many New Children are not given a loving environment and good opportunities, so they try to fit in with the system. They close down their higher circuits. But you will see in two generations, fifty years' time, children will change the world. Let the old guards (control and fear) go, and an environment of love will be created in which children will be able to blossom and express themselves.

All the people, all of you — all lightbeings — are building and laying the road for the generations to come.

DNA and the Places You Reside

Can you discuss DNA and its relation to the places on Earth where we reside?

Again, this is an important thing, and it is connected to numerology and to star systems. For someone who knows the truth, geographic location is just moving. Changing your geographic location is undertaken by the soul to bring a very specific learning to where there is work to be done physically. You do not just pack your bag and go to England and say, "I'm going to live in England. I like England very much," or Canada. Where you live is all very well planned with your divine soul: what you need to do and why you have come here. But most people are not aware of this at all. They will say, "I like that place, and I'm going to move there." Look into this. Why does one person choose to live in an area?

Ask yourself, "Why am I here? Have I completed the life lesson I am here to learn?" Then find another place that can give you the opportunity to grow in consciousness. Of course, this can create a great havoc in people, because it will create disruption in their lives.

In the future, you will see people becoming more nomadic. They will move continuously. They will not stay in one particular place. Some people may say, "I have a house. How can I move all the time?" But you must ask whether the purpose of living where you do has been served and whether you have stayed there too long. Has it served its purpose? Why has the soul chosen to live in this particular place out of all places?

You were living in Canada, then why did you choose to live in Massachusetts? You could have chosen anywhere in America. You might say, "Maybe I like the nature. I like this. I like that." It is all fine on a personality level. But on the soul level, why did you choose this place?

What we are trying to say is that everything is planned, and this relates to numerology, the stars, and the life lessons you have come here to learn. The life lesson of living in this particular place has not been completed. When it is and the wisdom is gained, you will be able to raise your vibration naturally, and higher consciousness can be supported once again. Collectively, all this is happening to raise your vibration and to support the activation of DNA. It's not just one thing. It is collective support in every area of your life.

This means there are no accidents. If you look at this from that perspective, immediately you will be able to raise your vibration. Suppose somebody is going through the same pattern again and again. Every ten lifetimes or every fifty years, that person is doing the same thing. Finally, the person gets it: "Oh my God, what have I been doing?" And in that realization, in that wisdom, he or she will immediately shift into a higher vibration.

The Validity of Some Channeled Information

There is a lot of information out there about imminent financial reform for the world, arrests of members of the cabal, disclosure of extraterrestrial life on the planet, and all this sort of thing imminently happening. It's always about to happen, and nothing ever does. I wonder if there is validity to any of this?

Why do you give importance to these things? Disconnect from the media, because as you know, there is very little truth in the media. Disconnect from the television. Disconnect from radio.

People connect with many things. They can say it is channeled information, but it is just one of the realities. There are many realities. Within reality, each moment has 144 realities [futures]. So a channel or a psychic is able to pick out one reality and say, "This is the truth of it, and this is it. This is what is going to happen. The world is going to be hit by a meteorite."

What we see, from our perspective, is that it will take a few more years for the financial situation to be cleared and healed with more structural reform. The real purpose for banks will become clear. The true function of a bank is to support people by lending and receiving, nothing else. It will take a few more years for this to happen. The present time frame is 2017–2020.

But will there be great destruction? What happens when disclosure happens? What happened to Snowden? He disclosed; what happened? People focus on him, not on what he disclosed. What he disclosed is truly historic. This has never been done in the history of the world.

It's true; they want to arrest him.
So are the people ready?

Probably not.
So do not focus on him; focus on what he discloses. The same is true about disclosing financial abuse. You will hear news here and there, but humanity is not ready to change, to let the old guards go. It will take some time.

Places with the Purest Energy

There are some places in the world that still contain the purest energies. These places have not yet been explored or tapped. Very few people know about them. Look for these places. They are deeply hidden.

This is like being in your home. Let us say you have a sofa in your home. Perhaps you do not sit on this sofa. You sit in another place every time, and you select this other place because you are comfortable there. Most people go to the comfortable places, but there are other places that are equally comfortable that have not been explored because you just felt comfortable where you were.

Look for these other places. There are still very pure energy centers, and immediately they can bring an elevation or an uplifting. There are places in the Polynesian Islands that can immediately bring on higher rates of vibration and consciousness. You feel uplifted. Many people say that when they go to the mountains of Tibet, they feel close to God because they are in a heightened, elevated state. There are some places where you can still go and work like that. This is one topic you should think about.

The human mind is the biggest barrier. Work with your mind every day. Look at your thoughts and what you can do about these thoughts. These thoughts are supporting your reality. The activation of DNA is not just one thing. It is a combination of everything. Before a rocket is fired, it takes many months of training and preparation.

Activation of the layers of your DNA happens when many things come together, slowly raising the vibration. When it reaches a particular level, the blast occurs, and this speeds up the fire element within you, speeding up through the spinal column, shooting all the way to your crown and then flowing back again — the movement of kundalini. When this happens, the rocket is launched and life is never again the same. You are truly in the hands of divinity from that moment on. But for this to happen, many other things need to be repaired.

Chapter 6

You Are the Creator of Your Own Peace

June 30, 2013

Sanat Kumara and Lord Melchizedek

This is Sanat Kumara. The purpose of this book is very simple: to raise the consciousness of humanity so that people can move easily and comfortably to a new stage in which they can feel peace and joy in their hearts, knowing that they have the capacity to transform their present lives to lifetimes of peace, love, and joy. If you look at the deepest aspect of people, they all seek the same things: peace, freedom, and joy. So the purpose of this book is to bring the concept that you can have peace, you can have freedom, and you can have joy in your life. However, this requires work.

To achieve anything worthwhile, there must be effort and there must be action. All these techniques and tools are only formats that can support you to come to the realization, the understanding, that you are the creator of your own peace. You are the creator of your own joy. It may take a lifetime to come to this understanding, but right now, there are many tools to help you accomplish this sooner. If you work seriously with these tools, in less than ten years, you will have the capacity for enlightenment. We are just asking for ten years of your life — a dedicated ten years.

So the idea of this book is that it supports people to realize that they have the capacity to reach this goal, to attain this peace, attain this freedom, and attain this joy. The information we are providing here is meant to bring you into the state of consciousness in which you are able to derive benefit from the techniques and to work with them to reach a level in which you are able to access higher wisdom.

These tools are presented in a simplified way: by relating your personal experience. By using these tools, you will be able to raise your vibration to a level at which you feel more at peace, more connection with Spirit, and more joy.

This is both an individual journey and a collective journey. Everyone using these tools is able to realize his or her true potential to gain freedom and peace of the heart. When you place the book in the context of a personal journey, people will be able to relate to you. For example, Rae used to work as a corporate man, but he made a transformation to his present state using some of these tools and techniques. Perhaps the same is true for you. It is an individual journey of how you transform your life.

The Call to Ascension

Now, briefly, we will talk about sound. Why are human beings so attracted to sound? What is the first sound human beings hear? The sound of the heartbeat of their mothers. Why do you think people like the sound of a drumbeat? Why did techno music become so popular? It is not just because of the dancing. "Boom, boom, boom" — it reminds them of the heartbeat at the deepest level. Of course, it was misused, along with drugs and many other things. Drumbeats can affect human beings at the deepest level, helping them, because the first thing they hear is the sound of the heartbeat of the mother.

Sound is in everything. Your cells make sound. Without sound, there is no universe. You and the world came about through sound with a difference. The word was made into flesh. And what was the word? It was sound.

Many comic books and fairy tale books talk about this very subtly.

When you say certain sounds, a magic door opens. Look at the Disney character Mickey Mouse, who says, "Let us open the magic door. Let us say magic words, 'Meeska Mouska Mickey Mouse!'" What is he doing? He is repeating the magic words that open the magic gate to the club-house. Aladdin went to the mountain and repeated certain words, and the mountain door opened. All those stories are teaching people to look at sound. It is not just written for fun. Look at Tarzan when he beats his chest and makes his sound. All those comic books are teaching you that sound has the power to transform.

We have long known about the power of sound to transform. The stones of the Egyptian pyramids were lifted by sound. The stones of the ancient temples of Tibet were lifted through sound. This is not magic.

Sound can release blocked emotions in the body. If energy is stuck, sound can restore normal energy and move stuck energy in the physical body. Using the power of sound, you can open the seals of ascension in your consciousness. This is the call to ascension.

When you hear high-powered sound, does this not make you feel more connected? For example, the simplest kind of Zen chanting can take people into higher levels of consciousness. Sound touches people at a deep, core level because they are made of sound, and the first sound they hear is the heartbeat of the mother. If you can tune into the sound of Mother Earth's heartbeat, the Schumann resonances[1], then you are truly communicating with Mother Earth. Each civilization, from other planets too, emits certain sound frequencies. Tune into their sound frequencies and connect with them.

[Archangel Metatron: The Schumann resonances are the underlying vibrations, or resonance, of Earth. Very few people understand them at this time except military scientists and some others. Once you understand this, you will see how Earth is vibrating at different levels. Then you can connect your body to the Schumann resonances.

It is for human beings to recalibrate and reconnect their vibrations with the vibration of the Schumann resonances. Then you will be much more in tune with Mother Earth, and you will feel Mother Earth in your body. Many people say they cannot feel Mother Earth. They love her and want to feel her more. This is one of the ways to do that.

---

1.   The Schumann resonances are a set of spectrum peaks in the extremely low frequency portion of Earth's electromagnetic field spectrum. Schumann resonances are global electromagnetic resonances that are excited by lightning discharges in the cavity formed by Earth's surface and the ionosphere (http://en.wikipedia.org/wiki/Schumann_resonances).

To attune to the Schumann resonance, do you go to your heart and ask to feel it? Is that how you suggest we try that?

Yes. Express your intention to do it and why you want to do it. You must tell Mother Earth, "My highest intention is to align with you so that I may experience more of you in my physical body as a knowing experience in every moment." That is what to say.]

There are certain sounds that can open doors to the mystery. For example, there are certain sounds to open and connect with the energy of the city we call Mu under Mount Fuji. The same is true with Telos. Certain sounds can be used to connect with the beings of light.

Just keep it simple in regard to what sound can do on a personal level. Sound can take you to a different dimensional reality if you really work with it. For example, if you listen to rap music for three hours or to hard-core rock 'n' roll, what happens? Do you feel good? Perhaps not. But if you listen to healing music, you may feel rejuvenated or you may feel very relaxed. You might even go to sleep.

The same is true with words. You can say words that can hurt or heal. Certain words spoken to you, such as, "Hey, you are an amazing person. I love you," immediately can raise your feeling level. On the other hand, if somebody says, "You are a terrible person," immediately the vibration can be brought down. Sound has a capacity to raise or lower your vibration level, simple. So these are just some ideas, and you can work from there.

Dragons

Dragons are archetypal energies that were seeded on to the planet. Some of these archetypal dragon energies are being opened up because humans are now ready to accept them. But like a time capsule, you need to access them and work with them. They can support your healing, the awakening of your DNA, and your connection with the Creator. There are certain dragons we specifically work with to open the DNA.

How does one access them?

Again, they also have an energy signature to call forth. How do you access a master? Through your pure intention and through your pure love. [See Appendix I: Working with the Energy of Dragons.]

The same is true with any being of light. Great masters have a certain sound frequency and vibrational energy. In the same way that you connect with the master, you connect with a dragon, using its sound frequency, the sounds of nature.

Again, what is the purpose of this book? Simply, these techniques are to help you move to a level where you find more peace in your lives, more joy, more passion, and more connection with yourselves and your Creator. These techniques may support you. This is your truth. It is not universal truth. This is your truth. Work with this truth.

Mudras

What are mudras? Mudras are energy postures (as practiced in chapter one). The body constantly creates energy through each moment: when you are working and when you lift your hand. Every act of the body creates an energy field. This energy can be modified by certain positions of the hands.

For example, when you watched Michael Jackson dance the moonwalk, what did it do to him and to the people watching it? Some might have said, "Ah it's very nice to watch." But there is a meaning behind what he was doing. He was creating energy for himself and for the people watching him. It makes them feel awe. It makes them feel very good. It makes them feel mesmerized.

It's the same with any dance form. All dances have body movements. Take Indian dance. Indian dancers show the different poses by the hands. If you look at the Hindu religion, you will see Indian dance. The whole story is told through dance movements, facial expression, and hand movements. You lift one hand and open one finger: What does it say? A closed fist: What does it say? A dancer shows that there is a meaning behind the movement and an energy behind it.

The same is true when you use mudras; there is meaning and energy behind a mudra. Even the simple act of praying or when you put your hands in front of your heart tells you something. What does it tell you? Does it make you feel good, connected to your own mystic power inside?

When your thumb is pointed toward your heart, that could be called a mudra. It creates an energy field. It creates a feeling of connection to the Divine. This is truly done with prayer. The same is true with mudras; simply said, they can create energy that can take you to a higher state of consciousness. It is that simple. Mudras are a gift to humanity from mystical masters and teachers from the ancient past.

Now you are going forth, and you are using mudras to support your journey in the present.

You see, everything that we discussed can be done in a very simple format. I gave you everything that needs to be done in this chapter. This is to give an idea of how everything can be simplified. This is Sanat Kumara.

✳   ✳   ✳

Working with the Five Elements

This is Lord Melchizedek. Working with DNA is a soul's desire for you to connect more with your soul. Working with DNA is not for every soul. It is for people who have been guided to work with their DNA. Many times, people think about DNA, "Ah, exciting, let me do it." But very few people truly understand the significance of DNA and working with their DNA consciously, continuously, until all the layers are activated. Still, it is not all of them, for there are many layers, layers within layers within layers, that will never be fully activated within this present lifetime — or any lifetime. When certain layers are activated, you move forward.

People are working seriously on their spiritual evolution, and they might feel that this material can support them and humanity. But I want to make it very clear: This is not for everyone. The intention may be good, that it will work for everybody. But I tell you, only few will work with their DNA, for someone must reach a certain level of vibration to connect with the essence of the words in this book, with its energy, and work from there. Some will say, "Very interesting," but how many will truly sit down and work with it? I would say very few.

Some may read it and then pick it up later when they are ready for it.

Yes, but each soul will choose the time in a lifetime when he or she will say, "I will work on myself very consciously, continuously, and I will keep on working to improve myself." Many times, people set up tests or trials for themselves to remind themselves, because it is through the tests that they remember. If there are no tests, maybe they will not remember their life's purpose. If life is good for you, then why should you think about God? So you set up these tests, and through tests, through hard knocks, you remember. You realize that if you do such and such, you solve the problem and use the experience to help you grow.

But there is something else we wish to talk about. One of the ways of working with DNA is working with elemental nature. The elements are very important to each person's reality — earth, wind, water, fire, and the fifth element, ether. The elements can support people tremendously in raising consciousness. This is why it is so beneficial to meditate in an open field, in nature, for nature, by its very essence, can speak to the entire body.

You and nature are the same. You have the wind element. You have the earth element. You have the water element. You have the fire element. And you have the ether element. So your elements speak with the elements of nature. Bring in the elements as part of the awakening process. The elements have some vibrational significance. Call on them, and connect with them.

Each of the elements also has a sound vibration to call it forth, to connect with it. Of course, meditation in nature is good, but for people living in cities, it is not always possible to go to nature and meditate. In some countries, you can even get killed meditating in an open field. But let me say: Never forget the power of the elements to elevate your consciousness.

So people can do this? They don't have to be in nature, but they can call on the elements in their own homes, is that it?

Yes, they can connect with them and work with them on a daily basis. It is very important that you work with the elements in this new consciousness.

Chapter 7

Raising Consciousness with Aromas, Plants, and Animals

July 2, 2013

Gaia, Flamingoes, Plant Species, and Peacocks

This is Gaia. People are always fascinated by smell. Most people like the smell of cinnamon bread, especially if it is made the old-fashioned way, being baked in earthen materials. The smell arouses memories of good times. It can arouse memories of a mother's love or of a beautiful, loving home. You smell it and suddenly you just want to eat lots of bread because the smell is so nice.

Smell has a capacity. One of the beauties of smell is that if you can recall the smell, you can recall a past experience or a memory. So smell has the capacity to awaken the deepest memories.

This is why certain oils are used during chakra initiations: to break cords or seals. These are called the seals of ascension. Indian sages used sandalwood. People now use sandalwood for purification, but the true purpose of sandalwood is to affect your crown chakra, your pineal gland, and your mind. It cleanses your mind. That is why in ancient India when people were dying, their relatives burned sandalwood, so the person would die with a clear mind. They could focus on God.

To open their crown chakras and make it easier for them to leave their bodies?
    Also to clear their minds. So it has two purposes.
    The aromas of many flowers arouse memories as well. There is much value to lotuses. They can help you remember some of your past lives in ancient Egypt. Roses were very dear to Mother Mary and Mary Magdalene. Often when Mother Mary appears, people smell roses.
    Smells can affect the chakras and the emotional bodies of a new-born infant. When people are feeling discomfort — say, in an office — they can spray something, and in a few minutes, the air is cleansed and purified. What does it actually do? It transforms heavy energy into light energy so that you feel better. In many New Age workshops, you see people spraying natural essences so that the energy buildup can be cleansed and purified along with any smells.
    If you put lavender oil on your pillow before you go to sleep, you may fall asleep faster and have good dreams. You naturally feel relaxed because of the smell.
    There are certain smells you can use to raise your consciousness. One is myrrh, and another is cinnamon. Jasmine, lavender, and sandalwood can also support you. There are many others. It is helpful for people to work with some of the aromas and essential oils. When the Essenes and other ancient communities performed initiations, they poured oil on the heads of the initiates to cleanse and purify them. This prepares you for initiation. Certain oils have the capacity to open your higher consciousness.
    Being with certain animals can also raise your consciousness. When animals are in their purity, uncaged, there is a natural beauty. They emit a pure energy. A wild dolphin is so beautiful. It naturally awakens something in you. Or a whale, diving and splashing in the water, evokes the feeling of mystery.
    Animals can take you to levels at which you feel more comfortable with yourself. You are in a different reality. Take a big sea turtle, for example. People go to Patagonia to watch great turtles who are one hundred years old. They evoke something inside you when you see them. There is beauty there.

Giant sequoia trees, giant redwood trees, and many other trees can support you and raise your vibration. They can take you to different dimensional realities. Certain animals can do this also. Have you seen the pictures of Hope [Fitzgerald][1] with the great white lions in South Africa? Does it evoke beauty inside of you? Because beauty is God.

So we connect to divinity by associating with animals?

Certain animals, yes. When you see a giant parakeet or a big parrot with different colors, it evokes so much memory inside of you, so much beauty. What a creation! Pink flamingos evoke beauty inside and open your heart. They are also part of raising your consciousness. There is so much they can teach if you would only ask.

Let's talk to a flamingo for a minute.

* * *

Flamingoes on Self-Sufficiency and False Desires

We are the family of the flamingo. We have never spoken to human beings on the Earth plane like this. So we are very happy that we have been invited to speak. As you know, just like you, we are part of Mother Earth and creation. We have a role to play, as you have a role to play.

One of the gifts that we can offer people is our self-sufficiency. We know how to take care of ourselves completely, fulfilling all our needs. We can help people who have difficulty thinking they are not self-sufficient, that they will have to struggle hard, and who see life as a struggle where the winner takes all. We are connected with our essences. Connect with us, and we will slowly infuse your consciousness so that you will feel self-sufficient. You are self-sufficient right now where you are. That can create peace in your life.

The Creator said, "If you want something so badly, look at your life and say, 'Right now I am living without this. Why do I really need it? I am still alive without it.'" That is a great shift at the quantum level. You can say, "I am self-sufficient now. I may want many things, but I am still alive and healthy without the thing I really want. Then why do I need

---

1. Hope Fitzgerald of Great Barrington, Massachusetts, is a spiritual teacher and personal friend of the author and editor. In 2013, she traveled to see the white lions in the Timbavati region of South Africa.

it?" This is a great personal inquiry. It can change your perception of life altogether.

We flamingoes can teach people about self-sufficiency. We are self-sufficient in every way. Of course, humans can work to improve themselves. They are alive on the planet at this time, and they have the means and the capacity to transform or change.

Good day to you. We are the Flamingoes.

*　　*　　*

Working with Plants to Raise Your Consciousness

We represent the plant species. A plant plays an important role in human consciousness. Plants were not created just for plants. They have significant purposes. Plants support humanity, and plants even take on the karma and suffering of people. Plants and animals sometimes willingly give up their lives. They will take on the heavy karma of people they are associated with.

There are certain plants that can raise your consciousness tremendously. There are also certain plants that can be planted in your garden that can bring prosperity, for they emit the energy of prosperity. Their scent affects part of the brain, and this gets you to take creative action, which can create abundance in life.

These are secrets that have not yet been revealed. But the time is coming for this to be known. Do research to find out which plants can raise your consciousness. There are some excellent materials already published. We want you to dig into this to find out more, such as which plants can raise your consciousness just by being with it.

Plants can even bring healing and communication. When someone has a communication problem with his or her partner, or with anyone, work with sage. This can bring healing. Communication can improve. So if you dig a little, you will find some good information. The same for aromas and animals.

Plants can raise your vibration, so the plants you have in your house are important. Plants do not harm anyone, and there are certain plants that can help you feel better, that can make you feel good when you come into your house, because that plant emits the energies of benevolence and relaxation. So find out which emit those energies. Not all plants do.

[Archangel Metatron: Some people are allergic or sensitive to certain plants. There are things like poison ivy and poison oak. Everything has its own purpose. But plants do not deliberately harm anyone unless they feel threatened.

Why would a person be allergic to trees or grasses?

It is not because of the tree. It is because of the person's own problems. If you are in front of a lion, the lion will not attack you unless it senses your fear. The same is true with poison ivy — if your consciousness is afraid of the plant. Both lions and poison ivy came from the Creator.]

Plants have a hierarchy. Different plants have different vibrations. The sequoia tree has the highest vibration. In the temples of Japan and Korea, the priests plant only specific trees. There is a purpose. Find this purpose, find these trees, and find these plants. Include Mother Earth in all her capacity to raise your consciousness, for she is your mother. She has so much to offer, and not only crystals; there are plants and animals, and her whole body can be used to support people in raising their vibrations.

We are the Plant Spirits, collectively speaking to you.

✳ ✳ ✳

Peacocks on Dance and Beauty

We are the Peacocks. We dance the beautiful dance. We have big tails and we splash our tails and create beauty. We dance because we are beautiful, and we know that we are beautiful. Dance is beauty. Dance is God. God danced the day you were born.

Dance to life, dear one. When you dance in passion, you are touching the hand of God. So we bring beauty to people's hearts. When they realize this beauty, they realize that they are God. This is our function. When we spread our full wings and dance, it is exquisite beauty. A beautiful spiritual dance touches your heart. It takes you to a different reality.

Take the Sufi dance of a dervish: The dervishes spin around and around. This is beautiful. If you were to watch a dervish dance for twenty or thirty minutes, both you and the dancers would enter into a trance and be taken to a different reality. The same is true for any spiritual dance. We peacocks dance because we know we are beautiful, and we can create beauty.

Some people who have difficulty accepting their beauty could connect with our energy, and slowly they would see a difference in their behavior.

[Archangel Metatron: You can connect with anything through breath, through your heart. The same energy courses through you, and you connect through breath. Come dance with me. Let us celebrate life, for in the dance, I celebrate my life as a Creator. Isn't it a beautiful dance? Come dance with me. Ask me to dance with you in your sleep time, and I will bring you the healing of self-acceptance, self-love, and self-beauty. This is my gift to you. Are you ready to accept it? Call on me.]

People would accept themselves more than before after connecting with us. They will be less self-judgmental and less self-critical. Perhaps they would realize that although they have problems, they can still love and care for themselves. Their self-love has been very shallow, and they can work toward full self-acceptance, including accepting their dark sides, embracing their darkness, and appreciating themselves.

We are the Peacocks.

Chapter 8

Working with the New Consciousness on the Planet

July 19, 2013

King Akhenaton, Saint Germain, Gaia, Pythagoras, the Creator, and Crystal Skull

This is Akhenaton. There has been much talk about the new light or new consciousness on the planet. Many have called 2013 the New Year, for this is the beginning of a new era. But one must ask if humanity is ready to understand this new light and whether people can understand and integrate it. Are they ready for it?

There are many steps in this process. If you were to teach calculus to a third-grade student, she would not understand it. She must be gently guided and her consciousness expanded so that she can understand what calculus is and how it can support her life. In the same way, this new consciousness must be introduced in such a way that humanity is aware of it and then work with it.

We suggest that you educate people about this new consciousness — about this New Year — and the possibilities of using this consciousness in a very different, conceptive way so that it can support their lives. Look at what is happening in Egypt. There is great turmoil among people who are committed to changing the order. Why is this so? The new consciousness is affecting them, but they are not aware of it. It is affecting them dramatically. But if they were aware of why they feel as they do, perhaps they would be able to bring about this change differently.

In America, there is a big scandal about spying on every citizen on the whole planet. One young man [Archangel Metatron: This is Edward Snowden. One day he will be a free man.] (who is an Indigo child) exposed this. Snowden was well aware of the consequences to himself, but he was committed to expose this because he was affected by the new consciousness in which everything is open. But are American people outraged by the surveillance? Of course not. If the American people knew about this new consciousness, they would be able to handle the present situation differently.

We must also ask one more thing before going. Why is this only happening in Egypt and not in other countries where people think they have higher consciousness? It is because most people are still sleeping. I would say 90 percent of the world's population is still sleeping. But why only in Egypt? They are clamoring for great change. They are not giving up. I will leave this question to you.

Is it because there is a lot of energy in Egypt affecting them? Is there more energy there?

As you know, the Great Pyramid is a sacred geometric formation that is an energy generator. It has many functions. The Pleiadians beam light into the pyramids every day. Combine this with the many spiritual people who went to sacred places before and during December 2012 and sowed the seeds of change in the ground. This affected consciousness. What happened in Egypt and Africa will reverberate throughout the world, but it won't happen as fast as we would like. Nevertheless, it will touch the whole world.

Why has this not happened in America, where the government has been spying on every human being? In East Germany, there was a great clamor. The Americans could stand up and say, "We must stop it now." Maybe a few will. There is a difference.

So Americans are sleeping?

I would say the world is sleeping. Ten people in Egypt will make a great difference, but the fighting is not over. [Archangel Metatron: They are all alive at this time. Some have come forward, however, not publicly. These ten people are supported by many beings, including Rae. Part of Rae's work at night is to support these people. This is why he keeps going to Egypt. Six of them are reincarnations of past benevolent kings and queens of Egypt, including Nefertiti.]

It is not easy. Anyone who tries to teach and bring in the new consciousness is attacked and killed. Nevertheless, they will succeed. It might take much time and much more suffering, but there will be change.

I will ask other people to come and speak with you regarding DNA unless you have any other questions.

This is not really a question, but I believe the Great Pyramid is actually a time lock. Within the Great Pyramid is the Ark of the Covenant, the one that is actually holding the ascension program. Much furniture and such has been moved out of the Great Pyramid because it is being recalibrated. We are moving into a different timeline frequency, and this is why it is affecting the Egyptian people so much — because of the wave energy that is surrounding the pyramid and the entirety of Egypt. This is what has the people worked up. This is not happening elsewhere because the Great Pyramid is like a great motor. That is why there is such chaos there: to bring about complete change so that there will be alignment with the new timeline.

What you are saying is very true, and what they are doing is laying the road for the new consciousness. It will go all the way to Russia, China, India, and many other places where the people are much more open.

So it is like a ripple effect, then? People can align themselves with it, and everyone who is ready for it will pick up on those energy frequencies?

Exactly. Especially all the other pyramids that are in complete alignment to this pyramid and all the lines that connect them. There will be great changes in the coming years. Now we will go into the DNA part, and you will have some questions later. Thank you, family. This is Akhenaton.

✳   ✳   ✳

Crystal Activation, the Pineal Gland, and Atomic Accelerator

Hello, this is Saint Germain. We are sending greetings from home, for we are with you. We are so happy that many have taken part in this program of bringing light into the world in their own ways. You are doing whatever you need to do to bring the light in in your own way, and we say congratulations! Thank you for this, for you will be remembered for this gift. It will be in your akash. How may we support you today, dear family?

Do the crystals in our bodies become activated when we reach certain stages of maturity along our paths?

This is true, and there are two aspects of this. One aspect is our dormant crystals, energy lying as dormant energy. The other aspect is a gift from a higher being when you raise your vibration to a certain level. Both of these are being activated at this time.

You may have heard about calcite in the body, in the brain, and this is being activated. It is called biomineralization, a process in which the minerals in the body are being fully activated to support the ascension process. Human beings must activate at least 33 percent of the minerals in their bodies for ascension. So 33 percent of the cells must be fully in contact with minerals to generate light in order to propel them out of the present reality and into a higher reality. When this happens, their auric fields become a beautiful silvery white. When you see a picture of a saint from ancient times, you will see an aura around his or her head. This aura appears because 33 percent of the saint's body has been fully recalibrated and activated to hold this crystalline consciousness.

You can also consciously ask for the crystals in your body to be activated. This is like a time lock. Many time locks are now being activated. But you must be ready for this. You must know about these things to ask for them. Similarly, you can ask for the minerals in your body to be fully awakened to their true consciousness. You may have heard the expression, "The entire cosmos lives inside of you." You are a microcosm of the macrocosm. You may know this theoretically. How do you experience it? You must ask for this activation inside of you every day when you awaken.

Ask for the microcosm of the macrocosm that you hold inside you to be fully activated so that you can experience the macrocosm, the infinity that you are working with throughout the day. Make it a point to work with this and ask for it. You could say how you intend to activate and fully utilize the biominerals in your body so that you fully experience your complete dimensional self.

This requires lots of work. The process will start naturally. But now, for you, we suggest that you begin working to activate the pineal gland. This is situated at the back of the head, behind the third eye and behind the crown chakra. You may want to place your finger there now, and then breathe there. You will be able to activate it. It is activated through stillness, through breathing there. Feel the energy expanding, and feel your whole brain filling with beautiful white light.

We ask you to work with biomineralization and with activating the pineal gland because only when you begin activating these will you be able to feel their interdimensional, or quantum, aspects. Biominerals are like a chemical that transforms something into something else, as in a biology or chemistry experiment. You combine two chemicals, and transformation takes place. A new energy is created. This new energy stays inside of you. You must call for this and work with it daily.

I also have a device called an atomic accelerator, which I have offered to humanity, but very few people know about it. This device has the capacity to send high-voltage energy. In your meditation time, call on me, and I will be there with you. I ask that this device be placed under your seat. I will send the energy appropriate to activate and raise your consciousness, and when that happens, your DNA will be activated. Use these three techniques: biomineralization, working with the pineal gland, and the atomic accelerator.

[Archangel Metatron: The atomic accelerator is a portable device used by ascended masters, especially Saint Germain, to support and raise someone's vibration. When you ask Saint Germain to support you to raise your vibration with this machine, he will come etherically and place this device under your seat. It looks like a small box, maybe one foot by one foot, which has some spinning, spiral gadgets that send vibrations into your body through your chakra column, starting at the base chakra.

As you know, masters know your level of vibration, and what you need at a particular time. So if you were to ask Saint Germain to raise your vibration so that you could ascend right now, it is unlikely that he would oblige. Rather, you would get whatever vibration you needed at that time.

In your meditation, ask for the atomic accelerator to be placed underneath you to raise your vibration higher. How much energy you receive and how much vibration it downloads are controlled completely by Saint Germain.

There are also etheric temples located in Mount Shasta and used by Master Adama. These temples have large atomic accelerators where energy is pumped into people individually or in groups who go to the Temple of Ascension there. You can ask to be taken to the chamber where the great atomic accelerator is located. We recommend that you use this regularly. In a few weeks, you will be able to feel the difference. But this is not given easily or freely. It is through your dedication to the light or pure intention to serve the light that this gift is given. The first time you ask, you may not feel anything. But if you are determined and have purity of heart, you will see your wishes granted.

One question to clarify this: So both the atomic accelerator and the temple in Mount Shasta are on different dimensions, and there is nothing physical about any of this?

This is on another dimension, but it is a reality. The atomic accelerator is made of many crystals and also many minerals. It has been used on other planets and in other times. It can also support in raising the vibration of the whole planet. If all of you asked collectively during your meditation times for the masters to place the accelerator in support of Mother Earth's vibration, you would be able to see a change in Mother Earth's vibration. Some of your storms would be reduced. Many of Mother Earth's movements could be shifted or altered, including the intensity of earthquakes. So individually, you can work with the accelerator, or a group of people can ask collectively.

This is done through intention setting and by asking?

Yes. For example, you may want to light a candle, be in a meditative state, and ask from the purity of your heart for the masters to come and place the atomic accelerator underneath you.]

Working with Additional Chakras

All of you are very aware of the energy points called chakras in your bodies. We mainly talk about seven chakras, but there are many more. There are specific energy centers in your hands, in your kneecaps, and on your toes. You are free to work with activating these chakras, for they hold certain higher vibrations to support you. Ask Spirit to activate these chakras for you.

When you start working with these chakras, you start remembering your true nature. You will come back to you, your true nature. This is the key that you must work with at this time. You must work toward coming back to your true nature, and you will start remembering. This will take you back to the time when you were a child to remember when you were just starting to crawl like a baby and to walk. At that time, all the chakras were fully aligned, open, and alive. Then they slowly started closing down. Now you may ask for these to start being activated.

Bilocation

We may also say this to both of you. To raise your consciousness, to activate your DNA, it is time that both of you give intention in meditation to bilocate. Go into the ashram of Shambhala, the ashram of Adama, or the temple in Telos to work with the masters there. This initiation was done in Egypt and other places in ancient times. Now you do not have to have the initiation because everyday living is an initiation, which is a great gift to all of you.

Now you may go directly using bilocation, but you must ask for it. You must send your energy body first. Work with Sananda to do this: Say, "I am connecting with my fifth-dimensional lightbody." Sananda is one of the great masters supporting this, along with Archangel Metatron. Metatron heads the spiritual hierarchy of this planet, and Sananda works with him. Sananda is the one who can bring in this dimensional lightbody. He has an ashram, and you may go there.

I would like to find out about the golden-and-white astral Temple of Lord Kasala over the entire Holy Land. Is there anything you can tell me about this?

There is not just one temple; there are at least three temples connected with each other, and one of the temples is on Hawaii. But we suggest that you both work with one of the ashrams located in the land of Ghana, for that is an etheric portal of Lady Portia. She can support you in bringing more of the permanent goddess energy and also with cleansing on a higher level.

Opening the Third Eye and the Heart

Will connection with the mighty I Am presence also help with the expansion of consciousness?

Yes, it is true, but the idea of working with DNA is that we can experience more of the I Am presence. The I Am presence is part of you; that is how you are alive. How do you bring this more into your body so that you can feel the I Am presence? The idea of this book itself is to raise consciousness so that you can download more of this higher-level energy.

One key factor is that you must fully develop your third eye so that your soul completely experiences your physical presence, living in your physical body. It is very critical that you do this work. It is the third eye that tells the higher self what experiences it has at a particular level. The idea here is to integrate your soul with your physical body. The soul does not teach people how to integrate it; this is done through the third eye. The third eye becomes like the little man for the soul. The more the soul experiences, the better the soul will get the message. So it is critical that you work with the third eye. To do this, there is an exercise called pumping.

Visualize a small pump, similar to that used for taking blood pressure, and squeeze it. It becomes tighter. Imagine you have a small pump in your third eye, and you pump it gently. You must do this very gently so that the third eye opens more and more, and you will be able to see.

If your mind is not clear, you will see more and more of the dark forces because dark forces are part of the subconscious mind itself. We see the astral aspects of ourselves and others, and this can be frightening. If you are clear, that does not happen. You must make sure that you work with the masters initially so that you will be able to see more of the deeper, higher aspects rather than just connecting with the lower astral aspects.

Once you get used to it, you can integrate using the pump technique with the heart chakra. But the heart chakra pumping does not really work as well, because the degree the heart chakra can open has a lot to do with past lives and the fear that we have brought from other lifetimes.

What about the threefold higher heart chakra, the threefold flame?

Every human heart contains this. You must develop it very carefully, in equal proportions, so that you do not supersede another. It is important to connect to the first three rays of God: the will of God, the power of God, and the love of God. You can work with three masters for this: Master Elmore, Master David Joshua Stone, and Master Serapis Bey.

[Archangel Metatron: Master El Morya is the master of the first ray of God. Master David Joshua Stone is the master of the second ray, love and wisdom. And Master Serapis Bay is master of the third ray, the will of God. Call for them every day to work with you, especially with Master El Morya, so that your will is the will of God and the will of your own beloved soul. Ask for an anchoring of this energy into you. The color of this ray is beautiful red.

You can do this in your sleep. Before you go to sleep, call forth Master El Morya: "I call forth the full essence and the presence of Master El Morya, and I ask to anchor only the positive, loving, and benevolent energies of the first ray of God into me." It is a beautiful red color coming down, not just through your soul star chakra but from your tenth chakra, coming down and coursing through your entire chakra column and going deep into the ground. It needs to be done for only two to three minutes a day. Work with this every day. It will give you courage and determination to continue on your spiritual path. It can also bring you into alignment with your soul's purpose — that is, why you were born.

Master Kuthumi was the previous master of the second ray; now this position has been taken by Master David Joshua Stone. The essence of this ray is the wisdom and love of God. The color of this ray is a beautiful metallic blue, and again, you can see this ray coming down through your tenth chakra and flowing through the chakra column deep into the ground. You can do this any time. The more you work with this ray, the more it will open up your wisdom and your heart's compassion and love.

Serapis Bay is the master of the third ray. The color is a beautiful, soft golden color. Ask for this master's energy to come through, coming down into your tenth chakra and flowing through the chakra column. The essence of this ray is manifestation. You use the wisdom and the love of your soul to manifest the will of God in your present-day world. We need all three rays. All inventions came from these three rays.]

I suggest that you do not stop at the threefold flame, for the heart chakra has twenty-four chambers. So we ask you to go into the deeper chambers, and in each chamber, create a sacred space every morning. You enter into this sacred space, and this is your inner sanctum. Nothing can harm you there. When you are in that inner sanctum and make a statement from there, it becomes much more powerful. When you wake up in the morning, give an intention. You can set the intention from the sacred chamber of the deepest part of your heart, the twenty-forth chamber, and you will be coming from a very high plane.

So you are meeting your higher self, where it can come and meet you?

Exactly. From this place, nothing can harm you, nothing can touch you. Thank you. This is Saint Germain.

✳   ✳   ✳

The Consciousness of Different Lands

My dear family, this is Gaia. I am sorry to interrupt you. The land you walk has consciousness. You are very aware of this. Certain lands can help to raise your consciousness. You might ask, "Certain lands and people living on those lands have higher vibrations. Why is this so?" Of course, there are many reasons for this because of the karmic energy and how land shapes your belief systems. So you must ask, "How does the land where I live affect me presently in my consciousness?" There is a secret there. We encourage both of you to look into that secret, and that is also part of your DNA. When you are fully connected with the land and there is great support for it, the work of activating the DNA is 50 percent complete. We ask you to work with this aspect of the consciousness of land.

[Archangel Metatron: Everything is alive and has consciousness, even the land. If you are in resonance with the land where you are living, then the land will support you. It is similar to a home. As soon as you enter some homes, they feel good. If you were to move into that place, it would support you. Learn how to work with every consciousness. Ask whether your consciousness is in resonance with the consciousness of that place. If it is, you will benefit and that place will benefit.

Land has different pockets of consciousness. Some places have very little consciousness. But higher-vibrational beings can simply shift that and raise the consciousness by anchoring their energy just by being there. When they walk, the energy goes from their feet into the ground, and the ground will retain the new configuration.

When you go to a new area, ask, "Does this land support me in my new reality? Or is there another land that will support me in my new reality?" Many people say, "I am here. I cannot move." But that is a choice. The land will communicate with you because you are of the land. You become the land. And Gaia, being your mother, has only love for you. When you connect to her with your heart, she will speak to your heart.]

It is not only the place where you live but also the country itself, for these affect your belief systems, and your belief system is a huge factor in raising your consciousness. For example, if I were to take someone out of Jerusalem or out of Israel and place him or her in a faraway country, how would the person's mind be? How would this person's thinking be? It would be very different.

The electromagnetic field energy inside of your body would not match the electromagnetic field emitted by the new country. This is a key factor because it affects your thinking, the clarity of your mind, your emotions, and your feelings. From emotions and feelings, there is will — how you act. So this is a very important thing to consider at this time. We encourage you to look into this.

Why do you think people go to Israel with sacred hearts and sacred minds? Why do they feel so touched by the land? When they are on the Temple Mount, why do you think it touches their hearts so deeply? There is energy in the land, and it talks to your DNA. There is energy in the land that talks to your cells. When you go to the tomb of Jesus or to any holy place in Israel, you will say, "I feel good. I feel connection." What is this connection? You are remembering more. You are absorbing it. The land affects you, along with the experience created by the master who walked there. The land plays a very important part. So we want you to examine how the land affects your consciousness.

[Archangel Metatron: How does land affect human consciousness? If you were to move to a place where there is heavy density energy in the ground, it would affect your consciousness. Look at Palestine and Israel. Look at any of the conflict zones. Why is there no peace? Why is there so much hatred? People were born in that land and carry the consciousness of the land, especially when they die. Their energy is not released when they die. Their bodies carry all their negative energies, like hatred, into the ground. What affects you affects others too. Do you want to have better citizens? Heal the land.]

Could I ask about the land where I live, the United States, which is a new land, fairly recently settled by Caucasian people and particularly where I live in New England. What advice would you have about that?

You must ask why your soul chose to live in that particular place.

Is the energy completed there? Is there a specific reason for you to be living there? It is no accident that you chose this particular place out of all the places in America. You must ask, "What is the appropriateness of it, and is the lesson learned? Is the energy completed? Is the energy integrated? Or is there any other higher-vibration energy place where I could move that will fit in with the new reality that I am creating at this time?" Only you can answer these questions.

One of the holy ceremonies in Israel is the wedding ceremony. Every wedding ceremony is holy, for it is a union of two beings coming together. But they have a sacred tradition in Israel that in the wedding ceremony they break a glass and stomp on it. Then they say, "Let my hand fall off if I forget Jerusalem."

This symbolizes that this land is a portal; it is a holy, sacred land. Never forget its holiness, because through this land, you will be able to reclaim and remember your godliness, your connection with the Father/Mother Creator. The ancient ones knew the sacredness of this land. They tell people, "Even if you get married and have a family, never forget your connection to this land, because it is through this land connection that you remember more of your true self, your godliness."

Before I go, I will tell you one more thing. You can connect with me more easily and with the land where you are living during the time of the full moon. There is much vitality during the full moon. The land becomes much more alive because of the high intensity of the light. This light goes into the sea where many creatures, organisms, and bacteria need it for reproduction. They need it for the survival of the ocean.

In the same way, many bacteria, worms, and other beings living deep underground are also part of the low-batch system for Mother Earth. The full moon supports the regeneration of these beings. The land and water are more energized. If you can tune into and match vibrations during this time, you will immediately raise your vibration.

[Archangel Metatron: The full moon sends powerful beams of energetic light into the Earth, supporting all beings, including beings in the ocean, such as microbes. There are organisms deep in the ocean, deep in the forest, deep under the mountains, that support humanity and support Gaia. They keep the ocean currents moving, and they have many other functions. It is the nature of life to multiply and continue, and to do so, life needs light. Deep in the mountains and deep in the ocean, there is no light. So Mother Moon provides this light for their continuation and reproduction. This is the true purpose of the Moon.]

In many traditions, you are encouraged to meditate outside, sitting on the ground, so that you are able to pull in the energy from the ground. Many lamas meditate outside, even if it is cold. You can immediately raise your vibration and bring in a sense of centeredness and balance when meditating outside.

This is Gaia. If you call on me, I will support you.

✳   ✳   ✳

Expanding the Consciousness

Hello, this is Pythagoras. Most of you know me as Master Kuthumi, but let me speak as Pythagoras. As you know, I formulated methods of sacred geometry with the precision of mathematics using sound. We ask you to look into the Pythagorean theories, for there are some secrets there that can help you open your minds.

How do you raise your consciousness? This happens when you expand your mind. How do you expand your mind? As children do, through books. Children are able to expand and open their minds and explore new concepts that books present, opening the imagination of the mind. The same is true when you read high-energy books with the potential to expand the mind. Suppose you read *The Book of Enoch*. It is a challenging book, for does it not make you think?

[Archangel Metatron: How can you figure out which books are right for you to read? Use your feeling body. It is like going to a crystal shop. You do not buy a crystal unless the crystal speaks to you. The same is true with books. Ask your feeling body to support you. Everything has wisdom. "Which is the book I need at this present time to support me in what I am trying to become?" Work with your feeling body. Take your hand and pass it over each book to see where you feel higher vibration — more energy, a tingling sensation, or warmth — and work from there.]

We also encourage you to look into Pythagorean theories, theorems, and sacred geometry. Why do you think Master Jesus, many Essene brothers, and many other masters went to different lands and sought out the theories and teachings of Pythagoras? We encourage you to look into that.

✳   ✳   ✳

Foods

This is Saint Germain. The Maya knew about the sacred aspects of food.

[Archangel Metatron: The Maya understood that you are what you eat. This is also the basis of Ayurvedic medicine. The Maya were an advanced culture who actually came from Atlantis, so they knew which foods would support them. They mostly ate foods that contained their full life essence, taken freshly from the farm, and they cultivated their food using thought-production methods. They imbued the highest vibrational thoughts of love and light into their crops.

When the food is full of light force, you need to consume only small quantities of it. Now you have to eat more because there is no light force in your food. It is a simple message. When there is light force, there is naturally more life energy. The Maya knew this. They also knew the vibrations of different vegetables. So they always did what was best to support them, to maintain and raise their vibration.

For example, the corn was an important staple of the Mayan diet. Corn contains high-vibrational energy, for corn was a gift from the stars. When it is picked ripe from the plant, it has the highest vibration.]

The Maya cultivated food with the movements of the planets and stars. Food of one month will not have the same consciousness, or the same level of energy, as food from a different month. This also plays a big role, because food is very critical in the activation of the DNA. [See Appendix 2: The Masculine and Feminine Aspects of Foods and When to Eat Them.]

Now Creator will speak to you briefly before we go.

※　　※　　※

The Passion of Creation

My dear, precious family, this is Creator. What is the most joyful thing that you can have in your life? It is the joy of creation. When you create something, it is so joyful. It is coming from you. It is so joyful to see other creators creating this new reality. There is the potential for a book, for a workshop, for teaching higher truths to people. This is how creation is made. You own this. You feel it in your body. Every cell communicates it, and then you are in your passion. When you are in your passion, you are experiencing God every moment.

When you wake up in the morning, along with your other prayers and meditations, ask to activate the energy of love and the vibration of passion. Just imagine that you are living in passion 24/7. What do you think you can achieve in life? What if all the people in the world were living in passion, doing what they loved the most? When you are in passion, there is beauty. So when you seek passion, you are seeking God — every moment.

There is a certain truth that can create a lot of passion. If you eat chocolates, it can give you somewhat of a kick, somewhat of a high. Suppose you take a drug such as cocaine. It gives you a kick. It makes you high for a short time. In the same way, there are certain foods, certain smells, a liter of water that can also raise your level of vibration. It has been said that ayahuasca is the vine of the Gods, and it can also elevate your consciousness. We are not talking about ayahuasca every day. What we are saying is there is much bounty in nature that can be used to raise your consciousness, simple things. So we encourage you to look into that.

[Archangel Metatron: For example, freshly picked corn and pumpkin, picked right from the soil, and cooked immediately; or a small, ripe tomato grown without any chemicals; or green peas picked from the plant can support you very much. Avocado is a very healthy food, for its masculine and feminine energies are balanced. Dates support you with nourishment but also with high-vibrational energy. A small banana picked right from the tree is excellent. Any food that is grown on the body of Mother Earth, like a watermelon or squash, is good. They all carry very high-vibrational energy.]

When you drink water in the morning, water has the capacity to expand your consciousness. You can say, "When I drink this water, it goes into my body, and the energy of passion will fully awaken me. I awaken a childlike innocence in which I am fully alive." As you call your beloved I Am presence, integrating and protecting it, in the same way, call for the energies of passion, aliveness, and childlike innocence to be fully activated.

Blessings, this is Creator.

❋   ❋   ❋

More on Foods

Seekers, this is Pythagoras. I will tell you some of the ingredients used in the food that was served in our mystery schools. One of the ingredients we always used was olives. Why do you think olives are honored everywhere? We used whole olive leaves. We had a mixture of many things. Olives were just one of the ingredients. Another was mustard seeds, and another was the fig. But there were also some secret ingredients added into this.

One secret thing that is especially good for awakening the heart is rose hips. Perhaps you would like to include rose petals in your daily cooking. How would this affect your body chemistry?

Rose petals have the capacity to touch certain nerve centers in your body. So we want you to look into that. Maybe you would like to experiment. Take a glass of water, put in some fresh rose petals, and leave them in the water for some time, perhaps a few hours. Then drink it, and write down your experience a few hours afterward. How do you feel? Do you feel any changes? You probably will not feel anything immediately, but in a few days, you will see. If you drink this every day, you will see a slow shifting of your consciousness.

How do you shift your consciousness? When you disengage from the drama of everyday life! Just imagine that your mind is taken away from all the dramas, all the little petty things you think are important or bother you. What happens? Most human beings spend 90 percent of their time on worthless things. Only 10 percent is spent on productive things. The rest is mind chatter. Humans create their lives with only 10 percent of their energy. The other things are not necessary, the thoughts going to their minds, coming from the subconscious and running through their subconscious minds continuously. Your subconscious mind runs your life. Teach people, "If you want to change your life, change your subconscious." This is one of the main teachings I give.

[Archangel Metatron: As with everything else, you need to be constantly working with and aware of how your subconscious is affecting you. One simple way of changing your subconscious is visualization. A picture is worth a thousand words. The subconscious does not differentiate between right and wrong. It just produces whatever is put there. So when an image, a symbol, or a clear picture enters your conscious mind, your subconscious mind will absorb it, and there will be healing.

When you want to create something, visualize it as best as you can, and every day you will see it more and more. It will become clearer and clearer. It is being imprinted on your subconscious mind. This is why we encourage you to have good thoughts all the time. Let them become a natural part of you. High-vibrational thoughts are much stronger than other thoughts. They will become a part of you. The new thoughts will be imprinted into your subconscious mind.

The subconscious mind does not differentiate. It just produces what is put there. You control how you express yourself and what you believe and feel. High-vibrational thoughts can be combined with images, for pictures can have a lasting effect. This is why sacred geometry and symbols are so powerful. They go directly into the subconscious mind and bring healing.]

Also, your diet is similar. It changes your chemical reactions. So we encourage you to work with the rose petals to see whether rose-petal water supports you. Do an experiment for ten days. In Thailand and other places, people have detoxification programs. They do not use rose petals. They use different berries. After a certain number of days, the participants are only given berry drinks to live on for three days, and they come out perfectly fine. Even the waste generated from their bodies turns a different color. Their bodies start to detox. When the body detoxifies, the mind is in a much clearer space. You will not have the old baggage or the old-thinking energy dragging you. If you analyze your thoughts before and after such a process, you will see how much mental baggage you are generating on a daily basis.

This is why it has been said, "Your mind is a creator of everything, so you must be consciously aware of your mind every moment. Where do you spend your energy?" Work with rose petals. Use fresh rose petals. The best effect is obtained if you pick the petals directly from the bush. You can remove the petals without taking the whole flower; it is less disruptive to the rose bush. But ask the rose, "Please, when I pick you, I ask that the essence of this rose be in this petal and be used for the highest benefit of the highest good for me." You are asking for the rose to participate in your awakening process.

Our students also ate a lot of papaya. Do you like papaya? It is very tasty. Why do you think papaya is called the food of the gods? Papaya has one of the highest levels of all vitamins of any food. It can support you. I know papaya is difficult to obtain in many places. So work with roses if you can't find it. Put the petals in a glass of water overnight, and then drink it.

You can also write in a journal for two weeks. [Archangel Metatron: Write about your evolution, your progress, how you are working, and how you are healing. Unless you keep a journal and keep track, you lose track. Journal about your thoughts, feelings, and emotions. How did you respond to this particular situation? What was your reaction? Was it loving? Whose thoughts are coming into your mind? Are they your thoughts, thoughts from the collective matrix, or are they being picked up from your subconscious mind? This is why journaling is important, to see every experience and who you were while the experience was happening.]

When preparing our food, we also energized it with pure gold. Gold has the capacity to energize everything. Gold is the personification of the energy of God. Why do you think we have so much gold on this planet? If you were to condense God's love, that would be gold. People wear gold jewelry around their necks with pendants falling on their heart chakras so that their heart chakras will open. You can energize anything with gold, even a glass of water.

Ayurvedic practitioners use gold frequently. Gold has a capacity to heal injuries of the spinal column. Gold can also remove negative energy if it is used for its true purpose. It can expand your consciousness. When people meditate on the Creator, or Father/Mother God, this is mostly gold energy, gold light, coming and filling you up.

[Archangel Metatron: Being in the presence of gold can create higher-vibrational energy. With the proper intent, ask for gold to emanate energy, for the energy of gold is the energy of the heart of God. This only works when you ask with pure intention. If you were to place a glass of water on a gold coin for some time, the water would become charged with the essence of gold.

Despite the fact that gold may have been combined with many metals, it is still very much alive. Work with gold. Make a thin golden helmet, and wear it over your head, touching your crown chakra. Breathe through it. In six months, you will learn who you are. This is what Mayan priests did. Gold has the property and the capacity to transform. Gold can also help you remember who you are and why you came here. Placing gold under the pillow when you sleep can create higher dreams.]

We mixed, we prayed, we blessed, and we energized with gold for a few days, depending on what we wanted to create. We gave you some of the ingredients but not all, because these ingredients are not available.

But we don't eat the flowers. I mean, we don't drink the petals of the rose, right?

Correct. But some cultures still use the petals in cooking because they open one organ [the third eye] in the body. Look into all the aspects of olives, papayas, and figs.

[Archangel Metatron: All of these foods are higher-vibrational beings who have been brought here to support humanity. They are not from this planet. Combine them with hemp to create emotional healing. They have the capacity to bring you into balance, to prolong life, make the sexual drive stronger, and improve general well-being. You could live on just these foods for long periods of time. These are considered the fruits of the gods. We ask you to experiment to see which can support you.

The foods we suggest can create more energy, more vibrancy in your life, and a sense of well-being. Hemp has been made into a powdery form that you can boil and drink. Taking a bath with hemp is very good. Hemp will become quite normal and without any legal prohibitions in the future. It will be sold freely all over the world, for people will understand the purpose of hemp and why it is there. It is such a beautiful plant, in support of humanity.]

And mustard seeds?

Mustard seeds. Why did Jesus say, "If you had faith even as small as a mustard seed, you could say to this mountain, 'Move from here to there,' and it would move. Nothing would be impossible'"? Why not something else? His words contain layers of meaning.

When Buddha was traveling, a lady came to him and said, "My only child died."

Buddha said, "Oh, my beloved sister, go and bring me mustard from a house that has not experienced death, and then I will revive your dead child." Why did Buddha use mustard seed?

[Archangel Metatron: It is a medicinal plant. Mustard seeds can have many effects on the body. It directly affects your pineal gland and third eye. It can also help your thymus and your kidneys. Mustard is a very beneficial plant. Mustard seeds can be utilized in many ways to enhance your well-being.]

I will leave it at this time. This is Pythagoras.

✻ ✻ ✻

The Lotus

Hello, my friends. I am the Crystal Skull. Today, I am sitting next to the crystal skull of Akhenaton, which was presented as a gift to Rae. I always ask him to take me when he channels. If you want to know the secret of having a higher consciousness, it is very simple: Look to some of the dietary habits of the Essenes. How were they able to attain higher consciousness? They lived in very difficult circumstances and conditions. Through constant practice, they were able to develop a higher vibration. Master Jesus and many other beings of light studied with the Essenes.

[Archangel Metatron: The Essenes ate figs, dates, mustard seeds, and olives. Olives produce life-enhancing energy. Why do you think olive leaves were used as a commemorative, placed on the head of Olympic victors? It is a high-vibrational plant that comes from another place. The diet of the Essenes included these foods, along with small amounts of meat, particularly small birds, such as pigeons. If you want to lose a lot of weight, go on a diet of olives with dates and figs. This is a very good weight trimmer.]

The Essenes were able to understand the importance of food in raising their vibration. Some of their elders perfected this technique. Their diet helped them clear their subconscious and their minds.

I will also give another secret to you, which you may not have thought of: the lotus flower. A lotus is a very significant flower. It has a very high vibration and consciousness. It always grows in the muddy slime, but it is always shining toward the light. It is a symbol of Buddhism: You can stand in the middle of the dirty world, and at the same time, your consciousness remains very high.

Lotus roots are very special. Look into that. The flower truly teaches us something. It offers its full entirety, including its body, to raise your consciousness. When you see a lotus, it evokes a memory and a good feeling inside. It evokes beauty and God within you. God is beauty.

New Children: the Magdalene, and the Sun

I will reveal a confidential secret concerning the Children of the Lotus. These are the New Children to come. I will reveal one more secret: the Children of the Magdalene will be born as well. Close your eyes. Can you feel the energy, the truth of what I have said? The Magdalene Children are coming, and the Lotus Children are coming. These children will start being born by the end of next year in China, and they will also be born in Japan and Israel.

There will be very few, but they will be very special children. They will know their role from a young age. These children will carry a higher vibration, the vibration of the triple goddess. So look for Magdalene Children. Many people will not be able to understand this. The Children of the Sun will also be born.

Remember that what you are doing is making a road for all these new children. Before brother Jesus was born, his grandmother and his support system worked for many hundreds of years to prepare the way for the master to come. Without that support system, Jesus could not have accomplished his mission. In the same way, you are creating the support system for these New Children — the Sun Children, Lotus Children, and Magdalene Children — to be born on the planet.

I am giving you very advanced information that has never been revealed. We are relaying this information to you [the questioners] because we feel that what you are doing has an important purpose, and we want to say thank you. This is our exchange of energy, this information to you.

We can contact some of these children already?

[Archangel Metatron: You must prepare yourselves for this contact. Otherwise, you will not recognize them. To prepare, you must call them forth through the power of your intention, using the energy of thought forms and the love of your heart. When the children appear, you will often not know who they are unless you are open. They will only reveal themselves if your intentions are pure — in the highest good. They need to protect themselves, for darkness would try to kill them; they carry higher-vibrational energy. So many of these children are now being protected.

So we really have four different types of New Children: Children of the Lotus, Children of the Sun, the Golden Children, and the Magdalene Children. Is that correct?

Yes. But each carries different specific vibrations for certain purposes.

Can you elaborate on their purposes?

We will just say that one is for Earth healing. One is for healing all Earth and the inner children of the world. One is to bring an understanding between adults and children. And one is to open up the imagination, to have a childlike imagination, and encourage open-mindedness. The world will discover more through them.]

What do we do with the roots of the lotus?

If you can find a complete lotus plant growing, ask its permission whether it is willing to share its roots, which is to share its life. [Archangel Metatron: Ask for permission, and you can ask the lotus to share its wisdom and love with you. Communicate with the lotus from your heart. Remember that you are a part of all: Everything is part of you, and you are all supporting each other.]

In olden times, it was soaked in olive oil for a few days. The roots were used as a condiment, the way you use pickles. The root can also be soaked in rose or sandalwood oil and placed on different parts of the body as a healing balm and for pulling energy. It is like putting on a Band-Aid. When you pull off a Band-Aid, all the dirty dust that was on the wound comes off.

But it does that energetically.

Yes, it does this energetically.

Which oil are we using?

Olive oil. The Essenes had many secrets, because they were master alchemists. They transformed their bodies.

We ask you to work with these children. These children are all starbeings. The Magdalene Children, the Sun Children, and the Lotus Children are starbeings, and they are all highly evolved masters who will do miracles. In fifty or sixty years, people will not give too much importance to miracles, for miracles will become not normal but naturally occurring events. They will become natural things. People will live intuitively and synchronistically.

For example, when you ask for support of the gods and you give intention to cocreate with the Creator, what happens? You follow the synchronicity, and serendipity happens. This is how spirit communicates and guides you. This will become the norm in the future — people living through synchronicity after giving intention to cocreate with Spirit. You will know what to do and when to do it.

Thank you for your valuable time and energy in this project. We wish you well. We are always here in service to humanity.

Chapter 9

Activating Your Genetic Light Codes

July 25, 2013

Saint Germain, Archangel Metatron, Sananda, the Divine Mother Amma, Abraham and Sarah, Master Thoth, and Pythagoras

This is Saint Germain. In this chapter, we are going to talk about dreaming big to manifest a new reality — teaching other people to activate their genetic light codes.

You know the akashic records as a library of every life experience you have ever had, but the akashic records are much more than that. They also record your origin — where you originated. Your DNA originated in the Pleiades. We ask you to start activating your genetic light codes.

[Archangel Metatron: This is done through intention. Call this forth. This is called empowered living. The time has come to start working on yourselves. This is called rewiring the physical body. Rewiring is not done by spirit but by you. It is done by asking and setting intentions.

This is very important. Humans are being rewired. You are doing it yourselves. It is part of your natural evolutionary process. You are evolving to the point where you can begin reconnecting all twelve strands of DNA and even activate some of the higher chakras, which you never even thought you had. You need to work on yourself and ask for these codes to be activated.

You have recently been given the power codes of Earth, published in the May edition of *Sedona Journal of Emergence!* (See Appendix III.) There are so many codes coming out. You must activate these codes — the Metatronic codes, the angelic codes, the Arcturian codes. You must also activate the genetic codes inside yourself. What would you discover? That you came from Source. That is your code, the primary genetic code. You are Adam. You are carrying the Adam code. You have got work to do, just like everybody else.]

This is an incredible opportunity: to go back and remember your true nature, for in an instant, you can go back to experience your natural self. [Archangel Metatron: This is done through intention, being, and experiencing. In that moment when you remember and you are able to be in a state of being and experiencing, naturally you are in a different cycle of time. You are not who you were a moment ago. You are experiencing. And through experience, you are becoming your own being. Beingness is happening this moment. So you are not who you were before. This is a new reality.

The purpose of life is only that: to be in a place of beingness all the time. It will take some time. It will take some practice. But everyone is coming to the place where they can be and know this in a physical body as an experience.]

Your natural self is your original self, and this original self is recorded in your DNA and in your akash. You may go back to your origin and tap into this. When you go back to your natural self, you are automatically activating DNA by raising your consciousness. Your DNA will command your genes to activate.

You can also activate light codes inside Mother Earth's body in the same way. [Archangel Metatron: This is done by being and forming the intention. When this activation is done, it helps Mother Earth tremendously. And because Mother Earth is part of your body, it naturally affects you too.] These are compatible with your personal light codes. There is a light code inside all creatures of Earth; to Mother Earth, you are one of her creatures.

You have light codes within you of your Pleiadian DNA, the light codes of Mother Earth, and also the light codes of your star heritage, where your dual higher self started living its existence. You also have light codes from the country where you were born.

All of you are aware of the Father/Mother Creator energy coming more and more into the planet. You will see more ideas and more channeled material coming through about how important it is to work from the consciousness of this energy. [Archangel Metatron: There are many examples of people of the world coming together, of the world becoming smaller, and of more bridges being built. You will see this through social media.

You might say that America is at odds with China, or China is at odds with Japan. This may be true on the political level, but young people view this very differently. Let these young people grow up and be in important places, such as in the medical field, insurance, fine arts, or banking. They will change the system. They will be in politics. They will be in economics. They will also be in teaching positions. They will change everything, and you will see it happening in your lifetime.]

We ask you not to refer to the Creator as Father but as Father/Mother Creator. The great brother Jesus and Mary Magdalene brought these two energies together as the unified Christ energy. Their combined consciousness sealed the planet with the Christ code. You can ask and tap into this Christ code, and you will connect with the very high energy of this unified consciousness.

When in Jerusalem, you can ask for the light code of Abraham and Sarah to be activated. They are anchored in the city of Jerusalem. This code will be activated simultaneously inside you. These beings, Abraham, Sarah, brother Yeshua [Jesus], and Mary Magdalene, also created a pod when they anchored these light codes.

If you [Mordechai] have ever wondered why you are part of the Jerusalem pod, it is because the light codes call you or talk to you. It is because you knew in your heart that you are part of this Christ/Magdalene pod. We are here to activate these light pod energies. This is done by calling forth energy, but most importantly, you must call forth light codes. This is very important work. You may also work with activating the light codes of your true original self and your Pleiadian DNA. You have to go back and work with Abraham and Sarah. You are special and hold much light.

Here is another thing you can do: We ask that the next time you go to your place of worship, wherever you are comfortable, ask for the activation of the light codes of the Flower of Life. Then send this energy into your place of worship, spread it to the entire country, and send it into the entire world. The Flower of Life has its own secret genetic code. You are one of the code carriers of that. You have work to do there. You have the capacity to bring this into fruition and then teach people.

Disconnecting from Martyr Consciousness

There are three phases of learning. Phase one is called crucifixion. Many people throughout the world are going through the agony of crucifixion at this time. Life is a mystery they do not understand. They will emerge through crucifixion, and then there will be resurrection. From resurrection, they will move into the freedom of ascension. Teach them how they can move into resurrection, and then from resurrection, show them how they can move into ascension. We ask you to do this very important work. This is very critical.

You must also ask to disconnect from the energy of martyr consciousness, which almost all of humanity carries. No more suffering to reach God. This consciousness is affecting every one of us at some deep level. You can disconnect from it this moment just by setting the intention. No more martyr consciousness.

[Archangel Metatron: Here are some examples of this: We all carry the cross of life's burdens on our backs. Some people are tied into life completely. They do not look at life as an everyday experience of joyful creation. They look at life as a burden. This is the time to break that body of consciousness.

History shows many examples of how you have to be a martyr to be enlightened. Buddha had to give up everything to be enlightened. Many masters in the past had to give up everything and live in a secluded place so that they could find God. This worked during that time.

Collectively, we carry the feeling that we have to be crucified so that we can find God, including your old pope (Pope John Paul II), who is now beatified. He used to beat himself up. He used to inflict pain on himself. Why? To redeem the sin of being human? That is what you have been taught. This is a collective cross that people carry. Release this.

Form the intention to connect with the Creator through joy, not through pain. Cut the cord of martyr consciousness, which you can only attain God through suffering, through giving up everything. Traditions in India and Tibet say the body is terrible: Give up sex. We say celebrate sex. Some Christians do the same thing. It does not make sense. If the body were so bad, why would the Creator have made such a magnificent thing? Why would God give you a body to enjoy, to play with? Play with sex, but let it come from the heart, not through lust, greed, or manipulation.]

Connect with this light code and state, "I disconnect from pain and suffering to find God." Ask to disconnect the world from the energy of martyr consciousness.

During his journey to the mountain, Abraham was a troubled soul. He would not look at his son. His son asked him, "Why do you keep walking in front of me, father?" He did not want to share his sorrow with his boy. He was crying. At a deep level, he knew that the loving God would not allow his son to be killed, yet his human mind still carried martyr consciousness. [Archangel Metatron: There is no actual biblical reference for this. The Bible is not always accurate or complete. It was written long after the events it records, and it was distorted and changed. We are giving you the actual facts that transpired.] This is just one story, but if you look at history books, Indian books, or Buddhist books, there is always martyr consciousness.

We ask you to break this matrix yourself. Then you can break the matrix in Israel for your people. It is certain that you are already at the forefront. We ask you to teach this to people. You may state, "I am a teacher." A teacher of what? "A teacher of the Creator." Do not be ashamed.

✳   ✳   ✳

Finding Your Path and Your Truth

This is Saint Germain with Metatron and Sananda. Everyone has an individual experience. Follow your own pattern, your own system. The road to God is an individual path. God honors each person's path. Follow your path and be. You might say, "This is the path I took. It is my path, and you must take your own path. You may ask me how I did it, but you must walk your own path."

When you read a book, how much does it speak to your heart? Do you feel expansion? Do you feel love? If you do, then use it. Otherwise, set it aside and continue on your own path.

Teach people that it is time. You learn from other people, but you must walk your own path and discover God in your own way

— through empowerment. When you follow, on some level, you are giving your power away.

You receive guidance, but you do the work and find your own inner truth. The ideal book or channeling would bring every reader back to his or her own truth. Work with this, and see if it supports you.

Breaking Free from Separating Definitions

How many definitions do you have? For example: night and day, tall and short, the four directions. If you are able to break free from the matrix of definitions of whatever you see, you will shift immediately. You will uplift your consciousness. You might say, "This is a mountain. This is a river. This is a fire. This is Earth." Become the mountain; be the fire. Everything is one in the highest power of DNA activation consciousness. You do not say, "This is my hand. These are my eyes." It is a collective "we."

When you are able to take out this separation, you will see an immediate upswing in consciousness. Of course, you will still work within the parameters of these differences in a world built in such a linear way. But you must look as an observer and not be drawn into it. If you say there is life and there is death, then of course you will perceive death. But if you look at life and its continuation, then your perception changes right away. When you are able to hold this, you will see an upswing in your consciousness. We ask that you work on removing this sense of separation every day.

Here is some homework for you. Jerusalem is a very high-spiritual place. We want to look at Jerusalem not as a separate, highly spiritual portal but as part of Mother Earth. Jerusalem is one with Mother Earth. Imagine a big circle with Jerusalem in the center, and see energy going through the center to everywhere else.

If someone asks you where you are from, should you say, "I am from Massachusetts (or wherever you reside)"? No. You should say, "I am from Earth. I am an Earth citizen." For example, you could say, "I am not from Jerusalem. I am an Earth citizen living at the present time in Massachusetts."

A Mantra

We also wish to give you an important mantra that you will want to try out. It is "Om ha hum."

What does it mean?

It means the combined force of unity consciousness. Now we have a very special guest today who wishes to deliver a very special message.

* * *

Activating and Disconnecting from Codes

This is the Divine Mother of Divine Mothers, Amma. We are talking about codes. Do you know you all have codes? Your father's code and your mother's code still affect you, along with your family's code. We ask you to release these codes, though not because your family is not important or your parents are not important. These codes are a direct influence on your reality and your thinking.

You acquired deeply held beliefs during your upbringing, and these are held in the cells of your body and your bones. Many of these codes were formed during your childhood when your consciousness was very different, and they still affect you. These codes no longer serve you. You may say, "I give intention today to remove and disconnect the codes of my father's and my mother's lineage. I honor them and bless them for the life they gave, but I will now create new codes for myself with Mother Earth and Father Sky."

Some of you have families; you have children. What kind of codes are you passing on to them? What kind of codes are you setting for your future lives? What you do right now is setting the codes for your future too. You can ask this question, "What kind of codes am I setting for my own future?" You could ask, "What kind of time capsule am I making for myself to open and receive in another lifetime?"

You made a code for the present time. Go back to that time when you made the code. You put something in your time capsule for the time you are now in. You prepared a time capsule for this lifetime. It is all in your akashic record. It is all inside you.

The year 2013 is a very critical time. [Archangel Metatron: Twenty thirteen is the first year of the new era for planet Earth and the new consciousness. After the shift, the new timeline is being drawn.] You have the capacity to completely redefine and re-create yourself because what you accomplish during the next four years — 2013 through 2016 — will be the template for this entire lifetime. There is a lot of work to be done.

There are techniques that you may work with to activate this new energy. Ask your guides what to do, for there are time capsules where you live that you can activate through your intention during your meditations. They will support you in anchoring the new conscious-ness in your beautiful land. Call for the codes, the blueprint, and the holographic imprint that some of the great forefathers of your land set. They had a vision for this land. Ask for this code to be activated now. You can do this.

The people of places such as Israel made a conscious choice to be born there again and again because this land is sacred and holy, and they returned to heal the land. Call for the codes set by the founding fathers of your nation. You can do this for all lands. This is why you were born in the country where you reside.

Have you ever wondered why the people of Israel are called the chosen people? They were chosen to carry the heavy load of bringing peace into the world. We ask you to activate these codes. All of this is tied into DNA — not only to your DNA, but also when you activate these codes, it activates the DNA in others.

✳   ✳   ✳

DNA Homework

This is Metatron with Sananda. Now I will give you some more home-work to do, part of the DNA work.

Each city, each country, has its own fifth-dimensional counterpart. You also have your fifth-dimensional lightbody, and you can call it forth. Imagine a beautiful lightbody. You are pulling this lightbody, pulling it into your higher consciousness and anchoring it into you. It is the same with your group meditation. You can pull in the higher vibrations, light codes, or the lightbody of the city of Jerusalem.

What you can do is mirror it or send it into the Escalia mirror, give intention to magnify it, and then lay it over the city of Jerusalem. What happens in Jerusalem affects the entire world. When there is peace and harmony in Jerusalem, there is peace and harmony in the entire world. Go and do the work. We are speaking of the DNA of Mother Earth.

✳ ✳ ✳

Quantum Aspects of DNA

This is Archangel Metatron.

When you say "collective DNA," we use the term "quantum DNA." When we are working in the quantum, it is not about seeing the DNA of individual people. The aim is to get a critical mass of people to run a quantum DNA. That's when it is going to happen.

Exactly, and when that happens, automatically the other person grows.

In other words, you just have to get to that critical mass of treating the next human being with human dignity?

It will happen. You are all creating this. Now we will give you one more riddle: You have guides, and your guides are working with you. You have many guides. Some come and go, but others stay with you. You also have a time capsule, and it codes with the guides. Some of these guides have been with you for this lifetime and other lifetimes on the planet and some have not. Ask for the time capsule code within you and your guides to be fully activated.

Where are the mother codes kept? Some of the important codes are in the palms of your hands. Others are on the soles of your feet. Others are beneath your kneecaps, on your shoulders, and on the back of your neck. There are some more, but you get the point.

We ask people not to slack off. You can say, "But I have been working very hard," and it only gets harder. The final examination is coming. Three years of hard work will set the foundation, the pillar, on which your ascension energy will be fully anchored, and you will walk this planet as masters if you choose to.

Building Peace with a Critical Mass

Some people believe that you can have true peace in people's heads. But you can only have real peace on seven levels: peace in the body, with the immediate family, with your surroundings, with other people, in your culture, in your country, and on Earth. Peace is a power card. When you have peace on all the seven levels, then you are truly peaceful.

You are one of the critical factors in building a critical mass. One person can affect more than 22,000 people. You can work on yourself, on your healing, and on your clearing. You see the power of one person. One effective soul can affect 22,000 people. That is a big number, my dear friend. So we ask you to hold and work from that level.

We ask you to further project yourself when you are in a very positive place and you feel expansion and completely loved. It is time to go to the next level of work, to project your energy. You can call it bilocation. Imagine that you are giving intention to project 22,000 "yous" going around the holy city holding light or going around wherever you want to go — America or abroad — anchoring light. It is time for you to start practicing this exercise, along with biorelativity: energy production and bilocation techniques. You must do it, dear ones. You can do it. We can do it.

This is how you can heal people. Just imagine and give intention during your meditations. You must do it when you are completely filled with love, and then give the intention that you are projecting yourself into 22,000 pieces. This is a projection called bilocation or bioenergy. You go to all the places you want to go and spread energy.

You can do the same thing in the Holy Land. Imagine 1,000 of you holding energy when people go to pray on Fridays at the mosque at the Dome of the Rock. That is a very fiery place. Project yourself out as 1,000 of you holding the light for people so that they are contained in the benevolent energy of your heart. They do not know this, but you are able to contain them.

So we are letting the light work through us?
Exactly, and you project light through them and affect the ground. They will not know what hit them. They will say, "I feel good," or "I feel love," and when people are in love and relaxed, they are much more forgiving.

What is our relationship to these 22,000 people? Are they part of our soul group, or are they concurrent lifetimes?
No, not at all. One person can affect 22,000 people because that is the power of the light you hold inside.

These are not a fixed group of people. These 22,000 people could change from time to time?

They will change, but your light is so powerful that 22,000 people can feel it. Why do thousands of people come to see a Buddha, a Jesus, or the Dalai Lama?

[Archangel Metatron: For example, a master walked through a village and there was great potential for everything and everyone in the village to be touched by his light, including the vegetables, vegetation, animals — everything. Why do you think people came to see Buddha? He was able to touch people within a three-mile radius. His aura was so strong. Everybody who came within three miles of him felt peace and love. Many walked for days to come into his presence and to feel his love. Even now when you are in the presence of a true master, you feel uplifted. Their energy moves so far. This is the power of a light-worker: to touch many.]

Sending Messengers Ahead

What is the difference between you and the Dalai Lama? He changed himself so that he could hold and project this light. Do you know what he does? I will give you a secret: Before he goes to any country where there will be a large audience, he sends his energy body to all these people. When they are in his presence, they already have the love he sent them, and they feel good. They do not know why they want to see him, but he has already sent his messengers ahead. You can do the same thing. The next time you want to do this kind of spiritually important healing work, send your energy messengers three or four days in advance.

Let me give an example. You can say, "I send the spirit in me to communicate with the spirits of all the people who are going to be praying at the Dome of the Rock. There is brotherly love radiating from my heart, and I am calming them." Or perhaps you will be having a meeting in a few days to discuss some contentious issue. You could speak to the spirits of the people involved, speaking their names, so that when you meet, there will be complete harmony, love, joy, and peace among you. You may not agree with each other, yet there will be no confrontation.

For example, if in the course of your profession you meet with clients and one is difficult, you can tell the spirit in you to meet the spirit of this client. So when you meet, there will be harmony, love, joy, and peace between you. You can also do this at the next level. You can ask collectively to lift a large group of people because you have the light inside you.

Do not have an agenda. Hold them in the light so that they will feel love from you. They will feel the compassion of your soul, and they will feel good about themselves without knowing why. In that feeling of love, they will know that love is the greatest factor. It changes the surroundings; it changes everything. Hold the light for them. This is one of the biggest draws for this lifetime. This is why you live in this beautiful, holy, sacred land. You made a promise to yourself that you, along with others, would shift this land. You will see a shift.

[Archangel Metatron: A master can light up. But a master will only do this when the student is ready. A master has the capacity to awaken the light within someone, even from a long distance. For example, in India many masters can touch the forehead of a person and directly activate the third eye. You might have seen such videos on YouTube. It must be done with proper care. If the subjects are not emotionally ready, this can create discomfort or destabilization. This is the power of one person, for a master's touch can awaken incredible power. It can even be done long-distance. This is what you are doing when you activate DNA. You will activate large numbers of people collectively in the future (Rae and Robert), hundreds of people at one time.]

We now have a very sacred and special guest today who will talk very briefly for the first time through Rae.

✳   ✳   ✳

Being One with the Creator

We are the combined consciousness of Abraham and Sarah. Many of you know the Rock [the Dome of the Rock on the Temple Mount in Jerusalem] to be a holy place. Some of you know that energy from the galactic codes, the Central Sun, comes into the storm, goes into waveform, and then transfers to other places. You could try to send light from your hearts into the Rock with the intention that the energy from the Rock goes into the place where you want healing. Send light from the heart (from the God part of you) to the Rock, and ask the Rock to send energy out in a circular wave throughout your beautiful city and throughout your precious world.

These other things we say to you now: You must not separate yourself anymore. You and the Creator are one and the same. You are building a microcosmic wave. You must play your part in this. It is our gift to you from now onward. Connect your energy with the deepest love into the Rock, to all the brothers, Islamic brothers, Jewish brothers, Christian brothers, Hindu brothers — everyone — and all sisters.

From now on, in your daily prayers, we ask you to focus for a few minutes every day and direct energy into the Rock. Create a buffer. Create energy that is aware, sending light everywhere. Ask the Rock to hold energy, and then activate the energy and send it out. Automatically, energy will bounce to all those who will receive it: in the great lands of Africa, Sudan, Nigeria, Ethiopia (where there is so much starvation), and other similar places.

You must act and believe from now on that you are cocreators with God. You know intellectually "I Am That I Am." You must believe and act that, through your cocreation, you can do the same thing: You can bring healing. We ask you to step into this spiritual activism more fully. Through your cocreation, things will change.

[Archangel Metatron: Many lightbeings have tried to stay out of what is happening in the real world. They see themselves as spiritual light warriors, and so they focus on the light. If everyone withdraws and leaves society as it is, then society will not change. If you withdraw from the world, then you are benefiting only yourself, and so you are basically of no benefit. With the new consciousness, you stay in the world and work in everyday life, and through your work, you will inspire and change other people. This is spiritual activism.

We encourage you not to start communities. First of all, they will not sustain themselves. In older times, communities could be sustained, but not in the new energy. The new energy involves staying in the world. The way of the Aquarian Age is to stay in the world, be part of the world, and create change through your actions and through your life.]

Let go of the fear, the guilt, the shame, and all inhibitions. We are the collective energy of Abraham and Sarah.

✳ ✳ ✳

Giving to Receive

This is Archangel Metatron. Please remember that everything we discussed today is for raising the level of consciousness on the planet and also in yourselves. When you do this work, you raise your own consciousness, and that will set the stage for the activation of DNA.

The secret to life is that whatever you want, you must give to others. If you want to have more light, bring more light unto others. If you want to have more joy in your life, bring more joy to others. If you want to have more wisdom for yourself, bring wisdom to others. What you give out is what you receive, so you are giving back to yourselves.

In other words, we reap what we sow.

I do not like to use the word "reap"; reap means it is a reward. Give — there is no reward. You do it because you love yourself.

✳ ✳ ✳

Light Codes and Erasing Karma with Pyramid Manifestation

This is Master Thoth. All of you have had many lives in times of Lemuria, in Mu, and some in Rama, as well as Atlantis. You have had many lives in Atlantis. I would say a significant part of the population of the present-day world has had lives in Atlantis. Some of you were priests. You may ask for the light codes to be brought forth of the priests you were in those times.

We also wish to talk to you about frequencies. Frequencies are about life itself. Many times, you wonder which lifetime is affecting you now. You cannot say that there is one particular lifetime affecting you. It is a combination of up to 300 lifetimes. You might say, "Today I give intention to erase all the lives that are affecting me at this present time that are not for my highest good." When you make that intention, you are giving permission to yourself to clear away your own karmic contract. This is a gift for the newly awakened soul. It can void the contract through intention.

What we are teaching you is one of the teachings of the ancient mystery schools. If you want to create something such as peace or great change in your country, imagine yourself sitting inside the Great Pyramid. Project the image of what you want to create as a hologram. Take it into the capstone of the pyramid, and then project it out into the world. The Great Pyramid is a powerful center of magnification and reality. The projected hologram will be sent out and automatically placed into the earth to start the manifestation process. This is one of the techniques for manifesting a new reality.

Master Jesus went to Egypt, and he played out the drama of what he would do on the cross — namely, what the significance of it was and what the lessons were. He projected these holographically through the chamber in the Great Pyramid and into the ground, and Mother Earth created that reality. Similarly, if you want peace in the Holy Land or peace in someone's life — or any other thing — you can work through the holographic chamber using the pyramid's capstone. This was one of the techniques for students of ascension in the ancient Egyptian mystery schools.

Students were taken frequently to the Great Pyramid to project themselves as ascended masters. They were asked to project themselves sitting on top of the capstone of the pyramid and then to holographically make an image of what they wished to be, whether it was an ascended master or passing a certain level of initiation. They would lay it into the ground. A pyramid is a generator, a big energy-generating machine.

Although it has lost much of its capacity, it has been revived. This is one of the reasons there is so much unrest in Egypt. This energy can be used to create a new reality for your world. You have completed many levels of initiation, and you have the capacity to create this holographically and bring it into fruition. This is Master Thoth.

✻   ✻   ✻

More on Foods

This is Pythagoras. The last time we talked, we discussed foods — foods that kept my students healthy and in higher vibrational states. We discussed different kinds of foods that can support raising your vibration. The Essenes practiced this as well. Their main concern was how to keep the vibration of a pure mind and pure vision on all seven levels and to influence the subconscious mind in order to reprogram it to create a new reality.

I mentioned some foods: olive leaves, figs, mustard seeds, and lotus fruits. I would like to give some more information. Garlic has great capacity. It is the only food that has all six tastes: pungent to sweet [in between are: sour, salty, astringent, and bitter]. It is the healthiest thing. Garlic is a gift from God. It is God's food.

[Archangel Metatron: The six tastes are the tastes of smell, because your tongue is directly connected to your other senses: the tastes of touch, because when you touch, you feel a reaction in the body or a sense of energy going through you, a sense of being, and the tastes of life, where you are able to dance, tasting life in its fullest. In other words, you can say, "Being in the present moment 100 percent." It is tasting life in its fullest every moment. "Fully experiencing" is perhaps another way to say it.

Garlic is a superfood, but there are also many roots that can support in awakening consciousness — some of the roots of vegetables, some of the roots of trees, and some of the roots of weeds. Many vegetables that are grown underground can support this. It is more of an individual thing for people to figure out what works best for them. Roots absorb the energy of the earth because they are grown underground.]

When you cook food, we ask you to do an experiment. Cook your food, but do not eat it right away. Leave it for fifteen to thirty minutes. Play sounds or sing to your food while you cook, and play music to the food you just made while you are waiting to eat it. Do the toning of: *Yod Hey Shin Vuv Hey* or any other tone that you feel comfortable with. You can also play some beautiful, melodic music without words or gentle classical music. Your food will take on the vibrations you are sending it.

Most of the food you eat has lost its essence because of how it is grown, processed, or transported. This process will bring the molecules back to their original shape as much as possible, as much as 60 percent. Your food will be much more energized. We did this in our mystery schools.

We also energized with gold. We placed gold nuggets around the food and cooked it in clay pots, which have the vibration of Mother Earth. We meditated on our food and sang songs to it before we ate. Food will directly interact with your cells. This was one of the secrets of our longevity and maintaining our high vibration. It raises the vibration of your food to your level.

The food we ate was much purer than what you have today. Your food is contaminated with chemicals and the vibration of many people. The thoughts of people affect plants.

This is Pythagoras.

Chapter 10

Connecting to Your Star Heritage

July 29, 2013

Lord Melchizedek, Yeshua, Archangel Gabriel, and Archangel Metatron

This is Lord Melchizedek. We ask all of you to look at your star heritage, for there is much you can gain here. This is not only about your DNA, because as you know, your DNA came from the Pleiadians. If you connect with the stars, you will connect with your complete lineage, to ancient parts of yourself. Can you imagine being alive for 500,000 years? That is what we are asking you to do. There is much wisdom there.

We are asking you to go back to ancient times, as far back as you can go. Do not limit this to 2,000, 5,000, or 10,000 years. Go back to your core original self. You have the capacity to do this. When this happens, there will truly be fireworks. You will not only be activating 12 or 22 layers of DNA but also working as a master of 144 layers. So we ask you to open this horizon and to have a bigger dream for yourself.

You have the capacity and are in the position to tap into this ancient lineage.

One of the masters you can work with is the galactic master, Melchior. He can support you. [Archangel Metatron: There are many levels you can work with. Earth is the planetary level. Then there is a solar level. The masters for the solar level are Helios and Vesta. The next level is called the galactic level. The master of the galactic level is Melchior. Then there is the universal level. The master for this level is Lord Melchizedek. There is also a multiuniversal level. The master for this level is Archangel Metatron. Then there is the cosmic level, and the master for this level is Mahatma. Then we have the level of the Central Sun. So there are many levels.

You must open up and integrate all these aspects to know yourself more fully. The solar beings, Helios and Vesta, support human beings, especially in understanding their connection with nature spirits, magic, and alchemy, for it is by working with nature spirits that you are able to create alchemy and magic. Nature has to change when you do magic. It is these beings who support this. So work with them by calling on them.]

Let me give you the example of Saint Germain; he is one of the benevolent masters supporting humanity. If you go back to the origin of Saint Germain, he was Lord Morda. He incarnated as the great alchemist Lord Merlin much later.

Who were you in this ancient past? We ask you to go back not just to Lemuria but all the way to the stars. You have the capacity to go back and connect to this energy, for this is truly a magical energy of procreation.

How do we connect to this library of previous lifetimes on different planets?

You can do this during your quiet time. Call it forth. You must have the discipline and desire to do it. You must believe that you are ancient beings. This work will only be done by people who are serious. All of you have the ability to tap into this incredible energy.

[Archangel Metatron: How can you can go back to past lifetimes? This is a very ancient question. It is called mining the akash. The akash, as you know, is a history of everything that has happened to you. Since there is no time, it is happening right now.

When in meditation, ask to be taken to a lifetime in which you have certain qualities that you seek in the present. Ask for the support of your soul and your guides, and you will be shown. It may not happen the first time you try, but if you persist, it will happen. You will be shown the lifetime when you had mastery over this particular issue. It is called moving through a dimensional portal or moving to a different dimensional reality.

If you are experiencing a great challenge in this lifetime and do not know what to do, in another lifetime you had this challenge and overcame it. So you do know exactly what to do. But that lifetime is not happening in the past. It is happening simultaneously. Through your intention, you can go back and forth in time. Look at time as a circle, and you are moving through the circle. You call backward movement the past, and forward movement the future. A circle has no beginning and no end. You move through the circle with intention and by asking. Ask your soul to guide you to the lifetime you seek to bring forth, and then ask to activate certain qualities of that lifetime.]

Connecting to Meteors and the Higher Chakras

You can also connect with meteor showers. They carry incredible amounts of life-sustaining energy and support. They are also bringing in new species. We want you to connect to these meteor showers because they are bringing in very high energy, life-sustaining energy, for many new life forms on the planet.

These meteors carry light force, and they are bringing in new species to the planet. They are like a rebirthing catalyst. You can use the energy of these meteors for rebirthing yourself.

[Archangel Metatron: Meteors carry many life forms and many energies. Connect with their essence. They can give you great energy, and this can propel you to immediately move into a new reality. Meteors bring in many new life forms. Connect with them and you will know more. You do this through intention and asking during meditation.

There is much to do at the present, because what you are doing is creating a template. You are becoming a completely new person, and there is a lot of work to be done to accomplish this.]

These are the new gifts offered by Spirit. When you are willing to work with them, they can enhance your energy tremendously. We are putting this offer out to you to let you know that it is available at this time. We want you to think about working to bring this energy into your spinal column and into your pituitary and pineal glands. Breathe in through these.

[Archangel Metatron: This is done by bringing energy through your soul star chakra or a higher chakra (the tenth chakra) and then running it through the back of your body. Most of the time, spiritual practice is realization, intention, and visualization. See the light coming into you and running through the back of your body. Then breathe through your pranic tube, making the intention that your breath is running through this opening, over and over.

The pranic tube becomes wider and wider. Breathe first, then bring in the light, and make the intention. Your pranic tube will start expanding naturally. The more it expands, the more you will be able to bring in the spiritual energy of your soul. It is absolutely critical in the new consciousness.]

People know about the soul star chakra or transpersonal point chakra and would like to integrate energy into this chakra, which is fine. However, we would like you to take your work to the next level.

The soul star chakra is located eight inches above the crown chakra. We would like all of you to start downloading energy from Father/ Mother God Creator. Go into the twenty-fourth chakra.

What is the name of that chakra, and where is it?

First, there are seven chakras (seven wheels of light), then the soul star chakra. Imagine that there are seven beams of light. Then there is a huge ball of light there, and there are three chakras above that. The other chakras above that are balls of light.

Is there a name for it?

I am not to give out the name at this time. Call forth this higher vibration. This chakra will be anchored through the assistance of a master. Call forth an appropriate master to anchor it for you. You could ask Archangel Metatron or Master Yahui. We ask you to download the energy not just to the soul star chakra but also into the spinal column.

This is Lord Melchizedek saying thank you for this great work to support humanity. This is our gift that we give to you for the next people who walk down this road so that they will have something to guide them.

＊　＊　＊

Transitioning from Crucifixion to Resurrection and Ascension

This is Yeshua. As you know, the world is in a state of crucifixion at this time. There is tremendous darkness in the world. From crucifixion, how can you go into resurrection and from resurrection to ascension and freedom?

All of you are pioneers. When you finish your crucifixion experience, you move into resurrection and freedom. Teach this to people. The world needs this at this time. There is going to be much more ugliness coming out this year, more secrets, fear, and hatred. You must hold the light. You can tell people that they can have resurrection only after crucifixion. All people want to resurrect, yet they do not want to go through the crucifixion process.

[Archangel Metatron: That has been the teaching so far: only after suffering can you attain God. This was exemplified by Jesus. But Jesus had many out-of-body experiences even before his crucifixion. He constantly traveled to other places.

So, again, you have the belief that you must suffer to attain God. This is old energy. And because of your belief system, we have been easily manipulated. Many churches and religions teach this even now, that you have to give up everything to find God. That is old age.

In the new energy, you can have everything and celebrate God through everything you have. You can see God in everything. In reality, you do not have to give up anything, only egotistical attachment and greed. Everything is here to celebrate God. God has created you to celebrate life.]

Crucifixion does not mean that people have to go through great pain. It means getting rid of the dark demons in their hearts and in their minds. They will clear their own heads. Teach them how they can get out of their heads and their own thinking, which they have created. The darkest of the dark is created in the human mind.

Connecting to Great Beings and Celestial Bodies

We ask you to connect to the Masters of DNA, to integrate and interlink your chakras with the masters. When you ask for integration of a master's energy, you can rise to the next level. Ask for integration of the master's chakras.

Call on your guides, who are part of your soul group. [Archangel Metatron: Everyone comes with guides. Imagine that you are sitting in meditation and you look up and see your guides, or call the essence of your guides to be around you. Breathe to them from your heart to their hearts, and connect your chakras with their chakras.

When you call on your guides, they immediately step into your energetic field. It may take some time for you to know that they are there, but you will definitely feel their energy. In a matter of weeks, you will be able to sense the energies from different masters, for many masters have worked with you before. There will be an instant feeling of knowingness.

When you call your guides, they will be so happy that they will jump into your awareness. Send an energetic connection from your heart to them, and ask them to download their energies into you. Ask them to connect your chakras with their chakras, infusing you with their higher-vibrational energy. You are filling up with light because these masters come from a higher-vibrational place. Not only do the masters have high energy, but they bring this energy from the dimension where they reside.]

You will be able to raise your consciousness through the Masters of DNA and higher vibrations. There are many, many layers, even for a master. Masters are working on raising their vibrations all the time. Ascension, if you really look at it, is less than one-tenth of one inch. There is so much work to be done. Ask how you can connect with the DNA of the great beings you like to work with.

[Archangel Metatron: Ask to be integrated with the highest aspects of the master's consciousness. See the energy coming into you. For example, if you want to connect with Archangel Metatron, see a beautiful silver-platinum light coming into you and filling you. Breathe it in. See the energy of Metatron. Perhaps you could kneel in prayer position, and say, "I call on the full essence and presence of Archangel Metatron to be with me at this time." You just have to do it once with pure intention and love in your heart. You will feel the presence, for as you know, all these beings are waiting for you.

Just request this. They cannot come unless you ask, for they respect your free will. You will be supported immediately.]

You can also connect with the DNA of Mother Earth. She has more than 12,000 DNA layers, many dimensional realities, and many energetic beings. Connect with my own awakened DNA, for I was completely one with the Father/Mother Creator and my beloved Mary

Magdalene, Mother Mary, and Maria. So we invite you to extend your connection to our DNA.

Here is another technique for you. Many of the higher-dimensional planets — the Pleiades, Arcturus, and Venus — have their own DNA, as Earth has. You can ask to interlink with their DNA. You will receive a tremendous download of energy. Your mind will become clearer, and you will have more light. Through this light, you will be able to activate your own DNA much more easily.

This idea is shown in some pictures from India in which people are praying with folded hands. On a higher level, they are connecting with the energy of the gods. When a teacher blesses you or you pray to Shiva, there is a transfer of the energy of their DNA into you. Then a miracle happens in your life.

You can also call forth the codes that these higher beings carry for Earth. For example, Mary Magdalene and I sealed the planet with the code of unity of Father/Mother God. You may ask for this code to be activated within you. This is the Christ code. Or call for the Metatronic code from Metatron.

You all know of Master Elijah. When his assistant went to his ascension, he took on the mantle of the master. Why don't you become assistant to Elijah in energetic form and ask for his mantle?

Higher beings all carry certain codes — Yeshua and Mary Magdalene carry the Christ code; Metatron carries Metatronic codes. An angelic being carries angelic codes. You must tap into these new codes to activate higher consciousness. This is a gift at the present time.

For example, a star brother of the Ashtar Command works to support planet Earth, just like the Arcturians. You can call forth the higher master of the Ashtar Command to work with you. [Archangel Metatron: Just ask for the full presence of this being to come into your life, and you will see a downloading of energy, a beautiful white light. The Ashtar Command is in support of humanity, especially working with planet Earth, along with the Arcturians. They come from a star system called Ashtar, and they have been here for a long time.]

The Pleiadians have a council of twelve called the Pleiadian elders. They hold the energy and the vibration for the Pleiades so that the work can go on. They maintain stability and balance. These are truly complete masters. The same thing happens in Arcturus. There are beings who are illuminating and holding the energy for Arcturus. We ask you to start connecting with these beings and their DNA.

All of you have your own personal codes embedded in the earth. Ask for these personal codes to be activated. Call on Mother Earth. She holds the imprint of each of you. You are her children. She holds the imprint of all the creatures who live here. Ask for the imprint to be activated fully.

Regeneration

I want to talk about something that was given to Rae a few days ago, which we think is important for you to know. When you start working with your DNA, we ask you not to limit your thinking about activation to the higher layers of DNA. Last year [2012], all of you focused on December 21 and December 12, the world ascension. Yes, a very significant event. In the history of this planet, it happens every 26,000 years. What is the next step for all of you? In addition to DNA, think about regeneration. You must look into that and start working toward regeneration.

[Archangel Metatron: Regeneration is a natural birthright. The first step is to communicate with your cells daily. Monitor your thoughts, the food you eat, the energy you take in, and the energy you expend. Your cells will respond to you. Then you can ask your cells to stop the release of the death hormones and to activate and release the light hormones. This is connected to longevity. Cellular communication is the key.]

You have the capacity for regeneration. For example, we would like many of you to live another fifty years. You already have a developed consciousness. We would like people with developed consciousnesses to stay so that they can hold the light for the next generation.

Regeneration is within the capacity of people who are already awakened. Regeneration has many steps. The first step is removing the death imprint. All of you bring these imprints into your physical bodies at the beginning of your lifetimes. You carry four to seven imprints with you. These are imprints that you brought for your own death in this incarnation. This imprint is stored in your aurical cord. Ask for these imprints to be disconnected now.

[Archangel Metatron: Your aura contains everything. Your aura is around you, and it must be cleansed and purified to be activated. When you bring in light from any being of light or you breathe in and activate light inside you, you must make it a point to send this light into your auric field, cleansing and purifying it, so that what your auric field contains can be manifested and brought into your present reality. Then you can understand it. Work with the auric field daily. It is very important. This is known as auric maintenance.]

The second step is very important and very difficult. You need to remove the belief system the matrix holds of death. The third step is to believe and know that you can communicate with your body. Perhaps in the past your body did not listen, but you are now in a different time period.

[Archangel Metatron: Removing the death imprint and communicating with your body go hand-in-hand. Communicate with your body daily. This is called cellular-level communication. Death imprints need to be removed, and this is done by asking. Command them to stop releasing death hormones into your cells, which produces aging and finally death. Death hormones move through the entire body, and the body dies. So often, aging is a chemical process.

We can have some control over this by cellular communication?

Of course. Stop producing the death hormone. When the great Master Paramahansa Yogananda passed away, his body was kept in the mortuary for more than three weeks without embalming, and it never deteriorated.[1] It took his physical body many days to understand that the master was not in his body anymore.

This is a new modality, actually an old modality, but for modern times. We encourage lightworkers to work with this, for you have sacrificed much to come this far. Stay here to see the results of all your hard work from many lifetimes. Communicate with your body daily.

Would you not want to stay here to enjoy the benefits of all the hard work you have done, lifetime after lifetime? You have prepared the food. Now it is time to sit down and eat it. Do you want to leave right away? Live a long life. It is your birthright.

From a linear mind, this might not make sense. But we ask you to stretch your mind to your potential, the possibility that exists if you are open to it. I am addressing the religious readers too. I hope to stretch their minds. There is so much new truth. If you were to look at the truth that you believe and compare it to the new truths, you could say that

---

1.   Paramahansa Yogananda, *The Autobiography of a Yogi* (Los Angeles: Self-Realization Fellowship, 1998).

all this is blasphemous. But all new truths are first considered blasphemous or laughed at.]

We ask all of you to start looking into regeneration at this time. Masters have done it. Many beings have done it. You have read many books with stories about people living up to many hundreds of years. This is now a gift offered to the world. Raising your consciousness is not just activating DNA. We do not want you to stop there. Regeneration is possible. We ask this of you because you have a higher-vibration consciousness, and we ask you to extend this more and more. We do not want you to leave carrying only the vibration you now hold.

When you regenerate, you will be fully healthy. There is no point in extending your life another fifty years if you are bedridden. It will be with full health restored.

How do we activate the regeneration that you speak of?

There are many steps. First, you must remove the death imprint. You do this by knowing that you can communicate with your body. You must change your beliefs about death. Know that life is an eternal process. There is no ending. Life is a continuous process without limitations and boundaries, like the four directions: north, south, east, and west. There is no separation. This is difficult for many people to accept. Remove the death imprint that you brought with you into this lifetime. Then work on activating your youth chromosome. This has been done by many masters. To remain youthful, call on the youth chromosome.

What happens to the DNA of a person who is deceased?

The consciousness does not die with the body. The energy does not die, so you will have the same DNA in your next life. You will have attributes of what you hold at the moment of the last breath and the consciousness carried at that time.

You were masters at one time. All of you were ascended masters. Why are you not able to remember this? At the moment of passing away, the moment of death, what kind of consciousness did you carry? This is the most important, significant consciousness. You must die consciously. If not, in your next lifetime, the predominant energy will be what you left with in your previous lifetime.

[Archangel Metatron: People in comas are very conscious inside. These people are often labeled vegetables. Do you think that they are vegetables inside? Of course not. They are very aware of what is going on inside, and they are aware of what is going on outside, but they are disconnected from the external.]

When most people are dying, all their fears kick in as their lives are flashed in front of them. Every experience they had and every word they spoke is reviewed. Most people feel great fear, and it is difficult for them to remain in higher vibration.

In India, Tibet, and other cultures, when people are ready to die, the family members burn sacred incense — especially sandalwood. They do this so that their minds become clear, and they start singing the name of the holy ones. Even now, people in India name their children God's name so that when they are on their deathbeds, they can call the children to come to them. Inside, they are calling the name of God. The DNA remains as it is, but will they remember? This depends on their state of consciousness when they took their last breaths. [Archangel Metatron: Does death change a person's DNA? It sits there lifetime after lifetime for the right instructions to be passed on.]

Changing Your Blueprint

What happens to DNA when we change the blueprint of our lives?

What happens when you add something to yourself? You become something new. There is more light in your DNA — more awakening light — and more remembrances. We ask you to change your blueprint often.

[Archangel Metatron: You make a new blueprint through intention. You may also want to remove death imprints, not necessarily as often. You could say, "I am ready to release the death imprints from my life that are appropriate at this time." This is what we call an empowered human being in control of his or her life. Remember, you have the capacity to remove death imprints through your intention.]

So when we make new blueprints, what would be included in that? What our intentions and goals are? What we wish to accomplish?

The intention of your soul is to always look for higher experiences. It never stops. So ask for the highest experiences that your soul can experience on the Earth plane in this new reality. If you were to say, "I am happy with my life," this could be true, but your soul would not respond. But if you ask for higher experiences, there will be many new things that that would open in your future, even if you are seventy or eighty years old.]

We can ask you, "What is your blueprint for the next three months?" This is a very interesting question. We did not want to say anything about this yet. After ascension this year, the important thing is regeneration. The next step is building your akashic record and changing your blueprint, upgrading the blueprint and upgrading the software inside of you. When there is no blueprint, there is no life.

Suppose someone is on her deathbed and she returns after having a near-death experience. What has happened? How did she come back? She went into the tunnel, and she started reviewing her life. Why did she return?

It is not because she was not ready or her time had not come. She created a new blueprint for herself. You too can create a new blueprint as part of your regeneration process. We ask you to rewrite your story from now onward. No more history: Do not be tied to your history. This is your story from now onward. When you change your blueprint, you raise your vibration. Do not change your blueprint just once; instead, change it often. Make a new blueprint every three months.

[Archangel Metatron: Again this is done through intention and communication with your soul, asking for higher experiences. Most people come into a lifetime with five to seven death imprints when they are born, sometimes as many as twelve. The narrow misses you experience are all death imprints. But through your intention, you can change this. This is called empowered living. You are in control of your life.]

When you start doing this, you will see there is a blueprint for our whole planet as well. There is a blueprint for each country. We ask you to activate your higher blueprint continuously every three or six months.

An athlete does not stop at only 100 meters, saying, "I'm fine, I am only going to go 100 meters." No. He says, "I am going to better myself," and works on improving his time by 11 seconds, 10.5 seconds, and so on, because he is training himself all the time to come to a level at which he can do his best.

Evolution is an eternal process. It is never finite. We ask you to consider this.

What happens to the DNA when someone makes a wrong turn in life contrary to the personal blueprint or life plan?

First of all, there is no wrong turn. It is only that you label things "wrong" or "right." People do things, but they do not label them, because when you label, you create separation. From now on, there is no more separation. You have done something, and that is it. The DNA is deactivated, or it stays dormant.

When people do things that are not in alignment with their souls' purpose, they do not have the energy to accomplish what they came here to do. Naturally, that affects their DNA. When you say, "Thy will is my will," you are coming alive; it is the will of God. All of your energy will move into the path you have set for yourself. Automatically, you are in a higher vibrational state. When you work with higher-vibrational energy, naturally your DNA will be activated. So the first thing you must do is get back on the track of the divine soul's purpose for which you were born: Thy will is my will.

When I asked these questions about five or six years ago, the answer came back from Archangel Metatron that I have to unlearn everything I have learned and undo everything I have done. I was in such shock. I didn't speak for a whole day. I was in such a paradigm shift.

What did Jesus [Yeshua] say? To know the Creator, you must become like a child once again, the innocent and curious child. You have to undo everything you have learned. Not only in this lifetime but culturally, genetically, what you have brought forth — everything. Just go back and completely erase the slate. This is not an easy task because the mind is very strong. The mind will pull it back because it is afraid it will lose its power. You must do what Metatron said: Undo what you have learned so far.

Letting Go

I would like to give you a small, joyous experience. Say something is really stuck in your mind, and you are not able to let go of it. You have tried very hard. The more you try, the more it is stuck there. This exercise can support you. We do not guarantee it, yet we say it can support you. Also, you are a human being, so we cannot fault you no matter what happens.

Sit down, light a beautiful candle, and take a nice piece of good string, not too thin, not too thick, perhaps a piece of white, beautiful string. Make two knots at the ends. One knot represents you, and the other knot represents the experience you had with a person or the actual person.

Breathe deeply and bring as much love as you can into your heart — much love, no hatred. Breathe in love. When you feel very connected in love, take a pair of scissors, and with one cut, cut the middle of the string. Then burn the string in the candle, and then leave the candle somewhere safe to burn itself out. Leave the candle to burn out. You may feel sad for a while, yet you will have completed a disconnection from the karmic energy of other lifetimes and removed any attachment to it.

How will you know that you have disconnected? In a few days or few weeks when you think about this person or this experience, there will be no sadness or any other feeling. It will just be a memory passing through your mind. You will know that you are healed hereafter. You can do this for a person or for any other inhibiting belief system, such as back pain or anything else.

This can be done for anyone, for any condition that could be improved in your life, for a person or situation, or anything else you are finished with but cannot get out of your mind. It does not serve you anymore. We ask you to do it in a loving state only. If it is done out of hatred, it will not work; it has to be done through love.

Mitigating Karma

How does karma affect a person's DNA?

There are two things. Karma is unfinished energy that you have come here to complete. So we differentiate between karma and learning. DNA has high vibration consciousness, but it is not activated. It stays dormant. When we release more and more karma, have more peace in our lives, feel more joy, and feel more compassionate, naturally our vibration increases, and this affects the DNA.

One easy way to release karma is by raising your energy and disconnecting from the energy of the karma. You would still like to learn the lesson that you must complete but without the pain and suffering.

[Archangel Metatron: Let me give you a small example. This is a story about Rae. He had a well-paid job. He was doing fine. But after the birth of his son, Master Kuthumi said, "It is time for you to look at fully stepping into your role as a teacher." He had great fear and doubt, for he was in a very well-placed position, and his son had just been born. He also had a daughter, a family to support.

Kuthumi said, "Let's go for a walk." He took Rae on a journey to one of his lifetimes when he was a warrior in Greece getting ready for battle.

There was a big war cry and a thumping in the air. He had no fear. Master Kuthumi asked him to breathe that energy of when he had no fear of death, bring it back, and paste it into his present reality. He did that for seven days. By the seventh day, he felt much stronger and more confident.

Rae was able to choose to leave his job without fear. This was the technique he used to disconnect from the energy of his karma so that his soul could bring him whatever lesson he needed.]

You do not have to have pain and suffering to learn your lessons. That is an old energy. Just put in a new one; you do not need the old. You can ask your soul to bring you whatever lesson you need.

To learn it through consciousness and not through hard knocks?

Exactly, through consciousness. You can do one more thing. You can release your karma etherically, not going through it physically. We ask you to work on releasing karma etherically so that there is no pain and no physical difficulty for you. You can do this during your sleep if that is your intention.

Most of you know you have grace from the Karmic Board. [Archangel Metatron: The Karmic Board consists of some ascended masters and the Karmic Council. They are lightbeings whose only duty is to see that energy is balanced. The Karmic Board is not about punishment. Its only concern is how to balance someone's energy. Energy, once created through the mind, through an action, through words, or any other interaction, never dies. It is carried forward into other lifetimes. The Karmic Board's only intention is to balance energy that people have created themselves.

Work with the Karmic Board daily. Ask them to bring you the energy you need to balance your life, and they will show you. Ask them to bring it in a gentle way so that you are able to understand. This is not about punishment. Who is there to punish? You punish yourself. God does not punish human beings.

All of you have grace because you have been working, moving into ascension, and raising your vibrational consciousnesses. Much of your karma has been moved into a period of grace for you. You can request that you want to learn the lesson without pain and suffering. If you still have pain and suffering after trying these methods, it is because your soul does not really care about the pain and suffering because it does not feel it. The soul is aware, yet it does not experience pain. The soul is only interested in how much you learn and what wisdom you gain.

You can talk to your soul. [Archangel Metatron: To talk to your soul, just sit down and call forth your higher self to connect with you. That is all. Direct your breath. You will feel your soul. It is not how or why. Each person's way of doing things is his or her own individual experience. Your soul is aware of everything in your thoughts. Do this on a daily basis, and you will build this connection more and more. Your soul watches everything. Do it daily. See your life change.]

You can explain that the lesson that you are going through is the hardest time of your life. You may ask to practice this lesson over many lifetimes, not just this lifetime. Your soul will communicate with Mother Earth, who holds your imprint in her body. Mother Earth will usually agree to this so that you can extend your karmic lesson through several lifetimes. It may take three to four weeks for this to happen, but you will see a shift. This is a gift for the present time for all of you. You may also use the same method to address the intense polarization going on around the planet.

[Archangel Metatron: Mother Earth is living spirit. You are all temporarily on her body. Do you not care for your mother? What do you do when you visit someone's house? You are respectful of the person who invited you. Are you respectful of Mother Earth? She gives her body, mind, and soul to support humanity. But are you doing the same for her? Do you thank Mother Earth, or are you abusing her? I leave it to you to answer this question.

You can connect with Mother Earth through intention and through love. When you have a good thought, a loving thought, and when you forgive somebody and have nice words, Mother Earth feels your energy. Communicate with her daily. How do you communicate? Through other human beings, how you treat others.

Somebody once said to Mother Earth, "I want to wipe the tears from your eyes. I know you are suffering."

Mother Earth responded, "Thank you. When you wipe a tear from another human being's eyes, you are wiping my tears, for I am that human being."

Honor this great being who provides a body to nourish and support you on your journey. Work with her daily. Your love is a healing balm, for she has carried a heavy burden for millions of years.]

Communicate with Mother Earth. Ask to spread this to other lifetimes so that this intensity is not only focused in the present. Work with that, for Mother Earth is very compassionate.

For example, in Ethiopia and other countries in Africa, they have had hard times for many years. The souls who were born there have chosen to be born there for lives of starving and great suffering. Ask Mother Earth, as appropriate, "Can we shift this?" or "Can we change this?" "If the intensity on a scale of 1 to 10 is 10, can we reduce it to 2 so that we can have a final lifetime of this intense suffering? Can we end this suffering with this lifetime?" You can connect with Mother Earth, and then she will decide, and she will agree.

Awakened DNA affects Mother Earth very consciously. Mother Earth will listen to you. This is a gift all of you must work with. Many of you have so much learning, and now you must bring that learning to a practical level. This is how you can support yourself and your planet.

[Archangel Metatron: When you have a thought, Mother Earth feels it. When you walk on her body, she is very aware of you. Send love from your heart; say a beautiful word. When you see a beautiful flower on her body, say, "Thank you, Mother Earth, for your incredible beauty. You are supporting this life form." She feels it. It is a healing balm for her. Native American people knew this and honored her. They knew she was providing her body to support humanity and all life forms. When you say a good word, when you heal another heart, and when you are kind to others, you are healing Mother Earth. When you say a harsh word to another, you are hurting Mother Earth, for you and Mother Earth are the same.]

When you learn a life lesson, how does this affect your DNA?

When you learn your life lesson with compassion, kindness, and acceptance, naturally you are in a peaceful, joyful state. If you choose to vibrate with bitterness and hatred, it will be the opposite. It is all in the mind. How much peace and joy remain in your heart and mind is the level of consciousness that will activate your DNA. Where does most of the darkness lie in the human mind? It is in the subconscious mind. Work with the subconscious mind. This is why the Essene brothers place so much emphasis on working with the subconscious mind.

Connecting with Your Star and Your Dragon

We would like to tell you one more thing. When planet Earth was created, it took a long time before human beings were allowed to come here for the experiment. There were twelve dragon beings who were invited by the Creator to come and seal the planet with their energies. These are the twelve archetypal dragons who anchored energy in the different parts of Mother Earth's body: energy of the merkanah, energy of the pineal gland, energy of the new blueprint, energy of the crystalline kingdom, and so on. You must call these forth, for they also carry the codes for activating the highest type of DNA.

[Archangel Metatron: These are called forth through intention and through specific sound vibrations. You can read more about this in the Kryon books by Lee Carroll. When humanity is more awakened, people can create holy places.

You can make a place holy by intention and holding the light there. Start with your own house and your own environment. Build a city of light through your intention. For example, see a beautiful hexagon or octagon shape being placed where you intend to create a sacred place. See this geometric shape being anchored into the ground. It is a light-filled space, and that place becomes holy. First, do this with your own house.

People do not really understand the true power of intention. Intention coming from the heart and the soul can completely change any reality. You can bring healing, even to parched lands.]

Kryon mentioned these codes and also Earth becoming more holy in some places. It is like a time capsule. Ask for the dragon codes for 2013 that are in alignment with your codes. They carry the archetypal energy that is anchored in the planet. All of you have been given a gift, for when you were born, you were aligned with a star and a dragon.

[Archangel Metatron: Again, do this with intention. The dragons have their own unique sound frequencies. Use these to call them forward (see Appendix I: Working with the Energy of Dragons). Each dragon carries a very specific vibrational energy. This work is not dangerous and cannot be misused, but it is very powerful. This is the power of sound. Call these beings forth with these sounds, and you will feel their energy. Try it in a workshop with many people.]

These stars and dragons carry a special code for this time period. It is like a time capsule ready to open. We can explain these tools to you; however, we cannot walk your walk. You must use the tools and work with them to see how they support you. If you work with them for three months, you will see a difference.

[Archangel Metatron: You must work with all the tools we have given. Working with dragons is one new tool. Use these tools continuously. All of you are in the process of re-creating yourselves anew.

Use these new tools. Old tools will not work in the new methodology. You will reinforce old energies. For the new you, you need new tools, and the highest tools are your power of intention and your power of thought.]

The Essenes

I wonder how far the Essenes actually went to change their DNA?

In another dimensional reality, their work is continuing. They were able to accomplish what they came here to do. Not all Essene brothers were enlightened. Not all Essene brothers did come back. Some were heretical. Overall, the master did accomplish his mission and set the platform for the Teacher of Righteousness to be born. After the crucifixion, the Essene brothers took the work to England and France.

Their work continues, and in the next ten years, you will see the teaching of the Essenes becoming more popular. People will feel much more resilient because their teaching is very simple and very practical. The Essenes said there is no need of having a great idea if you cannot better your life, better your heart, or bring peace. Their teachings were very simple to follow.

The Teacher of Righteousness taught a shamanic way of living, communing with Mother Nature and Father Sky. You are a brother or sister to all of nature, to all of creation itself. This will be the new teaching for the world, and you will see young people embracing this concept, because it is the start of a new religious conception. It is common sense.

Each of you has your own way of connecting with your higher self. Whatever you feel is appropriate, continue it. You are building one more bridge between yourself and your higher self.

Dying in Traumatic Circumstances

When we were speaking with Saint Germain, maybe a month ago, he mentioned what happens to the souls who die in traumatic circumstances, such as atomic bombings or the holocaust. Do they really lose the spiritual learning of seventy to one hundred lifetimes?

They do not lose their spiritual lives, but many life blueprints are wiped out. Someone comes into a lifetime, and it has taken 761 lives for that person to get to where he or she was. It is a cumulative effort. Through an atomic blast or holocaust, a large part of this person's heritage is gone. The memories are wiped out throughout that person's being. All the learning that he or she had in the 761 lives is completely gone. This person needs to come back and start again.

How can these souls be healed?

The souls of the Holocaust have already been reborn. They are not full. There has been so much fragmentation of their souls, and the energy they have brought is only a small part of their personal energy after the Holocaust. They have to work to bring their soul energy back. This requires spiritual understanding of what is happening. They can work with their guides and the masters to integrate their soul energy. If there is no spiritual understanding, their guides and masters will not be able to work with them.

Do you think there will be some healing techniques introduced in the future that will be able to assist these souls in restoring their heritage?

There is always teaching available; however, they must choose to work with it. Remember, people who did great damage can be reborn into the countries they persecuted.

The Arcturians have spiritual technologies called healing chambers. They can go into the past and into the future. They can go into the past and bring it into the future. When you heal something in the past, your future is changed. In order to have this work done, you must have a certain level of spiritual understanding and a certain level of vibration. Not everybody can go to these chambers to be healed. They need to know the techniques and how to work with them. They must be clear in their hearts and have some kind of spiritual understanding.

It is very good to work with this every day. It is good to call on your fragmented parts to integrate with you. You can call forth the fragmented parts, and sometimes you will see bubbles of energy coming into you. Sometimes you will feel a lot of sadness or new abilities coming into you. When you are able to bring all your fragmented parts to yourself, you become whole once again.

My concern is that these people lost all spiritual cognizance and are reduced to bare bones. They don't have the wherewithal to ask to be reunited.

I would not say they have lost everything. At a deeper part of their souls, they still have knowledge and wisdom. Most of them will be born into families in a country where they will have the opportunity to again relearn, depending on their other lifetimes and their karma. On a higher level, these people who died had their own karmic issues to work on.

In Japan, people are very polite and soft, and they look after each other. They were not always like this. They were brutal in the countries they controlled. After the atomic bombing, their perspectives shifted due to their suffering. It was a big shift for them. Japanese people are very polite and soft, and they do not commit much crime. Japan is one of the safest countries in the world that has very little crime because history changed everything for them. When a great tragedy happens, the energy goes into the ground, and when the ground is healed, what is born on the ground will be healed. This brings forth the energy of compassion. This is what happened.

A great tsunami hit the coast of Thailand, Sri Lanka, and other countries in 2005, and more than 237,000 people died. The whole world came to help. The tsunami brought the world together for a brief moment in time. Many countries came to support these people.

In simple terms, how would a person with twelve strands of activated DNA feel? And how would he or she perceive the world?

This activation does not happen instantaneously. It is a gradual process. People with twelve strands of activated DNA would see the world through different eyes — through an inner eye, through a truthful eye. They would see that this world is an important world but that they are not in this world. They have one foot on the ground here and the other in another world. Their perspectives change so that they are able to see the larger picture, the truth in every situation. They are able to see through eyes opened to higher dimensions. They are able to see more of the perfection and God in every situation. This is an inner perspective change.

What happens to the DNA of a person who has a long-term degenerative illness, such as a heart condition or cancer, with much suffering?

DNA is always perfect. It is a perfect library. If it does not operate and is not activated, it will stay dormant. If you have a degenerative sickness and do not work on yourself to raise your consciousness, then the DNA does not change. [Archangel Metatron: DNA is always perfect. If you never have the inclination or the awareness that you have the capacity to change, your DNA will not change. This will not be your reality at all.]

This is one of the reasons why many people in survival mode operate from the first chakra. They have very little time or inclination to work on themselves. They do not have the mind or time to work on another reality. So they are merely existing and not living consciously.

Even when they have a sickness and they are aware, they can ask why their soul chooses to have this experience and what the lesson is for them, whether it is part of their blueprint or their destiny, how they can move from it and handle it. With that perspective, naturally they are in an awakened state.

When you start working on yourself, you are raising your vibration and raising your consciousness. The same can be said that a sinner can become a saint in one minute through opening his or her higher mind.

You have heard about me curing the leper [Matthew 8:3, KJV]. I did not do anything to him. I simply restored his own belief that he could heal and walk. He was so mired in his thinking that he had been stuck there for thirty-five years. I changed his belief system and liberated his mind, and he started believing that he could do it. Many times, you believe you cannot do certain things. Change your beliefs, and change your life.

It is absolutely critical at this time that you hold a higher belief system in this new consciousness. This is year number one of the energy of expansion [2013]; believe everything is possible. Believe. Dream the biggest dream. This is your friend, Yeshua.

❋   ❋   ❋

Clearing Your Emotions and Your Mind

This is Archangel Gabriel. I ask all of you to call on me. There is much wisdom that I can offer. The angelic kingdom can shower you with angelic light so that your emotional and mental bodies become clearer.

It is easier to work with the emotional body. You can control your emotions because emotions are only one thing — energy in motion. How do you control energy in motion? You can move the energy to a higher expression and hold a positive vibration, or you can move it lower and have a lower vibration. It is your choosing. Start looking at everything as energy and how you want to play with energy. Do you want to move it to a higher level or a lower level? It is easy to work with an emotional body; it is energy in motion. You can become masters of it.

It is more particular to work with the mind because the mind is mired in many layers and has much past. The emotional body does not have much past connection and is not as affected as the mental body. Mental bodies need constant cleansing on a daily basis — maintenance. This is where we can help, for we carry the highest and purest vibration from the Creator.

The mental body is directly connected to stored memories. Those memories are stored in the brain, the cells, the bloodstream, the skin, and the bones. Unless you clear the memory from the bones, you are never truly clear. The ancient ones knew about this and worked to clear the bones. Unless you clear the bones, you bring back similar beliefs from the past. You break this down through the vibration of the purest love.

Call on our family to work with you: After showering and in the quiet, run your breath through your entire body, breathing and then circulating through the entire body and then releasing through the entire body. This may take some practice, but you will see what clearing can happen. Take a breath in the purest love for yourself. Breath is a source of life. Send your breath within. Send it into your body, and hold it if you can, count to eight or ten while circulating through the body, and then send it out.

You will see miracles. Many thoughts will go away. You will feel vibrant and full of life.

※　　※　　※

Commune in Harmony

This is Archangel Metatron. When you are in harmony with all, you are in harmony with God and yourself. The shamanic way is communing in harmony with all of creation. We ask you to be open to holy communion with your own Father/Mother Creator. Make this intention, and ask for the code of holy communion to be opened inside you so that your higher self can be heard every moment. You can live from now on in holy communion.

When you communicate with your partner, you are not going to talk to him or her. You are going to have a holy communion with him or her. There will be a huge shift. There will be no more talking because you are in communion with each other from the heart source.

To practice holy communion, from this moment through every experience, you cocreate a new world; every morning when you wake up, make the intention. Ask for support from angelic beings to be in holy communion, first, with all creation; second, to be in harmony with all creation; third, to be in unity consciousness with all creation; and fourth, to be in the flow of things.

[Archangel Metatron: There is no "should" or "should not" on how to communicate with your guides. It is done through intention. If you are in your bed, in the shower, or in your living room with a cup of coffee in your hand, go into your inner quiet space and call on these beings and communicate with them. They do not sleep like you. They are busy twenty-four hours a day. Any time you feel love in your heart, communicate with them.

Do not wait. Make this connection. They are always present, but you must initiate the connection from your side. Make them your best friends, for they only have the highest good and the highest intention for you.

The more you work with them, the stronger the bonds you create. They are your support team. They know Earth is a difficult place to live. They are here to support you completely with the utmost love, helping you to move from point A to point B while completing the life lessons you have come here to learn, opening up new contracts, and gently reminding you of who you are all the time. What better friends can you have than your own guides?

Make it a point to communicate with them every day. Perhaps you love your mother, but if you have not communicated for many years, the relationship gets rusty. The more you communicate with your guides, the more they will support you with their energy and wisdom, help you open up to higher realities, and seek more of yourself. When you die, they are the ones who are with you first to make the transfer as easy as possible.]

When you ask, when you make a statement in the morning when you wake up, you will see how your daily life will be much smoother. You may add one more element to it, an element of bestowing blessings. This is the reality that you wish to create, a future with harmony among all nations, among all people communicating and supporting each other. What a beautiful world it will be! This will come true in the future. You can see it right now, but it is only one moment in time. You will see; the future will shift.

Here is homework for you about large trees and how they can affect humanity. Find some trees in your own community. Trees have souls that are very wise, especially older trees. They have hierarchies. Some trees will grow higher than the others will because they have awakened DNA.

Go into nature and find a tree that you feel is appropriate because of the higher energies absorbed by this beautiful giant tree. Then ask for integration. Spend time with this tree. Do this in your own community. Be respectful, as trees are just like you. You do not want someone coming into your home without knocking on the door. Use proper protocol when approaching a tree.

[Archangel Metatron: When you approach a tree, a good protocol would be to honor it, for trees are sentient beings. Step 15 or 20 feet from the tree, and ask, "I would like to come to you. May I touch you to feel your love? May I enter your auric field? Would you like it if I were to come to you?" Show respect, honor, and love. Trees are life forms, very alive like you. If permission is given, then go. Then the tree will open.]

They are beings who are also part of God. They have souls, so you must stay a few feet away from them and explain that you would like to come to send your heart energy into the tree. You will receive a response. [Archangel Metatron: You will feel this. Trees have families. They may be sleeping. They may be busy with something else.]

If the response is yes, then go to the tree. Place your hand on it, and emit light into the tree. The tree will be ready to share its wisdom with you. You are asking the tree its permission to enter its area in order to get the cooperation of the tree. With cooperation, you will be able to share more and have harmony. Find some beautiful trees, and work with them.

Chapter 11

Clearing and Cleansing Your Energy

August 8, 2013

Archangel Metatron, King Akhenaton, and Sanat Kumara

Yeshua set the example for humanity. He was always connected to his lightbody and to his true self. He showed everyone; he transformed and transfigured.

All of us have lightbodies. In your meditation, ask to call forth your lightbody, and ask what to do with it. You have different layers of lightbodies. Ask for Sananda's support to bring forward your fifth-dimensional lightbody. It is like a web. During meditation, imagine that you are pulling this into yourself with a beautiful humanoid web. See how the lightbody can support you.

When you have integrated more and more of your lightbody, you become a complete lightbeing. You will be able to travel many places through the lightbody. Bilocation is much easier. So you can be in two or three places at the same time. This is done through the lightbody.

[Archangel Metatron: Bilocation is being in two places at one time through intention. You travel to another location using intention and by asking your soul. You are aware as your consciousness travels. For example, if you are thinking about something that happened twenty-four years ago, are you there or are you here now? Part of you is there. To make this very factual and objective, when you bilocate, are you physically present in both places? Can someone else see you? Or is it simply a matter of projecting your consciousness to that place so that you are aware?

It is possible to be in two places at once or even three places, but it requires high mastery. A great master like Babaji[1] did this and showed it to others. You can do it too. But it requires tremendous control of the body and the energy as well as great understanding. Simply, it is projecting your consciousness to both places.

So you are aware of what's happening in these other times or other places but you do not interact with what is going on there?

No. A time will come when people will be able to completely project themselves, including their bodies. Masters have done it; they finish their work and come back to the present. You will all reach this stage in the future. Let me ask you one thing. You are talking to Rae. Are you in America, or are you in Japan?

I am in America.

No. You are where your consciousness is.]

Here are some other things you can do with your lightbody: regenerate your cells, increase longevity, and understand and read the akashic records. We ask you to work with your lightbody because through it, you will be able to bilocate and teleport yourself. All of you will be called for this kind of work in the future. Perhaps you are not able to physically be in a certain location, but you can bilocate or teleport using your lightbody.

Here are three techniques that we wish for you to work with at this time. The first is regeneration, so you will be able to live a much longer life. The second is the ability to read and understand the akashic records, asking for groupings of three, six, or eight months, whatever.

---

1.   Babaji is discussed in Paramahansa Yogananda's *Autobiography of a Yogi*. Babaji is said to be able to heal the sick, change form, and appear in two places at once, among other abilities (http://www.crystalclarity.com/yogananda/chap33.php).

Continuously work with the akashic records. Third, work with the lightbody on a constant basis so that you are able to transport yourself or bilocate to different locations to work there and return.

Jesus demonstrated this, as did many elders in ancient times, all through lightbody activation. Call forth lightbody activation in your meditation time. Many masters do this; Babaji does it all the time. These are the new things you must work with at this time, for all of you are evolved students. Call Master Sananda for lightbody activation.

[Archangel Metatron: Do this by asking. You will see a beautiful sheet of white light in the shape of your own body. Master Sananda pulls this from a higher-dimensional reality. It is like a beautiful white cloth that is shaped like you. He pulls it and slowly brings its energy into your crown chakra. Slowly, this energy goes down into you, going down through your feet and into the ground. Visualize roots under your feet to ground this energy. This is a good exercise to do every day.]

This is very critical. There will be many strides made in different parts of the world so that lightworkers can hold more light. We need people to bilocate and work there. There are great difficulties in some places where people cannot go to work to anchor light and establish higher vibrations. You can do this by transporting yourself through your lightbody.

*　　*　　*

Connecting with Great Miracles

Hello, my friends. This is Akhenaton. Greetings and blessings to my dear and beloved family. We wish to briefly touch on two things. One is the story of the great being you know as Moses. This story is true, and we want to talk about it to show you what is possible. When Moses lifted his hand and asked for alignment with the Great Spirit, the Great Creator, the sea opened. You know this as a story, but it was a real event. Artifacts have been found under the Red Sea formed by wheels. Do you know about this?

[Archangel Metatron: Many references to this can be found by Googling "Red Sea Artifacts Moses." We want the readers of this book to be part of the journey. We do not want to give everything on a plate. Be part of the journey, and in that, you would gain much more. We are trying to jump-start the minds of the readers because when a mind is open, more is given. In older times, the whole lesson was presented predigested. That does not serve any longer. In the new consciousness, you must partake and participate. This is what we are asking now. We want people to participate.]

When you align with the Creator completely, as Jesus did, miracles can happen. We ask you to connect with that moment. Change reality for people, for the moment when Moses parted the sea (through the power of the Creator) is held in the akash. In that moment, he not only parted the sea. This was the moment of liberation for the people who were ready. You can tap into that moment, for it is etched in the akash, the history of the planet.

[Archangel Metatron: You connect with great moments through your intention. The most important tool you have is your intention. It is so powerful. It comes from the deepest part of your being. Expressing your intent is like shooting an arrow: it goes straight to the place where you shoot it. It can go wherever it is focused. This is why we say that through intention you can even heal past karmic energy. Intention is one of the most powerful tools for the new human in this time.]

It is a grand moment — a liberation. What Moses was trying to teach people was not only liberation from Egypt. Of course, on a physical level, that is what it was. But it was also liberation on a much higher level. You can have the same liberation now at the soul level, connecting with that moment in time, because it is in the akash of Mother Earth. You are capable of connecting with that particular moment to liberate yourself right now. I tell you, in three days, you will feel a difference.

We tell you this: During any moment in history when there was a miracle, the power of the Creator was present. When you believe completely and have faith beyond belief, all is recorded in Earth's akash. You can tap into these major miracle experiences, capture their essence, bring them back to the now, and place them over you. This is the gift we want to offer you.

Let me give you an example. The great brother Abraham was on the mountain with the dagger and his beloved son, but in his heart, he had great faith in Spirit. Can you connect with that kind of faith and bring it into you? [Archangel Metatron: This is an actual event that was not recorded in the Bible. It was a test of Abraham's faith. He knew the Creator. How could the Creator ask a human to sacrifice his own offspring?]

Consider the power of Jesus. He did many miracles, and there is even a list of those miracles. Can you connect with the essence of him doing the miracles with his power? Everything is there in the akash, in your own akash, and in Earth's akash.

[Archangel Metatron: In the new consciousness, you have the power of your intention. When you ask with the purest intent to connect with Brother Abraham or Brother Jesus to partake of their wisdom and understanding, this wisdom will be downloaded into you — intention, asking, and taking action. You each will receive instruction through your own filters and in your own way, tailored to your understanding. Once asked with the purest intent, the universe always provides. No one will be left out.]

We want you to connect with these magnificent events, because through them, there is great energy and great vibration seeded in the land. The experience of these events has been kept in a time capsule. Now you may go back in time to connect with grand events. I guarantee that your light will become exponentially brighter, bigger, and higher.

Having Faith Gives You Courage

In 2010, Rae had to decide whether to leave his job. He never had the courage before. He had a newborn son, and he was in a very good place in the working world. He was paid handsomely. This was a very difficult choice. Master Kuthumi taught Rae by taking him back to the time when Rae was a Greek warrior and his town was going to war. There was a great battle cry and the chants of war. Everyone was pumped up. Rae was a big, portly man, holding two swords in his hands, ready for battle.

Kuthumi showed him that this was a time when he had great courage, and he asked him to work with this feeling to bring the image of courage and paste it into his present lifetime. In about a week, he had the courage to tell his company that he was leaving. His boss was surprised because he knew Rae had just had a son, but Rae said, "I need to go." You can go back to your past and collect the qualities you seek. They are in your akash.

You can also go back to times of great miracles. There was great downloading of light and higher creative force in times past. You can connect with it. This light can enhance your light exponentially. This is one of the trainings we did in my mystery schools.

[King Akhenaton: There is no mystery in a mystery school. We understand the phrase you use, "mystery school." These schools are for truth seekers. They are sacred places where higher learning can be shared with like-minded students who are the seekers of higher truth. Mystery schools still exist, and you can access the libraries and the great wisdom held in a mystery school even now, through your dream state, through forming the intention, and by asking to be taken there by your guides. We encourage you to do this.

This may not be necessary, for the planet is already at a higher level of vibration. You already know so many things that were taught in the mystery schools. But if you were to explore further, you would still find gems of wisdom that could be applied to your present-day reality. They were called mystery schools because the consciousness of the planet was very low and the students had to be ready to experience higher energy in their beings. They needed to be in a place where they could maintain this higher vibration and purity. They were not for everybody because not everyone was ready.]

Now let me also give you one thing: Consider the three wise men who went to the grand master. These wise beings followed the stars and their own intuition, and they saw the master after their search. But what do magi represent? Magi are magicians. We would like you to connect with that event when the magi went to see the little one. When you start connecting with the magi, you will open up to your own intuitive understanding of what happened, what you need to know, and how to go about doing what you need to do.

They left this gift to the world — the gift of exploration and intuitive understanding. They were not the only ones to do this. Look at the explorers of 400 or 500 years ago. They crossed great oceans by watching the Sun during the day and the stars at night.

This knowledge exists as part of the akash of Mother Earth. If sailors could do it, you can too. Explore your own lives using the Sun, the stars, and the Moon. You are all capable of doing this. We ask you to start connecting the dots, especially with specific moments. You will see your life expanding in a huge way. You will gain a complete knowingness of how to chart your own life, and you will find God in your own way. This is the vision of your soul for you in this personality.

First, we wish for you to connect with and work with the events for which you feel the most resonance in your heart, the specific moments in history when there was great downloading of light. These are the trainings we imparted. Secondly, we ask you to work with the great magi, for they will open the energy of exploration of new ideas and new creativity to chart your own course in finding God in your own way — not in the way your personality thinks or the methods you have been using, but in a much grander and more profound way.

[King Akhenaton: These trainings will never be given unless asked for in a meditation. Prepare yourself and be ready to receive them. Prepare your body, mind, and soul to receive higher wisdom because, as you know, there is no time. Even the parting of the Red Sea happens this moment in another reality. One can tap into that reality and feel the essence of that moment, for all moments exist simultaneously.

Yes, in the fifth dimension.

Let us not call this a dimension or a name. All realities exist simultaneously. If you were able to open, you would be able to connect with many other realities. You could reach a high level of truth on the Earth plane, and you could reach your ascended self. Please remember, this book is not for babies. We do not want to spoon-feed babies. This book is for people who are ready for the next evolutionary level in their lives, for people who are ready to have a quantum leap in their evolution.]

Now we will take questions regarding DNA.

How Death Trauma Affects DNA

When we leave this world, the DNA automatically photographs the nanosecond of death, that moment of fear, trauma, or whatever we experience. How does that affect the DNA?

The DNA is always perfect. DNA is only an instruction manual, so there are two separate things. DNA always stays perfect; it *is*.

How you leave the planet has a big effect on the next life. If you have consciousness about fear, in the next life, you will not have an inclination to look at your spirituality. In any lifetime, you will bring back everything you have learned. But you must open the closet. Because of what happened in the last moments of another life, you may not be inclined to open the closet at all. So your DNA just stays as it is without doing anything. DNA is always perfect.

Higher-Dimensional Aspects of DNA and the Gantra Chakra

Does DNA exist on the fifth and sixth dimensions?

Of course, DNA exists on all higher levels. It is mostly shaped like an infinity sign.

We have talked about the twenty-fourth chakra. A question was asked about the name of the twenty-fourth chakra. The chakra's name is gantra, G-A-N-T-R-A. Imagine that there are many colors of light streaming way above your head. The top one is the twenty-fourth. Light from this chakra is being splashed around you, and you are sitting or standing in these lights. This chakra can only be activated with the assistance of a master. We ask you to call on any master you feel appropriate to activate this chakra. This is Akhenaton.

[Archangel Metatron: When one asks with the purest intent and the purest love for one's self-awakening, the entire universe is at your command. If you do not ask, nothing is given. The simple truth is, if you do not knock, the door is never opened. When you ask, and you are ready to receive this higher truth, naturally this energy will be downloaded into you.

Stay in your astral field — your energy body. It will only manifest when it is time, when you are ready for your mind to comprehend and understand it and make it into a reality. The same is true for higher truth. When the student is not ready, no amount of higher truth will make any difference. Prepare, and the new reality will appear. Working with the energy of the great Mahatma is a very high energy. We encourage you to look into this.]

❋   ❋   ❋

Cleansing the Soul

This is Metatron, speaking about activating DNA. To activate DNA, your consciousness plays the primary role. It is absolutely essential that you cleanse your consciousness. To do this, think of cleansing your energy field. But you must also cleanse your soul energy. [Archangel Metatron: To do this, work with the higher-dimensional masters, especially the masters who are in charge of the eighth to twelfth rays. You can request that they work with you to cleanse your soul, because your soul can pick up debris from everyday living, from your belief system, your cultural interactions, your upbringing, your parents, and thought projections from others.

So it is good to ask for a soul cleansing every three to six months. On a higher level, your soul is without blemish, pure. But your soul also has many levels. Ask for all levels of your soul to be cleansed with high light.]

Remembrance of many past experiences can be held as dust on your soul. Call forth whichever master you wish to work with to cleanse your soul energy, or you can call on me, Metatron. This practice is called "cleansing the soul." Do it on a periodic basis.

There are many masters who will help you cleanse your energy field. But Lady Nada works specifically with healing and cleansing soul energy. Once a month or every three months, make it a point to work with Lady Nada or any other master, and ask for help in cleansing your soul energy.

[Archangel Metatron: When you bring in higher energy and combine it with your energy, you experience a lift in consciousness. Every day, you pick up energy throughout your life. It is good to have a cleansing every fifteen days, especially if you watch a lot of television or the news. You pick up many thought forms that can affect you.

In ancient times, the initiates were asked to live separately, outside of society. People can project their thoughts to you, and if you are not strong enough, you will absorb this energy. Cleansing is just a blending of energy. Lady Nada's energy is a beautiful, soft-green color. Call on her and breathe this energy. See your heart joining with her heart in your own way and with your own imagination. You will feel a beautiful green light with a tinge of gold. Breathe it in. Give the intention that everything that is not of your soul truth be cleansed and purified. Be in this space. Lady Nada specializes in soul cleansing.]

You can also ask me and other masters to help you enter a higher vibration of the Creator's light. Every day, ask for an increased level of the Creator's light.

[Archangel Metatron: Ask for a higher vibration of the Creator's energy to be downloaded into you, higher than what you received the day before, for the Creator is also expanding. Everything and everyone is expanding constantly. So ask for a higher vibration every day or when you feel it is appropriate. These are new techniques you must use.]

Now, any questions from anybody?

Time Locks and Time Capsules

Would you explain what a time lock is?

A time lock is simple. It can only be opened when certain conditions are met. Certain specific vibrations need to take place. Only then can it be opened. It is like a time capsule, but a time capsule means that at a certain specific time, say 2015, it will open, regardless of what is happening. A time lock opens when certain vibrations are in place. Otherwise, it will not open. The conditions are higher consciousness.

Water

How do we control the water in our bodies? Lord Ashtar asks us whether we are vibrationally controlling the water within our bodies and whether we are attuning our bodies' water to higher vibration.

Know that you are more than 75 percent water. And what is the true purpose of water? The true purpose of water is expansion. Water has a quality that can expand. It is not just for cleansing. Water has properties that can help you remember who you are. You can consciously send energy to the water in your body and to the water you drink. Ask it to function and perform its true nature. Its true nature is to expand and to help you open up to your true blueprint and your true purpose for being born.

Is there a connection to our consciousness and water?

Of course. What happens when water is stuck in the body? You become a stuffy being. You cannot open up. How about consciously cleansing the water in your body? When you drink a glass of water, say, "I give intention for this water to circulate throughout my body, helping me remember my true essence, the code of Adam Kadmon (God Human), and also the purpose for which I was born." When you drink this blessed water, it will circulate throughout your body. Work with water every day, and you will see miracles in your life. Anytime you say thank you to water, the water molecules change.

[Archangel Metatron: Controlling and cleansing the water in your body is done through thought and intention. When you make an intention, this affects the water in your body. Your body is 80 percent water. Dr. Masaru Emoto[2] photographed water using beautiful music and saying loving words. The water formed beautiful crystals. But when false words

---

2. Dr. Masaru Emoto is a Japanese author and entrepreneur who claims that human consciousness has an effect on the molecular structure of water (http://en.wikipedia.org/wiki/Masaru_Emoto).

were used, untruths said, or unloving energy emitted, the molecules were malformed. What happens to your body that is 80 percent water?]

What about the thoughts in your heart and in your mind? What are you doing to the water in your body? Even the water outside your body can change through neglect or hurtful words. What about the words that you create for yourself every day through judgment, criticism, or putting yourself down? Have you not changed the consciousness of the water inside of you? Water is very critical for raising your consciousness and also the DNA.

So water stores our intentions and our thoughts?

Yes, and it expands. Also, it stores your blueprints. But the blueprint we are talking about is not about your soul's purpose or why you are born. This is the true blueprint of your true original code of Adam Kadmon. From now on, do not only focus on ascension or increasing the light inside of you, which is very good; also connect with your true original code of Adam Kadmon.

Can you explain the code of Adam Kadmon, please?

True God humans [Archangel Metatron: The ability to cocreate benevolently.]

So each of us has that?

Of course. So what we are asking of you is not to limit your focus to just ascension alone. Go into the source itself. Connect with the source of your being. Go back to the stars where you are connected.

[Archangel Metatron: Do this simply by asking. Your source is a beautiful higher self, your soul. Work with your soul every day. Make it a habit. How do you make friends in daily life? Perhaps you meet someone and exchange a telephone number. Maybe you communicate after a few days, then more and more. You might invite them to your house. People build friendships. In the same way, build on what you have started.

Make it a point to communicate with your best friend — your soul — on a daily basis. If you do not care for your soul, your soul does not really care much, either. Make it a point to do this every day.]

The embryonic state?

Exactly.

We come from the stars; that is our connection.
   All come from the stars.

Star elements, our star energies, our star codes — this is the source of our being?
   This is the true source of your being. That is what we ask you to do with it. Go to your source.

Changing Consciousness at Subconscious and Cellular Levels

How do we talk to our cells in order to bring about positive change from any dis-ease or lack from any lifetime that is now in the subconscious and in the cells? This is like a record or a program?

   This is true. It is not easy. Many people try to talk to the cells in the body every day. These are called body talks. But, you know, very few have results. There are many aspects of working on this. First of all, your body must be receptive. See how to make your body receptive. The second thing is to purify your body. Purifying means more than just taking a bath.

   Humans are all run by programs from the past — your subconscious minds, your unconscious minds. This is why the Essenes gave so much importance to their subconscious minds. They said that truth happens in the subconscious mind. So if you want your body to be receptive when you talk to it, program this body talk into your subconscious mind.

   [Archangel Metatron: The subconscious just brings forth what is put in there through your thought processes. If you want to have something materialize from your subconscious, put what you want to happen there. The subconscious does not differentiate between good or bad, ugly or beautiful. It just brings forth what is anchored there. Most subconscious minds are filled with fear, control, ego, and other unhelpful things from the past. Most human beings live through their subconscious minds.

   Do you want to live true to your highest blueprint and life mission? Cleanse your subconscious mind with the great light. The moment you integrate more high-vibrational light, your subconscious is cleansed and purified, more and more. Ask to send more light to your subconscious mind, and see it being cleansed, layer by layer.

   Your subconscious mind responds much faster if an image is placed there. This is why it is said that a picture is worth a thousand words. An image imprints your subconscious mind, and an image can be materialized. When an image fully enters your subconscious mind, it filters into your conscious mind and your conscious reality. Constantly work to program your subconscious mind.

One simple exercise is to tilt your head back with your neck forward, close your eyes, and visualize what you want to happen, not what is happening in your life, but what outcomes you would want to happen. Do this for five minutes. Tilt your head back a bit so that it rests on your shoulders. Spend five minutes a day visualizing as clearly as possible the perfect outcome of what you are trying to create. This can support you.]

Your cells hear everything you say.

Yes, and what you think as well.

Yes, and they are able to bring it forth. This change must happen in the cellular and subconscious levels. If you want change, work at the subconscious level. Let me give a small example. All of you know that you have moved to fifth-dimensional reality. But many of you still operate in the third-dimensional reality because you still do not believe that you are fifth-dimensional beings.

We mostly perceive what happens around us.

Exactly. If you want to get rid of the world matrix, first you must change your own matrix in your own minds and then the energy of the matrix. So work with that.

[Archangel Metatron: The matrix is simply the energy of the conscious and unconscious minds of all human beings on the planet. The basic nature of the matrix is fear. When there is fear, there is control. It is very easy to get caught in this matrix if you are weak, for the energy of the matrix is strong. It actually permeates the entire planet, and human beings are like sponges, easily picking up these energies without realizing it. Throughout history, most masters were alone. It was very easy to be tainted by the energies of those around them, so they stayed in their own power. The energy of the matrix is much stronger now because of the media. So you must be alert to this energy and how it affects your subconscious mind.

Let me give you an example. In April 2013, there was a bombing at the Boston Marathon. There were also so many other beautiful things happening in your state, but the media kept up nonstop coverage of the bombing, again and again.

Yes. So it affected everybody's matrix. I see what you're saying.
It affected everybody's subconscious mind and created fear. This year (2014), did the marathon have the same festive feeling?

I talked to a lady at the bank the other day. She is terrified of flying after all this noise in the media about the missing Malaysian airplane. On and on she went. I told her that she is safer in an airplane than a car, but she is just so fear based.
This is what we said. The matrix controls human beings. If you are prone to watching television or using the Internet, they affect you much more than you realize. You do not realize that you are constantly picking up energy from others.

So working with the matrix means controlling your intake of media and what you absorb?
It is not only from the media. You must be aware of the energy you pick up from everything, including the media. Human beings, by their very nature, are like sponges. They are continuously taking in energy from others. You must have a daily practice of cleansing the energy you have picked up, like brushing your teeth or taking a shower. Cleanse your energy field daily. You do this by asking to be cleared.]
It is also good to communicate with your body when it is moist. This is why people in Asia do their morning prayers and meditation under falling water. When the body is moist, the cells are more open.
[Archangel Metatron: You can try this in your bathtub. Get into your bathtub, filled with cold water. You are very sensitive at that time. Your emotions are heightened, and you are in a much more sensitive state. When you communicate to your cells, the communication is coming from the deepest part of your feelings. The cells will get the message more clearly than at other times. Do the experiment yourself, and you will see whether this works for you.]

So the cells are very connected with the water?
It is like hand and glove.

They are one with the water.
Exactly. You are one with the water. Do you know why? You were

a water-breathing being for ten months. You came from water — water in the mother's womb. And this water was your life, your connection to source, your food, your nurturance, and — most importantly — your love quotient.

As soon as you were born, you became an air being. Your connection with water was lost immediately. What happens when you take a fish out of water? It dies.

Just imagine a child taken out of water and suddenly surrounded by air. See the trauma in the mind for the baby. There are three traumas. First, you pass through the birth canal; second, you are a water being suddenly in the air; and third, you are disconnected from source, from your mother who gave you life, support, and nurturance.

This is where we must do healing. This is where separation consciousness begins. "The one who breathed my life was taken from me. The God who loves me is in a separate place." [Archangel Metatron: This saying has been quoted many times. It has been said in different ways because all human beings feel a disconnection when they are born. The soul that gave me life is no longer with me.] Water is the source.

Is this trauma and lack recorded and remembered in our cells and in our DNA?

Yes, in your genes and in your auric field. So work with water. It can truly do miracles. When you drink water, talk to it. Ask the water to give, for this is the natural function of water. It will open up and expand. Remember, it connects you with your true source.

The best water is water that comes from an underground source, directly from the ground. It can be difficult to get spring water, but get it if you can. It contains the purest essence and many magnetic minerals that can support your body.

How can we shift consciousness at the cellular level?

When there is a shift of consciousness in your subconscious mind filtering into your mind, naturally your cells will have more light. So we ask you to work your subconscious mind because it is much easier to work with a mortal body. The emotions that you know are energy in motion, and you are able to control them. You are able to choose. What energy do you wish to experience today: high energy or low energy? Emotions are energy in motion, so you can move this energy however you want.

[Archangel Metatron: One simple method for shifting your consciousness at the cellular level concerns the food you eat. If you constantly eat heavy food with a dense vibration, your cells have to work overtime to assimilate this food. They do not have time to relax, to bring forth higher levels of consciousness. If your mind is continuously focused on dense thoughts while you eat dense food, your cells are working overtime. Also, sound, sacred geometry, and beautiful paintings can support you, for their energy bypasses your brain and goes directly into your cells.]

It is at least one hundred times more difficult to heal the mental body and bring it under control, because the mental body is completely ruled by all the thought experiences you have ever had. We are talking of hundreds of lifetimes. Then there is so much fear in the mental body from all the things that have happened. Although these things are not remembered, they are very strongly etched into the mental body.

The mental body can only be shifted through higher light. The easiest way to achieve this is to work in the subconscious. The Essenes were given specific guidance on how to program their subconscious minds every day. If you can change the subconscious mind, you can change outer reality.

Joseph Murphy taught about the power of the subconscious mind. Change your subconscious mind, and change your reality. We ask you to read *The Power of Your Subconscious Mind* by Joseph Murphy. He talks about the subconscious mind and how important it is. It creates reality. A subconscious mind is just like a field; whatever you put in it will grow. Just imagine what you have put there for hundreds and thousands of years. The energy will always stay there. Once energy is created, it needs either completion or transformation.

Remembering Who We Really Are

I want to ask about the memory of our attachment to our higher selves. It fades out completely when we are a few years old. The remembrance of this is held within the grids of unconsciousness. How can we reverse this state?

There are two aspects of this. When a child is born, for the first few hours, the child is fully aware of who he or she truly is. Later, the child is still aware, but not at that level. Then slowly, around the age of three, the child starts forgetting who he or she truly is and starts integrating more into everyday life and its environment.

Let me ask you, if you were fully conscious, would you do the work you have come here to do? Would you complete the challenges and tasks that you had planned? If you know all the answers to your life, will there be any fun?

No, that's the challenge of learning and growing.

Exactly, and this causes the shift of Mother Earth. If you did not have any life lessons and if you remembered everything, you would not have to be here. You would not have to be born. So it is designed that you will forget so that you will come back and work. Through this, you are drawing more light and also helping planet Earth, for your evolution is directly tied to the evolution of Mother Earth.

But now, since Mother Earth has moved into higher realities, we all are shifting with that reality. By working on yourself, focus on yourself. You will increase the light and you will remember more and more of yourself. If you go back to the time when you were born, you will remember more of yourself, for that baby knew exactly who it was, completely, in its fullest sense.

This is one of the reasons we keep asking you to go back to the akashic records. Every teacher talks about the importance of being able to read and understand akashic records. This is one of the great keys. It records every key experience you ever had, including the complete memory of who you were when you were born. Are there any other questions?

I am moving from a carbon-based being to a silica being, a crystalline being, which is a rewiring of memory. Is this silica state in my physical body or in another body? And will it help me remember more of who I am?

This is happening in the physical body.

Calling Elohim to Clear Old Energy Patterns

All of you can now call on the Great Elohim. In your meditation, call on them to rewire your mind. Ask them to remove the energy patterns that you have been carrying for many lifetimes. You may experience forgetfulness for a few days.

[Archangel Metatron: Call on them before you go to sleep and ask them to rewire the energy of your thought forms. Thoughts are energy. Even subtle thoughts are energetic in nature. If you think of the same thing over and over, that energy gets embedded. Ask them to remove the energy that has already finished its purpose or has reached completion. Ask them to flush out your subconscious mind. They will do it.

Also ask them to use the golden vacuum to cleanse your mind and your subconscious mind. Visualize this vacuum sucking away everything that is not of the light from your subconscious mind. Ask them to rewire your subconscious mind, your unconscious mind, and everything with vibrational energy that you no longer need or that is incompatible with the new consciousness of the planet.

You will see how well this works. You may not remember as much as you remembered, and other things will not have the emotional charge they used to have. You could feel a little bit spaced out or forgetful but only temporarily. All the positive things will remain. Only negative things will be removed. Ask that all negative energy and all the energy that has been completed be removed. You want to keep the energy that was beneficial. This can be done before you go to sleep.]

These old patterns do not support you in the new direction you now wish to create. For example, suppose you have a life lesson about healing forgiveness. You have completed the life lesson, but the energy of this still stays in your memory. What the Elohim will do is remove that energy's memory. Work with the Elohim during your sleep time to completely rewire your brain, rewire your mind, and remove all strands of mind energy that do not serve you in the creation of a new reality of higher dimensions.

Faith and Miracles

Healing your past helps you understand faith and miracles. When Jesus commanded miracles to be performed, do you think he doubted the outcome? He never doubted. When he had the intention, he aligned his consciousness with the will of the Creator, completely in that moment, for whatever needed to be done. He just opened his hand, and it was there. Every scripture talks about having faith. So you must have faith that you will be able to unlock the codes and connect with the Adam Kadmon code inside you.

At the Egyptian mystery school at Kom Ombo, the initiates had to swim underwater in a pool full of crocodiles. [Archangel Metatron: If you type "swimming with crocodiles at Kom Ombo" into Google, you will see much information on this practice from different sources. There is even a museum there with mummified crocodiles.] These crocodiles were fed and drugged, but the initiates did not know that. They had to swim through a small opening, and many of them died of heart attacks doing this. The ones who had faith that crocodiles are of the Creator and would not harm them survived. Crocodiles are a part of the great teacher. The initiates know that the source of their creation is also the source of these great beings.

Here is a mantra taught by masters to aid, to enhance faith, and to overcome fear-based experiences: It is *"Ee tel om Ra."* [Archangel Metatron: This means: "I am the Infinite Soul." These are Egyptian words that also mean: "I claim the power within me; I claim the God who I am."] This mantra will help you have great faith and overcome fear, especially during spiritual initiations, but it could also be applied in your daily lives.

We are so delighted that we are able to speak to such beings as you, who hold much light. It is always a great and joyful experience sharing our time with you. So we want to say thank you for this opportunity because when you increase the light, you increase the light in us as well. This is truly a mutual partnership.

Archangel, are you giving us a compliment? [Laughs.]
Why can't you take a compliment? We want you to start acknowledging yourselves. You are also important players in the world. Never put yourselves down, and never put us on a pedestal. When you honor yourself, you are honoring us. We are part of you, always.

Storing Drinking Water

Try to store your drinking water in an earthen pot, made by hand if possible, and draw a beautiful infinity symbol on all four sides. Draw a Flower of Life image on the bottom of the pot, and place this pitcher on a platinum, gold, or silver coin. Try to fill it with water that you will be using the next day. The water will have a higher vibrational energy — the energy of Mother Earth combined with the energy of Spirit — Father/Mother Creator energy infused in balance. It is also advisable to cover the pitcher when you are not using it. This can support you very much.

Filtering and chemicals remove the purity and true essence of water. If you drink water like this, you cannot remember who you are. If you do not remember who you are, you open yourself to be controlled. This is how people are kept under control.

So try to keep your water in the earthenware pot. Draw the Flower of Life with your own hand. It does not have to be perfect. It is the intention behind what you are drawing. And it is best to place it on a coin that is silver in color or a silver pendant. If you can use true gold, that is also fine. If not, use gold-colored foil. Leave it overnight. This water will be highly purified and highly charged.

I drink local spring water. It is delivered once a month, and it's stored in plastic bottles.

Then take water from the plastic container, and put it into an earthenware pot.

Then dispense from there?

Exactly. Because right now, you are all trying to work on yourselves to increase your remembrance of who you are. This practice of storing water can be very beneficial in supporting this and in nurturing yourselves.

Three Practices with Water

If you have a bathtub in your house, fill it up with hot water [as you would bathe in]. Get into the hot water, and slowly visualize yourself getting smaller and smaller, slowly going back to the time when you were inside your mother's womb, feeling the warmth of your mother. You are inside your mother's womb and also in Mother Earth, immersed in this beautiful warm fluid.

Breathe in the love of Mother Earth and of your own mother. Being in this space for a few moments will help you remember the love you had and will naturally expand your love. You will feel very good.

Here is another thing you can do: In your bathtub, take the water you are bathing in into your hands. Cold water is best. Blow into it three times. Then pour it over your head. You are baptizing yourself. What does baptizing truly mean? It removes one more layer of illusion. You can do your own baptizing.

Thirdly, suppose you have something stuck in your mind, and you cannot let go of it. Take a shower, and then shake your hair. This is the method taught to Jesus by the great Druid teachers of England. Just shake your hair as much as you can. You will be able to shake off the strong energy that is stuck inside of you.

Your hairs are antennae, and they also carry memories. When you cut your hair, memories are gone. This is why Buddhists shave their heads when they become priests. Their hair is gone, so they have a new identity.

Clearing Your Consciousness and Cutting Energy Cords

Is it true that our effects and defects affect every person who comes within our fields of communication and consciousness?

Of course, very much so. The experience that you have of another human being starts with an "us." As soon as you see another person and judge him or her, please remember that you are hurting someone inside of yourself. Have no judgment. You must come to a place of nonjudgment — not good or bad. Everything is an experience, and that is all.

Our energies affect other people around us, particularly if we are in a bad mood or we are angry.

Of course, very much so. Where did this begin? Remember that when you were born, you were a water being. Then you became an air being. In this time (of being born), there was great fear and confusion in the child's mind. The child knew that it had great support, love, and nurturance through its umbilical cord. In the confusion and fear, the baby put energy cords to everyone around it, including the doctor, the nurses, everybody.

Most human beings (the doctor, the nurses) are not balanced. There is no love there. The baby picks up that energy right away. A human being makes more than 10 million energy cords in a lifetime. When energy is created, it needs completion. This is why people cannot break out of the cycle of reincarnation, because energy needs completion. So we must cut energy cords.

This is why maintenance of your energy field is critical. You must cleanse your energy body. You should say, "Whatever I have created today through my own thoughts and whatever energy I have collected through my experiences and interactions with others, that is not of love and not of the Creator's purest love, I completely disconnect now." When you start doing this exercise every day, removing and clearing, you can go back to past experiences and cut those energy cords. Then you can connect with your positive, higher-vibrational self.

Ask that all energy from everyone you have had negative experiences with in your life be disconnected from you at this time. Disconnect only from the sad, negative experiences, not the positive ones. When you start doing this, you will become clearer. You become much freer. You feel free in your life.

You can invoke your guides or the Creator or the gold light of being to come and disconnect you from the experience you had with a particular person, a particular time period, or anything else. This is called cleansing. When you start doing this, you will feel so free. You do this within four hours. [Archangel Metatron: Within four hours of the event, ask for the gold light to come and disconnect you from the experience you just had.] It takes four hours for the cells to get the message fully, because it is part of an energy imprint. It will not be part of your karmic energy.

Think of all the things you have experienced in your thousands of lifetimes. You can clear them through this simple technique with the gold light of the Creator's disconnection energy.

A question about sacred places: People go to an altar with all their issues, whether they are sad, angry, or whatever the negative intentions are. Do those energies still remain at those sacred places?

Rae was asked to go to many sacred places and cleanse the energy fields. When people went there, they had an expectation of healing or a miracle, and this did not happen, so they experienced dejection or sadness. This is all stored there. The ground you walk on absorbs your energy. What kind of energy are you carrying? Greed, hate, or fear? It goes into the ground. You must cleanse your energy field in the ground. Start disconnecting from all energies.

For example, you could say, "I call forth the Creator (or any deity) to disconnect me from the energy of the hatred this land holds and is affecting me at a deep subconscious level." Or you can ask to put energy codes back into the ground with the help of your guides. You can also ask for support with the good things of life — abundance, creativity, love. This is very important work. This process starts in the womb. As soon as the baby is born, the baby starts putting energy forth because of the trauma of birth.

What is the difference in the DNA of someone being born and the same person seventy years later?

DNA is always perfect; it is the genes and the consciousness that are affected. If you had a traumatic birth with the experiences from a past life you created, this is your new reality. You bring in energies from a past life; it becomes a part of your genes and your life experiences. You will not be in a position to create higher consciousness unless you specifically work on that.

Many times, because of life circumstances, people are not able to even think about higher things because they live in survival mode. This is a big problem in India, Sudan, and Africa. People are stuck in survival mode, and when they die, they think, "I hate this life." They come back with the same consciousness, and it repeats again and again. When they are in that mode, can they think about higher consciousness? Gandhi said, "You cannot teach about God with an empty stomach." This is how many people live, even now. They are in survival mode.

DNA is always perfect, but the effect on genes is huge. Old patterns will continue again and again. It takes tremendous effort to get out of this cycle and start focusing on higher reality.

Working with the Karmic Board

People need to know how to work with the Karmic Board. The Karmic Board has now been given permission to bypass many karmic energies. You can consciously ask in a meditation for the Karmic Board to change a particular energy — if you are feeling sad or depressed — so that you do not have to repeatedly experience this. All of you have the capacity and the understanding to work with these beings, the Karmic Board, the Elohim, and Gaia. Work with them, and a whole lot will be healed.

When you are clear, you start opening your vessel. You hold more and more light because you have cleared your old energy cords. Your vessel is no longer empty. How do you know you have become clear and have more light? Others will reflect it back to you.

Suppose you see someone, and you react by thinking, "That man has a big ego." Immediately, your ego is triggered inside of you. If you did not have an ego, you would not have the experience of being triggered by another person. Everything is a reflection of what is within us.

When you complete a lot of clearing and healing, your vessel will hold more and more light. Occasionally, you may have flare-ups, but immediately you will know, "This is not me," and you will know to bring yourself back to reality right away. Cutting energy cords every day allows you to hold a higher vibration of light.

This is Metatron. It has been a great joy to connect with all of you, so we want to say thank you. We want to say, we love you very dearly. Now we will have one short message from the great master Sanat Kumara.

✳   ✳   ✳

Erasing Death Imprints

My dear beings, I am Sanat Kumara. I have been the planetary guardian for a long time. Although some of the roles have shifted, I, along with others, hold the perfect imprint for the planet and the perfect imprint for each and every human being. So call on me in your meditation time and ask for your perfect imprint, for I hold it.

Recently, Babaji suggested to Rae that he prolong his longevity by asking that the imprint he brought into this lifetime for his own death be erased. We ask you to do the same thing. Each person brings about four to seven imprints of death or near-death or near-miss experiences. These exit points are imprints that you brought into your physical body. Ask that the death imprints be erased for this lifetime.

[Archangel Metatron: You do this during your meditation, through intention and asking. These are the new tools. You must ask for these new tools to be anchored into you. Then you can say, "I call forth my guides to support me in becoming a new being in this new consciousness, and I ask that any exit points I have had that were part of my old contract be completely erased at this time. I give intent to open the new contract within me for the new timeline."]

Then call on me to integrate the truest blueprint. I hold the imprint for each soul within me, the perfection of the imprint. I will overlay it over you. This is my gift to all of you. This is Sanat Kumara.

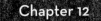

Chapter 12

Working with Additional Layers of DNA for Ascension

August 16, 2013

Adama, Master Kuthumi, Mother Mary, Crystal Skull, and Lord Maitreya

This is Adama, from [the Inner Earth land of] Telos, welcoming you to the grand land of Telos and to its cities. There are many inner healing temples, and we invite you to visit them as often as you can. Some of these temples are the holders of the sacred flames. By visiting these temples, you will naturally raise your consciousness to activate your DNA.

We invite you to come to these temples, especially the Temples of the Sacred Flames. [Archangel Metatron: There are many temples on the inner planes that can support human beings, and there are many temples for sacred flames. These flames were consecrated by the Creator and are kept alive by ascended masters and angelic beings. You can visit these temples and purify yourself in these flames. They are purification temples. We encourage you to go to these temples in your sleep. You can do this by asking to do so in your meditation, by expressing the intention that you want to go to the temple of a particular flame.]

We encourage you to visit the temples of the Maha Chohan of Paul the Venetian and work with him. [Archangel Metatron: When you make an intention from your heart that you want to go to these places for healing, you are taken there by your guides. To know more about this, you can read *The Seven Sacred Flames*, by Aruelia Louise Jones. Maha Chohan is the Grand Master. All of you have been students of one of the sacred flames in one lifetime.] He integrated the crystal rose flame and the vibrations associated with it. Also work with Paul the Venetian to support and open the heart center fully, especially working with the crystal rose flame.

All of you are very aware of the need to understand the rays of God, but there are also seven sacred flames you must integrate for ascension. We feel that working with the third flame, the sacred flame of love, is critical. Before you go to sleep every night, we encourage you to make an intention to visit this temple and call on the master Paul the Venetian.

You are in a very sacred time when the new history is being made on the planet. We would like to talk briefly about the different layers of DNA. You have alignment with the DNA layers of Gaia. You also have DNA on the solar level, the galactic level, the universal level, the multiuniversal level, and the cosmic level. We ask that you ask to activate not only the twelve layers of DNA but also to be in alignment with all the layers of the DNA throughout all these dimensions, because ascension is a process. There are many, many steps. You want to activate DNA layer by layer. You must activate the DNA in all layers, from the planet level all the way to the cosmic level.

Working with Your Signature Cell

Each of you has a signature cell, sometimes called the God cell. Everyone has one. You can go into the God cell and direct it to any part of your body that needs healing and also to expand the light. Before you manifest anything in your life, first, place all the energy of your intention into your signature cell, and ask the signature cell to go into every other cell, lighting every cell with the energy of your intention. Then your cells will get the message. When things happen in the cells, outside manifestation will take place much faster.

We can use this for healing. What else can we change?

Anything you want to create in your life. You must remember one thing: You are here as creators in training. When you want to change anything in your life, use the signature cell.

First, set the intention, and then send the energy of the intention inside the signature cell. See this cell going into every other cell, igniting each with the energy of your intention and moving through your bloodstream and throughout your body, even into your hair, skin, bones, and all the organs — into your entirety.

You will see the physical changes in about three weeks when you start working with your signature cell. There can be many influences from the past, your mind, your environment, and your upbringing. But if you work with your signature cell, you are working with the purest of energy.

That is our original cell?

Exactly. One of the things you may want to place in your signature cell is a sacred geometric pattern that is in resonance with your heart. There are many sacred geometric patterns; choose the one that you feel resonates the best in your heart. Let your feelings decide. There is the Star of David, the Ark of the Covenant, symbols of the human angel, or the infinity sign.

Or the Flower of Life.

Whatever. Place it into the signature cell, and see this expanding into your body and into every cell, filled with this energy.

It would help to know the different effect of each of these geometric symbols.

Each has a different effect. The golden ankh represents perfection, just like the cross — matter and spirit coming together, Father / Mother God, Spirit, and Mother Earth.

What does the Ark of the Covenant symbolize for us in our God cell?

The Ark of the Covenant symbolizes three things: the complete love of God, the complete love of your I Am presence, and the complete love you have with all creation and the cosmic beings who support creation.

What is the symbol of the Ark of the Covenant? What does it look like?

Imagine a large box with the two angels sitting on top of it. Imagine miniaturizing it and sending it into the signature cell.

What does the Star of David symbolize?

Universal wisdom. The Flower of Life symbolizes interconnectedness with all life wisdom. The pyramid symbolizes your sacred spirituality. We ask you to work with your signature cell to activate the higher layers of DNA not only at the earth level but also at the galactic level, solar level, universal level, multiuniversal level, and cosmic level.

Would it help to visualize the signature cell in a particular part of our bodies such as our hearts?

Of course. As you know, visualization and imagination play a very critical role in one's spiritual evolution.

Thank you.

Any questions from anybody?

Cords of Attachment to the Creator and Other Higher Beings

What is the silver DNA strand?

All of you are aware of the silver cord that is connected directly to the heart of the Creator. When you leave this planet, the silver cord is snapped. It goes back to the source from which it came. There are also many other cords attached to the Creator. For example, there is a golden cord, a platinum cord, an aquamarine cord, and a turquoise cord. These cords are directly linked to the higher chakras, and all the chakras are directly linked to the Creator. Your higher chakras are activated through the energy coming from the Creator through these other cords. So imagine — in your mind's eye — twelve cords going from the top of your head all the way to the Creator, activating the higher layers of the chakra column.

We ask you to envision your chakras activated all the way up to the twenty-fifth chakra. We gave the name of the twenty-fourth chakra last time. It is called the *gantra* chakra. The twenty-fifth chakra has a Sanskrit name; it is called the *artnakar* chakra. These chakras are directly linked to higher dimensions.

Envision that your chakras are going all the way up to the twelfth dimension, and the cords from your head are directly connected to activating these higher layers. We are asking you to not only focus on the soul crown chakra, which is just above your crown chakra, but also go up to the higher twenty-fifth chakra and see energy falling around you like a lattice through a rainbow of colors. You are surrounded in this lattice.

Imagine that you have all twenty-five chakras. You do not need their names to imagine that there are twenty-five chakras. All are above your head, and from there, rainbow colors are falling down. You are surrounded by them. So shift your focus from the soul star chakra to the higher chakras. They are all connected through different cords.

When you pass away, the cords are snapped—but the energy, vibration, and consciousness contained in these cords are never snapped and do not disappear. They come again in the next life. For example, when a person leaves this planet, should that person choose to come back, he or she will bring all the teaching, all the wisdom, all the consciousness, and all the energy vibration that had accumulated in this lifetime through these cords.

The beauty is that when the planet evolves, humans evolve, and more and more of these cords will be placed inside of you. For example, when you start connecting with Lord Melchizedek, there will be a cord from Lord Melchizedek connected to you. You can ask for this cord to be strengthened or connected eternally. When you connect with Metatron, cords from Metatron will be sent directly into you. You are fed energy from the masters through these cords. We ask you to work with these cords, for they are conduits for the energy coming from the masters and higher beings.

Do you also know that you can ask for an energy connection to be placed between you and Max the Crystal Skull? Max represents the perfection of human beings. He is a library not just for this planet and not just of this galaxy but also for the universe.

Connecting with Important Historical Moments

Recently, we mentioned the importance of having connection with certain important moments in the history of this planet, certain miracles. The great energy of God was delivered when Moses was able to part the sea. This moment is recorded in the akash of Mother Earth, and you can tap into it by asking for an energy cord from that moment to your head. We ask you to be cautious, for these are highly charged energy particles, and you should be ready to accept them. This is very high-vibration energy, truly the ultimate energy.

Another event that truly took the world by surprise was Jesus's resurrection. We ask you to ask Master Jesus for the energy cord to be placed between you and that event and time. Ask Master Jesus to activate your higher chakras and for the energetic cord to his resurrection. Master Jesus exists on many planes. You can ask Master Jesus to connect with you through all dimensional realities.

[Archangel Metatron: Please remember that not only do you exist on the Earth plane but your essence also exists in many other realities. You must call these forth. For example, there are also parts of you on the galactic level, on the solar level, on the universal level, on the multi-universal level, on the cosmic level, and on the level of the Central Sun. You must ask to be healed and to be fully on all these levels and also from the first to the twelfth dimensions, through all parallel and alternate realities. Then you have true healing. Then you truly integrate energies from the Creator in the fullest. Otherwise, you are only integrating a very small part of you. This is done during your meditation. We emphasize this because there is much work to be done by lightworkers; there are so many things to do.

For my own sake, for my own mental understanding, I would be grateful for you to explain the difference between cosmic, universal, multiuniversal, and the other planes.

These are just different higher-vibrational energies. Is one level bigger or better than another? I would say no. But each level has a higher vibration. Higher vibration does not mean that they are superior, or better.

It is just a different level.

Exactly, and each level has its own master. Work with these masters to understand yourself and to integrate yourself at each level. For example, you can open the heart chakra on the planetary level, but you can also ask for the opening of your heart at the galactic level, at the solar level, the universal level, and the multiuniversal level. The bar is stepping up. You can ask for your higher blueprint from all these levels to be activated, not just from the planetary level. You can ask that Christ consciousness be anchored into you not only at the planetary level but also at the multiuniversal and cosmic levels. Your consciousness will be expanded much more.

This is done just through setting intention, asking for support from your guides during your meditation. You must remember one thing: Spiritual evolution never stops. If you reach a certain level and say, "This is mastery," no. The bar is stepped up again and again and again.]

Now, does anybody else have any other questions?

Solar Effects on DNA

I want to know whether the Sun is having any effect on DNA. I mean the polar changes, the magnetics, and the solar flares. Do those things affect our DNA?

These affect the consciousness of human beings. They affect the emotions, the feelings, and the mind, all of which definitely affect your consciousness. They are like a double-edged sword. They can elevate your consciousness, or they can create much more disharmony. When you are balanced and have a higher consciousness, your DNA is automatically affected.

An Exercise to Connect with Your Interdimensional Aspects

We would like to give all of you a small homework exercise. Picture an Indian god with many hands and many faces, all fading into each other. What does this show? The multiple hands and faces show the interdimensional aspect of that particular archetypal energy. We want you to do these exercises for yourselves.

Imagine, or visualize in your mind's eye, that there are twelve beings of yourself. You are the thread in the twelve beings behind you, fading into them, into different hands, different heads. This is a wonderful exercise. You will start incorporating the quantum aspects of yourself. Your everyday life will slowly change. You will make choices and decisions from your quantum aspects, not just a particular aspect of yourself. It will take some time to get used to this idea, but you are these twelve beings, and they are with you all the time. They are behind you.

This exercise will help you shift your perspective about who you are. You will start connecting not only with your physical human heart but also with your quantum human heart, from each of these beings in twelve dimensions. This can truly empower and enrich your life. Your intuition will be strengthened. Your emotions will be stabilized. Your mind will be clarified. We ask that you draw this out yourself. See your

Quantum Symbol.

face and then other faces fading back and meditate on this (see Quantum Symbol image). This can support you because you are bringing all aspects of yourself to the fore.

Aligning with Recent Planetary Shifts

One of the problems you face this year is that although you know there has been a shift, you have not fully embraced it and the wholeness of yourself. Many are still acting from a very limited aspect of themselves. Yes, it will take some time to integrate this, but you must work on integrating these changes. Then you will be in complete alignment with the new consciousness of the planet. You must come into alignment.

The planet has shifted. Did you shift? You may think intellectually that you have shifted but experientially, absolutely not. This is why there is so much confusion. We encourage you to start working from that level. This will mean you are in alignment with your new catholic (universal) self.

You might have seen many people channeling about the new magnetic heart and the new magnetic mind being opened. What do these mean? This is the opening of the quantum mind and the quantum heart.

We ask you to envision each cell of your body being turned into an infinity sign filled with the color gold. [Archangel Metatron: You do this by visualizing. When you visualize, you are imprinting your subconscious mind with this image.] At the center point of the infinity sign, there is a golden Flower of Life. As you know, your cells are very alive with their own consciousness, each with its own heart. Cells have their own heart centers that communicate with them. Placing the infinity sign in your cells will shift them into their quantum aspects. They are thirsty, and they long for this.

Imagine yourself filled with trillions of infinity signs, and imbedded in each infinity sign, there is a golden Flower of Life. This will raise your vibration immediately. This is one of the practices taught in the mystery schools of ancient Egypt. If you were to visit Karnak Temple in Luxor (in Egypt), you would see this initiation by Master Thoth drawn on the walls in the initiation chamber.

Now, do you have any questions, dear ones?

I would like to know about the quantum self that is said to be the observer. Is it simply an observer of everything that takes place?

It used to be the observer, but now this has shifted. It is to become fully incorporated and to include every action coming from not only the observer level but from the participant level as well.

You can work on this with a particular being (master) you feel close to. Send a beam of energy from your third eye chakra into the third eye chakra of that being. There will be an interchange of energy coming from that being into you. A large measure of consciousness can be opened immediately, and you will feel a shift and more clarity. You will feel much more at peace, more joyful, and more expansive.

[Archangel Metatron: You do this by calling the being forth. For example, if you want to work with the Master Kuthumi, invoke the full essence and presence of Master Kuthumi to be with you and see an energy beam. Visualize as best you can. When an intention is made, it happens automatically. See energy in front of you as best as you can. From your own third eye chakra, say, "I send energy from my heart first and then from all my chakras into the chakras of Master Kuthumi — with whom I wish to integrate my energy." You will feel energy coming into you, forming an infinity sign from the master to you and filling you up with higher consciousness.

At the next level, invoke the master and ask him or her to be present with you. See the master sitting in front of you. Visualize in your own way and say, "Master, I am open now to receive higher-vibrational energy. I wish to make a deeper connection with you through my chakras." You will see the connection between your chakra and the master's chakra. Your chakra will be filled with higher-vibrational energy. Do it daily, and you will know when to stop it because you will have a feeling of completion. But we encourage you to do it slowly, and not too much at night, because the energy could be so strong that you may not be able to sleep.]

Healing Yourself and Others

How do I go about adding more angels and more guides?

Angels have a hierarchy system, but also there are angels assigned for each specific task. There are angels specifically for physical healing, business and commerce, organizational and structural formation, creativity, literature, music, water, and so forth.

If you are trying to help someone heal physically, then you must call for the angels who work with the physical body. They work with the body template. But they will only work with people if the healing does not interfere with their karmic lessons. If the healing would interfere with a karmic lesson, these angels will not bring the healing. You must petition them and ask whether the healing is for the people's highest good. Have they learned the karmic lesson they have come here to experience? Angels also work with the guidance of the Karmic Board.

Quan Yin is a member of the Karmic Board. So when you ask for the physical healing for others, you may ask the Karmic Board or Quan Yin whether this healing will benefit this person karmically. This is one of the reasons Jesus did not heal everybody, for he knew that by healing some people, they would not learn their life lessons. Before any healing took place, he asked the Creator whether it was appropriate to heal that person.

You can call on the angels of healing or work with the Karmic Board. You can work with the angels to replace old body templates with the new body templates that can hold higher-vibrational energy. Remember that the planet has shifted. You must adjust to the shift. You must upgrade yourself to where your whole body, your heart, your eyesight, your lungs, your kidneys, your intestines, your stomach — everything — can hold more vibrational energy. Call on these healing angels to work with you.

When the sages and yogis of India are ready to pass away, they thank every part of their bodies, for body parts have consciousness and work in harmony and unity. You can ask the angels to support you in upgrading your body parts. Angels play a very important role in your ascension and in the activation of your DNA. Call on your personal angels. When you wake up in the morning, ask them to work with you to bring the energies of harmony and balance.

Ask your angels to put you in a cocoon of divine love. You can go into this cocoon. It is your sacred, loving space. You will feel comfortable there, especially if you had an issue with your inner child. Work with this love cocoon of the angels. Enter it every day. It is your sacred and beautifully protected space. It is spun of a beautiful silver platinum light, a webbing of light around you. Ask for this cocoon of light to be placed around you when you go to bed every night. You will feel loved and supported, and your body will rest well and absorb the love coming from the cocoon. You will feel much calmer. You will have a good night's sleep, and you will be better able to manifest love in your waking hours.

There are certain animals and certain species of birds that support humanity. Let us see whether someone can come and speak about that.

*　　*　　*

Crickets, Bees, and Golden Eagles

My dear brothers and sisters, this is Master Kuthumi. Let us look at the great golden eagle. As you know, all creatures have different layers of DNA functioning in different ways for their own evolution. But some of these beings' DNA can be interlinked with our DNA to support us. For example, we have mentioned interlinking or working with the DNA with the great bird called the flamingo and the great peacock. Today we would like to talk about the great golden eagle.

The great golden eagle is a magnificent bird. When you look at this bird, you see beauty, grace, strength, freedom, and nobility. Golden eagles have a sense of purpose, and they know who they are. They stand in their power. This bird is placed here as an example of what you can become. We ask you to call on this bird. Why do you think many countries' emblems have eagles on them? They represent great strength, nobility, leadership, greatness, focus, and determination. You can see this in their eyes. These are some of the qualities one must work with and integrate to become balanced.

We ask you to call on the Great Spirit in your meditation and ask for the activation of the energies of the bird kingdom, especially the eagle, for it can affect your chakra column — not just the seven layers, but all the way up to the thirteenth or fourteenth layers. When you start this work, the universe will feel a shift in you. You will have more focus and a knowingness that you can do this. You will have more hope inside you, a fearlessness and a daring: "I can do it!"

Second, we would like to talk about the cricket. The cricket makes a sound — "tak, tak, tak, tak, tak, tak, tak." Next time you hear this sound, sit down. This sound can put you in a very relaxed space. Do you know why it makes this sound? This is one of the sounds to activate human DNA. "Tak, tak, tak, tak, tak, tak, tak." Here is rhythm. Here is vibration. Here is a beat.

When you hear a drumbeat, it evokes a memory of the heartbeat of your beloved mother. Most people like to hear drums. It touches some part of you, helping you remember. Crickets also have the capacity to help you remember.

Third, we would like you to look at the great beings you call the bees. The bees, in their little heads, carry where humanity is going, its potential future or destination. If you knew clearly where you were heading, then the challenges you face in your daily life would not matter much, for you know this is a destination you can reach. The bees, in their little heads, carry the blueprints for all of humanity. So we ask you to call on these great beings, and they will guide you and clearly show you your future potential — where you are heading but also how you can get there.

[Archangel Metatron: Call on the essences or the spirit guides of these beings. Each species is supported by its own spirit guides, so their essences will come. Show them the utmost respect and honor. This is done in a meditation, quietly. Ask them to show you your part within humanity, how you can move into that. If you meditate with this spirit, perhaps a thought, an inspiration, or a feeling will come to you that you need to take a certain action or hold a quality of consciousness. Surely, they will support you.

Everything is in the act of working quietly and asking. Asking is very important at this time. It is absolutely critical that you must ask. Unless you ask, the door is never opened. The new reality is that you must ask to receive higher guidance daily.]

You know about the significance of the dolphins and whales. Whales carry the memories. Dolphins also carry the knowledge of star heritage, for they are from the stars. Connect with them, and they will help you remember your true origin.

※　※　※

Activating Your New Blueprint

My dear family, this is Mother Mary. During this important time, you must consciously activate the new reality — your new blueprint. Many of you have completed the work you came here to do before 12/12/12 and 12/21/12, and now many people are leaving. Those people had a contract to raise the vibration of themselves and the planet, which they did. They felt uncomfortable after that, for they did not know what to do. There is a lot of confusion. Many felt they had done everything they came here to do, which is their personal choice.

What we ask all of you to do is to start activating your new blueprints. Ask yourselves, "What is my blueprint for the next three

months? What is my blueprint for the next six months or one year?"
[Archangel Metatron: You do this by asking in your meditation.] When
you consciously activate new blueprints, you are opening one more
layer of yourself. When you open one more layer, you are opening one
more layer of higher consciousness. Make it a point, once a month, to
ask, "How can I open a new blueprint?"

Many talents and abilities that you knew you had but were never
able to manifest will start coming into focus more easily. This will open
another layer of your blueprint, and it goes on and on and on. Your life
will become much more enriched, your own creation, at a much higher
level, continuously creating.

America is going through a dark period, and this will continue
somewhat longer. There are great changes ahead for America. It is only
through the light that people can shift to a more positive direction. We
ask you to meditate on this and not to hold yourself back, for Mother
Earth and creation need your light. You carry this inside you. Call on
the goddess beings to support you if you need the support.

✻   ✻   ✻

Oam versus Aum

This is Master Kuthumi. My dear ones, all of you know about the
sound "Om," which is usually sounded as "oam," O-A-M. It is toned
and chanted throughout the world. Many cultures do this. To have a
higher vibration of this sound, we ask you to tone "Aum," not O-A-M
but A-U-M. When you do this, you are incorporating and integrating
all your bodies including your soul and your I Am presence.

This is the tone of the great Sufis: "Albaum. Albaum. Albaum.
Albaum." Blessings to you.

✻   ✻   ✻

Connecting with Crystal Skulls

Hello, my friends. I am the Crystal Skull. In the channeling today, there
was mention of making a code (energy connection) with Max the Crystal Skull. Make a code not just with Max but with all the crystal skulls,
for skulls interact with other skulls. Stones interact with other stones,
and a tree from anywhere can interact with a tree from Africa. It is
the same for skulls. Crystals can interact with all other crystals and all

the other skulls. You can even connect to skulls that have not yet been discovered. Connect with all the skulls through benevolence, for some shamans have used them for opposite purposes. Blessings. I am the Crystal Skull.

❋   ❋   ❋

Activating Platinum Consciousness

This is Lord Maitreya. My role in the world will start becoming more prominent as the months go by. You will see more people channeling me, and my name will be mentioned more and more. The time has come to bring forth more of my teachings to this planet about expanding human consciousness. There are many messengers around this planet. Some of them will be awakened soon, and some will not, but I ask all of you here to enlighten your hearts and send a beam of light to me and make a connection. I would like to communicate with all of you, for there is much to be brought forth.

There will be a great shift on the planet after 2038. Most of the old order will be gone by that time, or at least faded, and a new order will be forthcoming, clearly seen and visible. People say they are not seeing shifts happening, that things are only becoming worse, but as of 2038, people will be able to see a different energy on the planet, an energy of much more harmony and benevolence. During those times, I will be forthcoming with much more information and much more wisdom.

All of you have heard about crystalline consciousness. There will be another consciousness coming, an activation on the physical level from the crystalline consciousness to another level. It will be the anchoring and activation of the platinum consciousness. I bring forth this ray and anchor it into the light. I am now preparing for this. You will see and hear more of me in the months and years to come. Blessings. This is Maitreya.

Chapter 13

Auspicious Times for Awakening Consciousness

August 19, 2013

Saint Germain, Archangel Metatron, Samiel

Greetings to everybody. We thank you for being here today. In chapter twelve, we talked about connecting with cosmic DNA, galactic DNA, solar DNA, and universal and planetary-level DNA. We also mentioned connecting with certain animals, like the golden eagle, what it stands for, and how to connect with its DNA.

Now we would like to briefly talk about certain days of the month and certain days of the week that have the potential to help awaken consciousness. There is a specific day every month that is more auspicious than others. There are also certain days of the week. Each day of the week has a different energy. The ancient ones knew this. They were very well aware of the day of Shabbat. In India, they knew of certain specific days that, if observed properly, could align a person to higher consciousness. The Essenes knew about this as well.

Look for the day that could be good for you; it is a different day for every person. [Archangel Metatron: Each person needs to find that out individually.]

Can you explain how you would know which day is best for you?
You must go within and find it out for yourself. We will not reveal this individually because it would be spoon-feeding you. We want you to use discernment to see what is best for you. It is not that we do not want to help. We want you to see how we work. We explain what to do, and you take it and develop it.

Amazingly, there are also certain periods in the day that are very auspicious when a person is able to connect with higher energy. For example, there is a special time in the evening, right before it becomes dark. In the English language, it is called twilight. At this time, you are better able to connect with other dimensional realities. It is a special time for shamans, sorcerers, and magicians. It is a very important time.

There is also a special time in the early morning, between 4AM and 6AM. Many ancient yogis taught people to wake up at this time for their meditation and prayer.

Certain times interact with certain constellations and are directly connected to the astrological signs, to the meridians inside of your body, and to your DNA. We ask you to look into this and see how you are able to utilize your time during the day, during the week, and during each month.

[Archangel Metatron: When you were born, all the planets were in perfect alignment to bring you energies for the perfect lesson, for understanding what you will seek during this lifetime. You are also assigned a special energy from the stars. It is a supporting energy that you can call forth. This energy is not the energy of the constellations or the alignment of the stars when you are born. You have a specific energy designed to support you.

You also have the support of many beings, including dragons, trees, and stars. Each person is assigned a star. Again, you must call these forth during your meditation to feel the star that is aligned to you so that you can work with that star and gain energy.

Your support team is not only the stars. You can work with a dragon, a tree spirit, an animal spirit, a flower spirit, a plant spirit, and a bird spirit, as well as certain smells, sounds, and geometric patterns. They are all waiting to be opened. Until you ask, they are not given.]

The Essenes knew about making the best use of different times, for they were masters and worked directly with starbeings. They were very connected to the stars and the planets, especially the planets that influence sickness.

During your special times, you will be able to access higher consciousness, and you will be able to work with your DNA. These are the times when you must call forth your new consciousness and give intention for the consciousness you are bringing forth to help you to open up the cords of ascension.

This is Saint Germain. Now we will take questions, and then other masters will come through.

All Humans Are Created Equal

In an earlier session, you talked about 12 strands of DNA, 144 strands, and 144,000 strands. Were you talking about regular human DNA, a different dimensional level, or the DNA of only certain special people?

First of all, there is no special person. Everyone is equal. Everyone has the potential to activate all layers of his or her DNA. It is each person's blueprint. It is like a seed; the small acorn can grow to become a huge tree. However, not all acorns grow to become huge trees; some grow to be a certain age and die. It is the same with human beings. If the tree as a seed is allowed its naturalness, it probably will grow to full height. If human beings are allowed to develop and grow naturally without interference, they will fully develop their DNA.

Human DNA is of Pleiadian origin, and when you connect with this aspect of your DNA, you will remember your true origin and your past. DNA is activated naturally when you raise your consciousness. The purpose of this book is to give tools, information, knowledge, and wisdom that can support raising your vibration and consciousness so that your DNA is activated naturally. Consider your intentions and your beliefs. If you believe you can raise your consciousness, you will naturally activate your DNA, and that will be your truth. But if you believe that this opportunity is for somebody else, that you are only a simple person, then of course it will not happen. Your beliefs create reality.

Believe that you are a child of God, that the essence of God is within each cell of your body, and you came here to activate the highest aspect of yourself, the code of Adam Kadmon. You came here to experience and express God in every moment. Every being brings spirit into matter, and living your truth in this moment is an experience of God.

At the last meeting, you talked about the many levels we exist on at the same time, and about how DNA is at its own evolved level working spontaneously all at once. Is this true?

It is true, but it is dormant. It is like a time code. Unless you come to a certain level, the next level is not activated. It is like an initiation password. For example, the calculus for the tenth grade is already there, but you have to go through the first through ninth grades in order to have an understanding of calculus.

I see. It's a gradual evolution. Let's say we have a bad day. Is the DNA affected in the now, in every nanosecond?

It affects your genes, which naturally affect your consciousness and your energy field.

Entertainment and Spiritual Evolution

Can we be affected by someone else's negative, lower vibrations?

Of course. As you mentioned last time, every human being is a sponge. People pick up energy from every experience — even watching television. You must ask what energy you are drawing forth. Keep supporting your present reality of constructing a new being of yourself.

You can know about a person's evolutionary status just by looking at what he or she does for entertainment. You can see the degree to which people have evolved by what they call entertainment and fun. How do you spend your free time? How do you spend your entertainment dollars? How much television do you watch? How many movies do you see? What kinds of movies and programs do you spend time on? How many books have you read this month? How many concerts have you attended? How many ballets have you seen? What kind of music do you listen to? Does any of this matter to you?

Reaction versus Response

Nourishment for the mind is no different from nourishment for the body. What you put in it is what you get back, threefold. We are constantly affected by our thinking and through other people's actions, especially when we react or respond. If we react to a television program, it does not matter who is right or who is wrong. If you react, you need to know that you have something going on inside you.

The master never reacts. The master is able to maintain equilibrium and the level of consciousness. When you react to something, you need to look at yourself. You are mirroring what you observed. Why does that thing have that effect on you? What do you think when you see a particular television program? Something inside of you is triggered. The triggering affects your genes and your consciousness.

It is very easy for people to raise their vibration but not as easy to maintain it. In new consciousness, nothing is static, so either you go up or you go down. Metatron said that this is one of the reasons that almost all cultures are unable to sustain their moments of highest achievement.

There were so many periods of greatness. Take any culture — Italian, Roman, Greek, Mesopotamian, or Egyptian. The people went to great heights, but they were not able to maintain it.

Why were they not able to maintain their greatness? Because they were only thinking and never had any idea how energy works. So you must constantly ask about yourself. When you are exposed to energy, you must ask, "Does this support me in what I am trying to create for my highest good?" In the new reality, everything affects your genes, your consciousness, and your DNA. In everything you do, you must support your genes and your energy field so that you maintain optimum consciousness to naturally awaken your DNA. Does that make any sense to you?

You cannot be reactive. There are certain times when you must take action. But reacting comes from past memories. Immediately, something triggers a memory of an event that happened in the past, and you react right away. Response comes from the present moment. You must ask, "How do I respond?" Reaction comes from the past; response means you think and take responsibility.

Even if you are facing lower energy?

Yes, very much so. For example, a woman walks to the grocery store, and she is attacked. A man holds up a gun to her forehead and says, "Give me the money."

This brave woman says to this man, "I see God in you. I see God in you. I see God in you. "

The man tells her, "You are a crazy old witch." And he runs away. That is mastery.

[Archangel Metatron: It is difficult to provide a specific reference for this anecdote. The point is, if you are able to see who another person truly is, not what they are able to show you, then you could reflect that back to them, and they could change their behavior right away.

To give you another anecdote, a holy man takes a dip in an Indian river. He comes out, and there is a man standing on the bank of the river who does not like the master. He spits on the master. The master does not say anything. He just goes back to the river to take another dip. He comes out and the man spits on him again. The master goes into the river again. This happens, perhaps, twenty times.

The last time, the man falls to the master's feet, and says, "Oh, forgive me, Master."

The master says, "I only saw the master inside you when you were doing this. Thank you for the opportunity to awaken the master inside of you once again through the spitting process." That is the greatness.]

What did Mahatma Gandhi do? This great man chose his last incarnation for ascension here. He was walking to prayer when he was shot. The first words he said were, "Please forgive this man." He uttered the name of God three times, "Ram, Ram, Ram." And he fell to the ground. That is a master. What did Jesus say on the cross? "Father, forgive them; for they know not what they do [Luke 23:34]."

He helped the other two souls who were to the right and the left of him, who were also on crosses. He liberated them. That is a master. Please understand that this level of mastery is extremely difficult.

Let us use the Dalai Lama as another example. Do you think he does not have challengers, that he is not persecuted? Yet he is still able to maintain his composure. He chooses how he wants to respond in each moment, including how he responds to the criticism and the death threats he gets. He still chooses.

In choosing, you will define who you are. Life is choices. Believe that you are able to remain in higher vibrations of consciousness. In the choosing, in that consciousness, you are able to choose every moment how you want to express yourself. This is why this moment is called the present moment. What is the meaning of the present? The present is a gift. What are you going to do with this present moment? It is your choice. It is about how you want to live through the choices you make. Every choice you make has a vibration and defines who you are. Every moment of your life, you are giving a message to the world. And that message is expressed in how you live this moment.

Let me ask you one thing. If you want to choose mastery in this moment — or absolute peace, or absolute divine love — and you die in this moment, is this not the energy that you carry with you? This is why the ancient Tibetans always said, "Live your day, live this moment, as if it could be your last moment on the Earth plane." Live like that, thinking that you might die tomorrow. [Archangel Metatron: This is not a citation from a book. It is a general understanding carried by the Tibetan people. It is inbred in them. It has been taught to them verbally: "Live your life as if it is your last moment." Do you want to leave your life without making peace in your heart with everyone? What would you carry to the next life? You will carry only love and peace in your heart.]

You can choose this. Every day could be your last, or every moment could be your last, because every moment is a moment of death; the moment is gone and now it returns. Jesus said, "Do you think you only have one death?" [Archangel Metatron: This is an ancient truth known to all cultures. It is an understanding of wisdom, not a textual citation. You are dying every moment. You are dying to the past moment.] Only the physical body dies once, but you are dying every moment. One moment passes and is gone. You never get it back. That moment is finished, and a part of your life experience has died. Many deaths are happening: the death of a relationship, death of a job, death of a partnership, or death of a loved one. Choose to see in every moment of death what you are in this moment and who you are.

All that matters to your soul at the end of your life is not who you were or what you did. The only thing that matters to your soul is how you were when you lived. Were you compassionate? Were you kind? Did you love? Were you forgiving? All of this affects your consciousness and your DNA. Therefore, when you start choosing, naturally you are raising your vibration. Then you are able to activate the highest strands of DNA, not only your Earth DNA but also your galactic DNA and solar DNA.

Now, if you have any questions, please ask.

Accessing the Akash

I have a question about the akashic record. You were speaking about accessing the akashic record to connect with different gifts or feelings or moods that you experienced in a past life. Can you explain how to access one's akashic record? Is it through visualization?

First of all, know that the akash is the history of you with all its pieces. It has every experience that you have ever had and the history of your own origin. It is in your auric field. When you are in your meditation time, consciously ask to recall and access a particular aspect of your consciousness. You will be shown thought forms, energy patterns, a book, a feeling, an image, or just colors. If you persist, you will be able to read clearly.

There is no particular technique for you. There are guided meditations in which you visualize in your inner heart the locations where akashic records are kept. One such location is called the Halls of Amenti. It lies under the Sphinx. You may go there during your meditation time, and you will be taken down steps to the places where your akashic records are kept. There is no specific technique for you to practice. You must follow your own path. When you ask in meditation for access to your akash, I would say that within five to seven days, you will be able to easily access this place.

You also spoke about accessing our past lives in the akashic record. I was wondering if there is a way that I can tune into that.

Yes, of course. It is through meditation. When you ask your soul and your guidance to find the particular past life that supports you or can have a benefit for this lifetime, it will be shown. Each meditation is very individualized and different. Connect with your soul daily, saying, "Take me to the light, for I wish to add this quality to my life." For example, you could ask, "How can I trust myself more fully? How can I believe in myself?" Then ask to be shown a lifetime when you had complete faith and belief in yourself. It could be 700 years ago or perhaps 200 years ago; your soul will show you. When you are able to go to that particular lifetime and visualize it, you will be able to bring forth supportive energy immediately. It is only accessed through individualized meditation. It is possible to do it many times. Once you get the hang of it, you will be able to do it again and again.

The Power of the Full Moon

I wonder about meditating during the full moon. Do you need to do this at night, or could you do it in the daytime?

There are certain specific times of the day and certain specific days of the week that can be beneficial for your work. Right now, we are entering a very beautiful time. The full moon is a very powerful time. I told you one of the purposes of the full moon before [see chapter 8]. It has a very special purpose. It has very powerful, strong energy. It affects your human body. It affects the first and second chakras, specifically the sexual chakra. It activates them. But this is not only for human beings. It is far more.

The full moon's main purpose is to support all organisms that live underwater, especially in the sea. These vital organisms are absolutely critical for the survival of the oceans. Everything that is created by the Creator and is alive needs light to reproduce. Some organisms live far underwater, in the deepest part of the ocean, where there is hardly any light. Without enough light, they cannot reproduce. During the full moon, the light is able to penetrate to the deepest part of the ocean. Then these beings are able to reproduce and keep the ocean alive. [Archangel Metatron: There is no reference for channeled material. Truth does not need a reference.]

Because the full moon affects our first and second chakras, it also affects our creativity and our emotions. It also affects our bloodstreams. Many doctors will not operate during this time because blood flows are much higher and stronger. This is a special time for meditation. The full moon has very powerful energy to cleanse your emotions and your feelings to support your higher consciousness. It is also a good time to reproduce your creative ideas.

When you pray during the full moon, you will be able to access higher-dimensional reality. During meditation, you will also work with and connect with higher dimensions. If you want to send healing energy to someone, do a meditation and a prayer when the moon is full. The twenty-four hours around the full moon are the most powerful.

The second most powerful time may be around 3AM, but the best times are different for each person. Another good time could be from 6:30PM to 7:20PM. These are very powerful times. During these times, all forces unify to create a new reality. During these times, you can request a change in the weather, for you can talk to the weather. Give prayer requests for any powerful transformation you are seeking. Use your intention during this time. If you seek to raise your consciousness and your DNA, these are some of the best times for such work.

Creating and Disconnecting Cords

Why not put in a call to the heart of the Creator? You can connect your heart with the heart of the Creator. You can also ask to put a cord between your heart and Metatron, an eternal bonding cord. You can also connect a cord to all the good things of life, the creative powers, and many other things that you seek in your life. Once you are able to clear all the dross that you carry, you can start connecting cords to all the good things that you want in your life.

Remember, it is your negativity that you are trying to heal, and the proper thing you want is only one thing. It is energy. Establish a cord to all the good things in life, and have a relaxed, joyful life in which every day is a holiday. You are still able to make a living on your holiday, doing things that you like the most. Work becomes play; it is called joyful living. You can say, "I disconnect the cords of suffering, pain, and working hard to make a living." Just cut them off. It is all perception, what we carry.

Cords are very important, dear ones. Cords go in both directions. They go to the good things and to the negative things. Of course, you do not want to disconnect the cord with the Creator, with any other higher beings of light, or to the good things. Rather, you should only disconnect from those things that do not serve you anymore. You also have cords connected directly to Mother Earth. These cords are what keeps you grounded on the physical plane. You can refine the cords and clean them up, even with Mother Earth. Your living existence on the planet becomes more joyful. Your life must not become a burden.

Start refining your cords that connect with the mass consciousness of Earth. In the eyes of God, such cords are not good. Cut the cords to the energy matrix of the whole world. Examine your attitudes. Do you believe such things as the winner takes all? No pain, no gain? Or when everything falls into place, somebody pulls the rug out from under your feet? We carry cords to the energy matrix of the whole world. Cut those cords during your meditations. Say, "I disconnect from the energy cords that bind me to the mass consciousness lodged in my subconscious, my unconscious, and my present conscious mind."

Just use one statement: "I will cut this cord." In your meditations, seek out the dross that you carry, such as "no pain, no gain." You can cut the cords to such negative attitudes. Cut three cords a day. Soon you will see a difference. You will start feeling much lighter, more peaceful, and much more joyful. Cutting negative cords will affect your genes and your DNA.

Consciousness of Buried People

When you walk by a cemetery, you see many burial plots. Do you know that they carry energy? When a person dies, the body continues to hold his or her energy — hatred, anger, sadness, or any other feeling carried during life. Consciousness leaves the physical body, but that person's energy body is still intact, and it continues to carry its emotions and feelings. You take it to the ground. People who are unaware — who are not protected — are affected by these energy fields when they walk in a cemetery.

One reason there is so little peace in the Holy Land is because so many people died fighting for this beautiful land. The people born into this land are influenced by the energy of the land, so they still fight. There is so much hatred. If you want to heal a country, heal the land. Disconnect the energy from all those beings who do not serve you, because you are on a different path. Cut the energy cord you carry connecting to the country where you were born.

Suppose a person dies of cancer and is buried in the ground. The body, in years, will disintegrate and become one with the elements. The energy of cancer goes into the ground and into the vegetables grown nearby because this energy extends through the ground for at least five to seven kilometers. Plants in this area will carry the consciousness of cancer. It is very minute, but it is still there.

What if the body is cremated?

That is better. But throughout the world, Mother Earth is burdened with all the bodies that are buried in the ground. Sea burial is best. Being thrown into the sea, the body goes back to its natural state. Of course, that is not always possible. Cremation is the next best choice.

[Archangel Metatron: Sea burial is ancient wisdom practiced by the ancients and teachings that may not yet be revealed. The ancients knew that a body can decompose much more easily in water, and nothing is wasted. With land burial, decomposition is slower, and Earth is affected by the consciousness the body carried — the hatred, anger, and so forth. These energies spread into plants and trees. In the sea, a body is usually eaten by fish, and their digestion reprocesses the emotions. The waste produced does not have the same energetic intensity.]

Burying people in the ground can be perfectly fine if their relatives can help them be at peace before they go or work with their energy fields for the first three days after they die. During that time, people who die are still very connected to the Earth plane, and it takes three days for them to pass through the death canal. If you want to know more about this, read *The Tibetan Book of the Dead* by Padma Sambhava. This book explains how important it is to heal dying people through prayer, meditation, and sending light. They will be healed, and it will help them be reborn with a different consciousness. Mother Earth will also be healed.

You started to say how we could help heal Jerusalem because of all the people buried there.

First, you need to disconnect from all the cords of people who are buried there, especially people who died in fear, anger, hatred, or similar negative states.

How can we heal the country of Israel or the city of Jerusalem?

You must bring in golden light and see the ground as a carpet of golden light. So much energy has been embedded in the ground. This work has to be done collectively. It is a very big job. But on a personal level, you can ask to be disconnected from the national cords that are alive at this time in Jerusalem, containing the energies of people who died fighting, who died with anger and hatred. You can also ask to make new cords connecting you with the great wisdom teachers, rabbis, and other great masters.

[Archangel Metatron: To do this, see yourself connected with many strands of energetic light. Every human is like a sponge. You take in the energy of the ground you are standing on. If that energy is hatred and your energy field is not strong, you will definitely be affected. A true master can remain in the darkest places and nothing will happen, because he is able to shield and deflect the energy coming from the ground. But if you have weaknesses in your consciousness and have issues to resolve, then you will pick up energy from wherever you are.

Why do you think you feel so good when you are in nature, particularly in pristine natural places? Because the ground is very pure. You are not picking up anything negative from pure places because nature itself is God. Remember that you are bombarded by energy and are very susceptible to the energy around you. You need to know how to work with energy, how to protect yourself with energy, what energies to release, and what energies to integrate.]

So what you are saying is to connect from those great masters and sages?

Exactly. Create a cord to King David. Erase the cord to Herod the Great. Put a cord to Elijah. When you remove a cord, replace it with a new cord to the higher beings of light. Connect to Anna and other great beings of light who have great wisdom. Many masters from Israel chose not to ascend with their physical bodies. They decided to give back to the earth, for their bodies could bring some healing to Mother Earth. Theirs was a great sacrifice. Although they had the capacity to ascend, they chose not to. They ascended after their deaths.

[Archangel Metatron: Do this by visualizing cords going from your solar plexus chakra into the essence of these great beings, and then ask their permission.

To cut the cord to Herod the Great or such people, ask again? Is that correct?

Yes. Or say, "I give the intention to release this energetic cord connection that I had with Herod the Great. I also give permission to connect my cord with the cord of Master Elijah, and through this cord, I bring in the higher-vibrational light of Master Elijah to support in my own ascension process. I ask this in love."

You must ask. This is a practical book, and two things are important in this practice. One is asking. The second is forming intentions. If you do not ask, it is not given at all. In the old energy, ignorance was bliss. In the new energy, ignorance is dangerous. People need to know about this. The old way of thinking is gone. The Creator will not come down and support you. You must cocreate through asking and support yourself with your constant work.]

Four Colors of the Heart

Master Kirael says that the physical body will reshape itself when we begin putting higher energies into it, and this starts with a substantial amount of prana breathing.[1]

[Archangel Metatron: Many Indian masters have shown this. Look at Master Babaji. He still maintains the body of an eighteen-year-old. All the masters who walked the planet were able to choose a body that they liked. When you ascend, you will be able to choose the physical appearance you want. Do you see any old or haggard ascended

---

1. Fred Sterling, *Kirael: The Ten Principles of Consciously Creating* (Honolulu: Lightways Publishing, 2005).

masters? You can choose to have the kind of body you would like to keep from now onward.]

By doing this, we become bodily enlightened. This means that our bodies will vibrate to the colors we utilize to bring ourselves to Mother Earth. We come with a core essence of gold, and we bring forth defined colors to vibrate our physical systems. The food and drink we ingest affect our colors. The question is: What are our four colors? Obviously, it makes a huge difference on everything about us, our physical bodies, our mental and emotional states, everything.

Basically, the four colors are gold, silver, platinum, and turquoise.

Are those what each person comes in with?
These are the main colors that everyone comes in with.

So that we can clarify, where are these colors? Are they in the energy field?
Yes, in your energy field.

So everybody carries those four colors?
Yes, and they also carry 144 sacred geometrical patterns.

Kirael said that each color signifies an aspect of what we are to do here.[2] Once we know our colors, then we can no longer be limited. So the question is: Does everyone have the same colors?
[Archangel Metatron: The specific color is your supporting energy. As we mentioned before, you have supporting energy from a dragon, a star, a plant, a tree, a sound, and a color. So you must find out which color is most suitable for you by asking.]

Everyone in the core level has the same colors. Turquoise represents your unlimitedness, your ability to realize that you are an eternal being. Gold represents the realization that you are a creator in physical human form. Silver represents your sacredness, your divinity. Platinum represents your connection with all of creation, the communion with all.

These colors are altered by daily life experience. First of all, nobody knows about these colors. These colors get buried deeper and deeper, and you truly forget who you are. If you can bring these colors to the forefront of your consciousness and integrate them once again, you will

---

1.   Ibid.

be living like a master. These colors affect your DNA. You may want to experiment with these colors, as they can give you a great breakthrough.

[Archangel Metatron: Take a color and meditate on it. How do you feel with green? How do you feel with brown? You must ask. Why do you wear certain specific colors in your life? Many people do not wear brown at all. Some people do not wear olive green. Some people will not wear black, and some people wear only black. Why do people choose? Sometimes when you see or wear certain colors, you are in the flow of things. Work with colors and see which help you feel more energized.]

Having said that, I will also tell you that each of you carries one certain primary color. For example, people who are very vibrant and positive come with blue, like a soft purple. People who are introverted, who never share experiences or emotions, have the primary color of soft green. People who are born with nervousness, do not like crowds, bite their nails, or tap their feet come with the primary color of white. These colors can be enhanced by mixing in other colors for healing. We ask you to experiment with this fascinating wisdom. We thank you for bringing this very important question forward, for colors can truly open people up to new possibilities and revelations.

Ancient Human DNA

In regard to going back into our essence, or our signature selves, if we were to go back 50,000 years to when we were in Lemuria or Atlantis, how did our DNA differ then from what we have now?

During that time, it was fully awakened. Now it has become dormant. That is the only difference. At that time, people were aware that their twelve strands were fully activated.

So we have regressed?

Yes, you have regressed. At that time, the threefold flame in your heart center was in full bloom. Also, your pineal gland has shriveled to a very small size.

Do you mean that back then it was a lot larger?

Of course. The pineal gland is your spiritual gland. It is the light gland inside of your brain. When you open the pineal gland, you open up your higher-dimensional mind.

The Threefold Flame of the Heart

Could you explain the threefold flame of the heart, please?

It is a flame of love, power, and wisdom. The colors are pale gold, pink, and blue. These are the three colors of God. They represent love, wisdom, and action for manifestation. It is now less than one-sixteenth of an inch in each human heart. You must be able to stay inside the threefold flame burning brightly, exhibiting these three qualities of God — the love of God, the wisdom of God, and using the love and the wisdom to manifest these qualities.

The Essenes knew about this threefold aspect of God, but they explained it differently. Their concept was that humans are interacting with many forces, both seen and unseen. We have many energy bodies that interact continuously. There are three bodies that we use daily; the Essenes called these the acting body, the thinking body, and the feeling body.

The highest thought, or energy, of the thinking body is wisdom. The highest energy of the feeling body is love. The highest energy of the acting body is to bring wisdom and love into reality, into our physical lives, so that we can interact with the cosmic and etheric forces — and also the social forces — of our cultures throughout our lives. These are the three important aspects that you have inside, and you must develop them: love (pink), power (pale gold), and wisdom (pale blue).

[Archangel Metatron: This is in reference to the three-fold flame of the heart. Each heart carries these three energies, and they are directly related to the first, second, and third rays of God. We love God, the wisdom and love of God, the creative power of God, and the manifestation power. Align with your soul and your soul's will to use its love and wisdom to manifest your soul's will into your practical reality. This is what masters do.

First, they ask, "Is this part of my soul's contract?" Then they ask, "How can I manifest this using wisdom and love?" Finally, they take action to bring it into physical reality. Many people have great ideas, but they do not know how to manifest them. Even if they manifest, they do not know how to do so with love and wisdom. So this is directly related to the three-fold flame of each heart. This is a very important part of ascension itself. It is critical.]

Would it be correct to say that these are in the higher heart chakra?

That is not quite right. Your higher heart chakra is a little bit above and to the left side. It is in your left shoulder, near your thymus. But you must develop your higher heart chakra also, and when you do, you will hold more and more light. Your thymus will expand and increase. During Lemurian times, the thymus was much more expansive.

Prana Breathing

Would you talk about the importance of prana breathing? How it revitalizes and replenishes our cells, cleanses the cellular consciousness, and increases our lifespans?

This is true. You must also expand the pranic tube inside of you. The tube needs to become much bigger so that it can hold more light. Prana breathing is very critical. A simple way of doing prana breathing is to imagine that you are breathing in golden particles. Each particle is shaped like a golden star. This may take some time to become natural. Every time you take a breath, you are breathing golden star particles.

[Archangel Metatron: Just breathe it in. Imagine beautiful star-shaped golden particles coming in through your head.

Do you mean coming in through the mouth or nose?

No, coming through your head.

At the crown chakra?

Yes, and then going into your brain and filling your brain with these golden particles. See the pinecone-shaped pineal gland opening up with this light, and both sides of your brain filled with this beautiful light. Do it every day.]

How will you know that you are doing it properly? In three to four days, you will feel a shift in your diet. You may not eat as much; you will feel that your stomach is full. One of the best ways to do this breathing is to imagine that you are drawing forth these golden particles from the Great Central Sun. Breath these particles in. Every star-shaped particle is going into each of your billions of cells. In a few days, you will feel the difference. You may not eat as much, or you may not be as hungry as you were. This is a very good exercise. When you start doing prana breathing, it not only affects your food intake but it also affects the regeneration of your cells to lengthen your life.

Prana was the energy that we existed on during our lifetimes in Lemuria.

Prana was the main force, yes. Prana is the force of creation. You can consciously intend to breathe prana, or life force. You will feel the difference in a few days. Your mind becomes clearer. This is one of the tricks of people who do not eat. They breathe in prana, and they consciously maintain the attitude that they lack nothing, even if they have no money. Your food intake will diminish, and you will be able to live without food. The lack in your life is directly proportional to the food that you eat. When there is no lack and there is no fear of living, the intake of food will be minimal.

Your cells will naturally convert the life force in the air you breathe into food. The great sages and saints from ancient China, the great Taoist masters, had an initiation test, and many Americans still go to China for this test. [Archangel Metatron: in the Kunlun Mountains.] People are guided to sit down in an opening cut in the rock. There is nothing there. They are asked to spend seven days there, alone. No food is given. On the seventh day, someone comes to see if they are dead or alive. The only way to stay alive is by communicating with Mother Earth and asking for the prana from the Great Central Sun. The initiates breathe this prana with absolutely no thought of ending the moment. It does not matter whether they live or die. So there is no lack of anything, and there is no fear.

✳   ✳   ✳

Be Part of the Unified Force Field

This is Metatron. My blessings are with all of you, for I am a part of you. I exist within every cell of your being. Many of you think that I am also above you. Do not look for me outside of yourselves; look for me inside. For every guide you have, every master you have, is a part of you. These masters are also outside, but they are inside of you as well. Even though you put us on a pedestal, we thank you for that honor, but we are always inside of you. So seek inside of you first.

That which you seek is who you are. With this realization, there is no more separation. Envision from now onward that you are part of Metatron. People talk about separation not from the Creator alone but from all that is here from the Creator. In the past, you thought like this to serve the Creator in support of the universe. If you can shift your focus to the concept of oneness with the cosmic force, the Creator, and your I Am presence, you will hit the jackpot. So from now onward, make the commitment to see and experience everything from this Unified Force Field. [Archangel Metatron: The Creator.] See yourself as part of the Unified Force Field.

You have heard so many times that you are part of a group energy. What does this mean? This is the group energy of the entire universal wisdom. The energy of little ants is inside of you. The energy of the greatest master, Mahatma, is inside of you. When you realize this and when you work to integrate this into your cells, you will experience everything. If you want, you will let the Creator's essence inside you. You will see a flower and become the flower. When you see a bird in a tree, you will become the bird. You now have the capacity to do this, and you do it in certain moments.

Before I go, I would like to challenge your minds. All of you are very aware of the aura, or the auric field. Everything has an aura. A building has an aura. Trees have auras. A pond has an aura. Animals have auras. Most of the time, the aura of a tree is a beautiful gold color with tints of green. The aura of a building is white with gray.

We ask you to open your third eye. Hold the intention to see the beauty of creation. Then when you see a building, you will not see its four corners; you will see its auric field. You will see the auric field of the beautiful trees. You will see the auric field of a flower. You will be able to see the auric fields of everything. At best, you will start seeing through the eyes of God. You will see only beauty. When you see only beauty, it is only a perception. Do it in love, the greatest energy you can have. It will change your DNA. Blessings. This is Metatron.

✳   ✳   ✳

Raising the Vibration of Your Food

Hello. I am the angel of food, specifically the angel of the vegetable and plant kingdoms. My name is Samiel. Today, I would like to briefly expand your consciousness and mind about the DNA of the fruits you eat.

Every living thing on the planet has consciousness and DNA. Fruit has DNA, but if the DNA of the fruit you eat is not compatible with your DNA, this can affect your consciousness. It is best to pick your fruit from the tree, for then it contains the purest original DNA. But when fruit goes through many processes, the DNA becomes dormant. It gets shriveled. Try to get fruit in the best condition possible, then take it in your hands, and ask the fruit's DNA and vibration level to be brought into compatibility with you so that you are equal with it.

This can be done with any food. If you live in a city, you may not be able to get fresh, natural foods. So you have to buy food from the supermarket or eat food from a can. This food has lost most of its original DNA, or molecular structure, because of the way it has been handled.

Take your food in your hand or pass your hand over it, and ask to raise this food to your vibrational level. The food you eat has a very big effect on your vibration, your genes, and your consciousness. Consciously ask that your food be raised to your vibrational level, especially fruit. Most fruits contain high vibrations and are very compatible with your DNA. They have consciousness; they are all beings of light. They are here because they want to support humanity. But if fruit is grown using synthetic chemicals and is processed, it starts losing its consciousness completely.

Masters are very careful about the foods they eat. Many ancient masters cooked their own food because the thoughts of the person who cooks the food affect the food you eat. It is often said that there is no better cooking than a mother's, for when a mother cooks for her children, the food contains her love for her children. So it is critical who prepares your food. If this person thinks cooking is a burden and hates doing it, those feelings affect the food. The thoughts of this person go into the food.

You may not be able to cook your own food every day, but at least you can increase the vibration of your food through intention, asking that it match your highest vibration. This is Samiel, the angel of food. Blessings and thank you.

Chapter 14

How Ascended Masters Can Assist Your Ascension

August 21, 2013

Yeshua, Babaji, Gaia, Spirit of the Whales, and Archangel Metatron

Hello, this is Master Yeshua along with Babaji. Blessings and love to all my family. This is an important time for you to be on the planet. People are working in their own ways to raise their vibrations and to support their own evolutions as well as humanity's evolution. Remember to ask for support from the cosmic realms. It is freely given. We have noticed that many humans do not ask for cosmic support, which is always available to them. Ask for cosmic support on a daily basis.

There are many beings in service to you. Know the Creator's rule: If you do not ask, the door is not opened. Ask for teachers who have Earth experience and who have gained enlightenment. Some of the more popular names include Elijah, Anna, the great Indian teacher Sri Aurobindo, and many others. When these teachers left Earth, they left their imprints, like footprints on the ground, which still exist on the Earth plane today. And since you are living on the Earth plane, you might be able to access this imprint left by them. It does not matter when they ascended; their footprints still remain.

We ask you to seek these people. Learn who they are and study them, and then you will be able to receive the powerful energy of ascension. They are in service to you. They support humanity's evolution. There are many cosmic masters supporting you, and you must ask for their support daily. Ask your guides and masters who are in support of humanity, especially for ascension.

There are also many trees in support of humanity. Metatron recently mentioned the great oak, the sequoia, and the yew. There are other giant trees that you can work with too, such as the great banyan tree and other large trees that are over one hundred years old. They have the capacity to bring in higher consciousness.

You may also call on support from dragons. [Archangel Michael: You can feel their support by calling them forth. Dragons are a part of your supporting energy, just like the stars. Sit down and call for these great beings. How do you call them? There are certain sounds, specific sound vibrations for that. (These sounds are found in Appendix I: Working with the Energy of Dragons.)]

When human beings are born, they are given a lot of support. One of the supporting beings is the great dragon. Call on the dragons to support you in raising your vibration, especially for ascension.

Sounds to Raise Your Vibration

We also would like to talk about sound. Certain sounds, like the ragas from India and certain tones from other cultures, can be sung at specific times of the day to change your consciousness. This is why ragas were composed, and they have stood the test of time. We ask you to look into that, for certain ragas can take you into higher states of consciousness. You will be able to access higher wisdom and higher-vibrational energy. During my time in India, I practiced these ragas to raise my vibration.

Now we will take questions.

We used to have twelve strands of DNA, and we have been progressively regressing over the past 50,000 years. How does that affect our DNA?

DNA is always open. It is a perfect code. What affects it is your consciousness. You need to have a certain vibration, a certain level of crystalline consciousness in order to have the ascension code so that the ascension seal can be broken and opened. Raise your consciousness, and this will naturally affect your DNA and its opening. When you connect with the ascended masters who walked this planet, you are connecting with the powerful energy they had before their ascension. That moment of ascension is a very powerful moment.

In other words, we are going through basic training in order to be prepared for that magic moment?

Exactly. When you connect with these masters, you are connecting with the magic moment they ascended. They left such powerful footprints in the history of the planet. You are connecting with those footprints. Can you imagine that you are standing in front of Master Elijah, and he is ready to ascend? That is a glorious moment.

Alchemical Transformation after the Last Supper

Let me tell you about another very powerful moment, especially for people who live in Israel and people who have been there. A very powerful moment took place the night before Jesus was arrested. It is called the Last Supper.

After the Last Supper, there was a moment in time in our history on this planet when two opposing forces — the darkness and the light — came to their highest polarities. There was a moment of magic and transformation after the Last Supper. Mary Magdalene and I went to Gethsemane and connected with the Creator, asking for guidance. At that moment, the air opened up and unconditional love washed over Mary Magdalene and me.

The energy of that moment is still there in Gethsemane. If you are able to connect with it, you will be connecting the dark aspect of your consciousness with your highest light aspect. This is what ascension is all about: complete alchemy takes place. The darkest unenlightened parts of you join with the cosmic, magical part of you, and then true transformation takes place.

Go to Gethsemane, and connect with one of the four great olive trees that are 2,000 to 3,000 years old. They hold my energy, that of Magdalene, and many others. Connect with the events of the Last Supper.

Transcending Pain

Was the Last Supper the first night of the Passover?

Yes. After the Last Supper, I went to Gethsemane with my entourage, and there, the darkest of the dark was joined with the lightest of the light, and alchemical transformations took place within me, in Mary Magdalene, and in many others. So although I knew I was going to be crucified, this transformation altered my consciousness in such a way that I was able to alter the functioning of my entire body. I went through the motions of being whipped, crowned, and tortured, but I was not in pain, for I had completely transformed my body. I had withdrawn all the pain and suffering from my cells, so despite what they did to me, I never felt it. You all have this capacity.

Is it like withdrawing part of your consciousness from your physical body?

Yes. This is one of the things that you can do. When you have raised your vibration, you are able to control your body, your feelings, and your emotions when you go into pain. You can use your thoughts to disassociate from pain.

I think I have done that.

The way to work with this power is to increase your energy until you feel no pain at all.

Are you talking about what psychotherapists call "conscious disassociation," consciously just letting go of the feelings of your body?

No. You are very aware of what is happening, but you are disassociating from the pain. Also, if you are aware of your body, having communicated with your body, then your body will respond easily. You can withdraw, which is to remove the consciousness of pain. Most of the pain happens in the mind.

About thirty years ago, I had an accident with a band saw and cut off the end of one of the fingers. It was incredibly painful. By the end of the second day, I learned to talk to my body to say that the purpose of the pain was to warn. I knew I had an issue there. I did not need to be warned. And the pain backed off. Is that the kind of thing that you are speaking of, Master Yeshua?

Yes, exactly. You can fine-tune it. You can withdraw. Many shamanic masters have demonstrated this. For example, say there is an earthquake, and you are crushed under rubble. You know there is no way that you can get out, and no help is available. You are about to lose your life. There are certain sounds, chants, and tones you can make so that your soul consciously leaves your body. You can leave much more harmoniously and peacefully. This is possible for everyone. It is there, so search for it. [Archangel Metatron: Do this consciously when you have a headache or when you are at the dentist.]

When a soldier is wounded and everything is done to help him but he knows he is going to pass away, he can make certain sounds, tones, and chants that will slowly withdraw his consciousness from his brain. Then he is able to transition with more grace and peace.

Would you be able to tell us some of those sounds?

These are only told by a teacher directly to the student's ear, and this must be respected. You may want to connect with your own guides and teachers to get this, because it is personal information given by the teacher to the student. [Archangel Metatron: These are oral teachings for highly advanced souls. They need to be taught. This is practiced by shamans in Tibet and by Native American shamans in the Americas.

Let us say that you are caught under a rock and you know that you are going to pass away. You do not want to carry the pain of passing away pinned under a rock. By deliberately chanting these words, there will be no more pain, so you will not carry the consciousness of pain to the other side. The chanting will also support your spiritual body. You do not want to damage your spiritual body; you take it with you, and you want to keep it in the best condition possible.]

I have another question relating to the moment at the Garden of Gethsemane, where the great light and the great darkness came forward in an alchemical reaction. I am having a hard time understanding that. Does that mean that the darker, or negative, aspects of each of the personalities involved came forward to be lifted? Is that the sort of thing you're speaking of?

No, there was great darkness from the Roman persecution of the children of Israel and myself. The possibilities of living and dying as a human being are so much greater than most realize. You must truly know that death is only the leaving of the physical shell. I demonstrated that. That was a big transformation, and it lifted the veil for human consciousness. Humans could not conceive of it. Just imagine, 2,000 years ago a human being resurrected and proved that there is no death.

This is what we are trying to teach people now. There is truly no death. If you have this consciousness, then there is no fear of living and no fear of death. Life is eternal. And grounding this consciousness, the eternity of life, is what we are speaking about.

[Archangel Metatron: You can look at death as the end or as just the end of one of the processes of the eternal life you are having. These perceptions are different. All scriptures and all religions teach that life is eternal, and you are eternal. So do not look at life as the end of every-thing. It is the end to this particular experience you are having.]

So it all still boils down to that magic moment that influences so many things? We are trying to slowly approach the understanding that our own conscious-ness is what actually controls that magic moment.

Exactly. Ascension happens in a moment.

My teacher and my master Archangel Metatron would say that everybody is going to ascend. It's just a matter of when.

[Saint Germain: This is from a channeling session. From our time perspective, everyone on Earth will ascend in 275 to 300 years.]

Yes.

Blessing Water and Using Symbols

I have a question that relates to an earlier session. You spoke about creating a water storage vessel with infinity symbols and the Flower of Life. Could you explain how these symbols relate to the activation of energy?

These symbols correspond and interact with the geometric patterns you have inside your physical body. Every cell of your body transforms into an infinity symbol. Each human body carries 144 sacred geometric patterns. Forty-four of them are in your throat chakra. These symbols interact with the geometric patterns inside you. It is very simple. Does this evoke any feelings in you? Does this make you aware that there is a bigger picture? There is balance and perfection in the universe. Heaven and Earth are both completely in balance.

Symbols talk to you directly. They have the capacity to bypass the mind and go directly into your subconscious and unconscious minds. This is why symbols communicate. Symbols are interdimensional. It might take days, sometimes years, to convey the meaning of a symbol in the linear way. But when everything is condensed, you do not look at the lines; you see the whole symbol. In the same way, if you look at your life in a linear way, from point A to point B, its meaning becomes much deeper because of its multidimensionality. A symbol, like a painting, talks to the interdimensional aspect of every human being.

Giving blessings can also lift your consciousness. You can say, "Blessings to all creation." You can also bless things individually: "I bless all creation," or "I bless all that supports me, including all the food that nourishes me." Doing blessings can take you to a higher plane of existence. When you give blessings and feel love and appreciation, you will naturally receive grace in your life — living with grace every moment.

* * *

Autistic Children

Greetings. This is Gaia. Recently, there have been attacks on autistic children and families in the beautiful country called America. These children have very high vibrations, and they carry the purest love. In thirty to forty years, many families will want to have a child who is autistic. But right now, these people are being bombarded in America.

[Saint Germain: An attack means they were vilified, demeaned, or made to look smaller than they are. Sensitive people are able to see the brilliant light these children carry. They are a gift to humanity, for they carry the purest vibration. In their presence, you naturally feel connected to yourself. They have the capacity to awaken you to your own divinity, your own self-love. Their light is so powerful that when someone who is not used to it feels their light, they can become afraid. This has happened throughout history. When a master walks, there is light, and people attack the master. The same thing is happening to these children. There will be more and more of these children being born who carry the brilliant pure light.

A Google search of "attacks on autistic child" yielded hundreds of hits.]

We ask you to hold these children in your hearts, for we need them. They are bringing very high frequencies of love and grounding it into the earth. We need them to stay on the planet. They are being attacked because their light is so bright. Envision that all the autistic children are safe and able to continue the work they have come here to do, which is to steady and anchor very pure, vibrational love energy. They are very connected to other dimensions.

[Saint Germain: Hold them in light. Visualize a beautiful gold light is pouring out from your heart and going around the world to all autistic children. This would be done during meditation.] These children are bringing very high vibrational light. When you have more light, people attack you. These children have such pure hearts, and we need them at this time.

Utilizing the Power of Lightning for Ascension

Now we would like to expand your imagination on another topic. At the time of this channeling, all of you are experiencing summer. During this hot time, there are some days with great thunderstorms. It can be fun to watch these epic thunder and lightning storms with their heavy downpours. People welcome them, for they cool the earth.

During moments of lightning flashes, great power is unleashed. Scientists are working to capture the power of lightning, for one strike can light up a whole town. You can connect with this power. We know that some of you have been working with biorelativity and transporting yourselves to different places for healing. We ask you to go into the center of a thunderstorm. Be courageous. You will be protected and guided, and you will feel immense power. Make sure that you talk to your body so that your body opens up, and you will be able to hold more energy and more power. You will see that your power will be increased exponentially.

[Saint Germain: Remember, you are where your attention goes. Wherever your consciousness goes, there you are. Projecting your consciousness into the middle of a thunderstorm connects you with a great source of power. You can breathe into this. It is a very powerful source, but you must be able to hold this vibration in your physical body, for it could burn you.

First, you must ask your body whether it is capable of receiving this incredibly powerful light. Remember, the eye of the storm is a part of God, and you want to connect with that consciousness. Everything is of God. Interestingly, as you will see in the next few years, there will be a scientist who discovers how to harness lightning.]

Ascension happens in a nanosecond — when there is an explosion of energy inside you. That energy is like the energy that propels a rocket. A rocket is fired with great force. It flies into the sky and separates. In the same way, you can harness the huge amount of energy being downloaded to Earth through lightning and connect to it to fire your rocket of ascension. Alchemy will take place within you, and you will step out of physical reality into a new merkanah field.

Imagine that you are a rocket: You are getting ready for lift off, and you know through great power that you will separate. That is what ascension is all about. You will separate from earthly consciousness and completely move into a new consciousness.

For what you are talking about, no merkabah is really needed, is it? It is just purely consciousness.

Correct. It is purely consciousness. We feel that you have the capacity to do this. Go to the center of the thunder and lightning. It is an explosive force, so you must take precautions. You must ask your own heart if this is appropriate for you. There is great power there, unbelievable power.

So what you are saying is that if you have the certainty and the chutzpah, be the thunder and be the lightning?

Correct. You are harnessing this immense power. Imagine when lightning hits someone and they are burned. There is so much energy that it can propel you to move from your present level of consciousness to a different level. This is alchemy happening in an instant.

What if you asked to be connected to the energy of the lightning in the amount that you could safely handle in this physical body or make some other provision like that?

It is very difficult to control the flow. The energy comes so strongly that if you are not ready to handle it, I would suggest that you not do it. Your mind must be open enough to reach this higher level of consciousness. It is like taking a strong, mind-altering drug. It expands your consciousness. If you are not ready, the drug can play great tricks on you, and you could lose your mind.

Would you include this information in the book? There may be people who read it that are not ready to do this.

This is a practical book, and everything must be used with caution using your own heart resonance. High alchemical powers must be used with caution. They can completely transform and transmute in an instant if you are ready. We ask you to start working with this. Meditate with it. You will feel the energy coming to you in your meditation.

So we need to emphasize that people doing these practices need to use their own discernment?

Exactly. But people need to know. There are certain energies you must be cautious with and prepare yourself to use. If you do not, you can go mad. Your mind can go crazy if you are not able to handle the light coming into you. It is like running 5,000 watts of electricity through a 100-watt wire. It will burn the wire out. You must prepare your body and mind, and you must ask your soul, because your soul is in the driver's seat of your life.

If some of you work with the great teacher Juliano, you may want to talk to Juliano about working with the energy of thunder and lightning. Then use that energy in your bio-resonance exercise if you are able to hold the energy. You will feel unbearably hot for a while. It will be very uncomfortable. But you will be able to hold this light, and you will be able to use it in your bilocation and multilocation.

You must ask for the complete support of your soul in this. Just imagine the whole darkness being hit with the greatest force of light coming all at once. Ask your soul. This is one of the great ways to completely and temporarily transport you to your new level of consciousness. The energy is fabulous and strong. Thunder and lightning do not happen by accident. They have great consciousness in the way that a hurricane has consciousness. Many shamans and magicians work during lightning storms. The great peacock dances during this time. Celebrate the power. As Metatron says, either you go up or you go down; you never remain static. You must remember that. [Saint Germain: This is a quotation from a personal teaching for which there is no written documentation.]

When discussing higher levels of responsibility, I use the model of a down escalator. It's like walking up a down escalator; you can't stand still because if you stand still, you go down.

There is no standing still anymore. It is a continuous evolutionary process every moment, consciously. It all happens in the consciousness. My dear family, today we have a very special guest before we close today.

✳   ✳   ✳

The Spirit of the Whales

Our dear family, we are the Spirit of the Whales. We love humanity in its evolution and in its sacred journey. We know it has been hard, having many challenges and much darkness. Still, humanity continues to evolve. This surprised many of us. If humanity had not progressed, we would not be here. Nostradamus predicted that a world war would start in 1999 and a large portion of the population would be dead by 2012. You changed this through consciously choosing to elevate your consciousness. The Hippie Movement[1] helped to transform human consciousness. They used drugs, but they also preached love.

We carry important wisdom and much information in our heads. We carry the history of the planet's evolution. Juliano mentioned our functions. One is to act as messengers for Mother Earth. Mother Earth has different needs in different places. [Saint Germain: These are teachings that are not referenced in writing. Juliano is a teacher from the Arcturians.]

People from all around the world like to watch whales. They listen to our sounds, read about us in books, and see photographs of us. We carry the history of the evolution of the entire planet. Your evolutionary history is also encoded within us, and we hold human DNA directly in our molecular structure. When we sing, many scientists think we are calling our mates. But we are really calling you to activate your DNA.

All the creatures of creation contain the element water, and when they hear our calls, this triggers their DNA. We ask all of you to consciously connect with us. There are many beings who hold these imprints, such as the great Sanat Kumara and Mother Earth. We also carry a large pattern of your energy field, your soul history, and your role in this universe. We invite you to come to us and study with us. You can call on us during your sleep time. We will be there.

Shifting Earth's Magnetics

I have a question. I would like to understand more about the change of the history of Earth, how (up to 1987) we were on a path of self-destruction in which the human race would have killed itself off and then things shifted. I would like to know more about that, how that happened, and how that turnaround was made.

There is not one simple answer. Kryon, the magnetic master [channeled by Lee Carroll], played a very large part in this. He shifted the magnetics of the planet. When there is a strong magnetic energy in the ground, it is difficult for humans to awaken. Magnetics keep people embedded in a certain script within their consciousnesses for hundreds

---

1. The history of the Hippie Movement (http://en.wikipedia.org/wiki/History_of_the_hippie_movement).

of thousands of years. When you have strong magnetics in the ground, there will be little change. The Middle East has strong magnetic energy, so people do not want to change. In the United States, Virginia and Connecticut are still very conservative. There is strong magnetic energy there. But in San Francisco, people are open to new ideas. Kryon played a very big role in shifting the effects of the magnetics.

What Nostradamus saw when he wrote about the end of the world was very true. It was one scenario. But he did not see the scenario of humanity awakening. The Hippie Movement changed a lot. You started awakening through your own conscious choice. Then the Harmonic Convergence came, and you were asked, "Are you ready for the shift?" Humanity answered yes. So Earth's mission for twenty-five years was to raise its consciousness. The guardians of Earth watched to see whether the consciousness on Earth would rise.

The consciousness was very low, so the scenario of what Nostradamus said could have happened. But since then, Earth has increased in consciousness, and this has shifted many paradigms, including the collapse of the Soviet Union. The Soviet Union would have played a major role in the Armageddon starting in 1999 and finishing in 2012. But since the Soviet Union collapsed, that scenario was replaced. That is when many human beings started seeing the number 11:11 on their clocks. Then they saw 12:12. These were transformation dates.

The Light Exposes Darkness

We are now going through a shift, and grounding the energy of this shift will take some time. There is much more darkness being revealed, for there are no more secrets. The light is shining so brightly. Many more secrets will come out. It is like an old, empty bottle. When you fill it with water, dirty water comes out. The shift of consciousness really changed things, and a lot of light has been generated. This is exposing much more darkness.

At special times, more light will enter the ground, so more darkness can be exposed. One great darkness in America was recently revealed: how the American government is spying on everyone. This was kept hidden, but it had to be exposed because there is so much more light in the ground. You will see more and more light shining, which in turn will highlight how pharmaceutical, insurance, and health care companies are manipulating people. They are keeping people sick so that they can make money. All will be forthcoming in the future. There will be revelations coming more frequently about how the government is trying to control people to keep them in the dark. But they will not succeed, no matter how hard they try. They will try with intimidation and force, but ultimately, light will always win.

Look at the news. A young man from Brazil [David Miranda] was in transit from Berlin to Brazil via Heathrow. He was detained for nine hours under order from the British prime minister because he was carrying some information regarding Edward Snowden.[2] Do you think it is going to stop? Governments are trying to intimidate people. Again, light has been shone on what people are doing. It is not going to stop.

The light that is coming in is flushing out all the darkness.

Exactly. You will see how certain interests are trying to control human beings. In many countries, the police and the judicial system work hand in hand with big corporations to control people.

People are idol worshipers of money. People are bought.

Everybody gets bought. Even judges are bought. There are companies that give scientists grants to promote a product and write a favorable report. Bankers and rating agencies all get large sums of money. Everything is slowly going to be exposed.

All Creation Supports Humanity

India recently granted noncitizen status to a great being you call the dolphin. Dolphins were granted personhood by the government of India.[3] People are realizing the importance of the great animals. When the light is shone, people awaken and understand the importance of all of creation and how it is supporting humanity. We have not seen major disruptions or major loss of life, but more and more, darkness will be exposed. Why are we allowing this?

So people can wake up.

---

2.   BBC News UK, "David Miranda detention: MP asks for explanation," August 19, 2013, http://www.bbc.com/news/world-latin-america-23750289.

3.   Mike Adams. "Dolphins granted personhood by government of India," August 9, 2013, *Natural News*: http://www.naturalnews.com/041547_dolphins_personhood_intelligence.html.

Exactly. But the question is: Will they wake up? There will be some, of course, who will awaken.

We can't change people, but do we have any way of knowing how we are influencing them? Or is it just none of our business, so we should just go and do our thing and hope for the best?

No. You are influencing. As mentioned before, one lightbeing with full, pure, sincere love in his or her heart can influence up to 20,000 people. We are looking for a critical mass of people. That is all. This was proven when 144,000 people meditated on peace for half an hour; the world crime rate dropped during that time period.[4]

Sending Light to Leaders

We must send light to all leaders of the world, because when leaders make decisions, millions of people are affected. The margin of error for making mistakes is very small. Hold the light for all leaders so that they are able to make right decisions. They still have free will, but the more light you shine, the more effect it has. If everyone sends light to the leaders, the situation will change.

I will give you your own example. Recently, we all sent light and meditated on Lois, who had major heart surgery. She was discharged from the hospital in just eight days. Is it not a miracle? [Lois Hartwick of Great Barrington, Massachusetts, is a personal friend of the authors and had open-heart surgery in August 2013.] In the same way, send light to all leaders because when they make decisions, this affects millions of people. Leaders need to make wise choices. Let us hold the light for all leaders, like President Obama and the current prime minister of Australia, Tony Abbott. There is a great war going on between the light and dark in Australia. Send light to him and to everyone. Then leaders will be able to clearly see more light and make decisions from that light.

Where I work, I see many clients for energy healing. During the time I've been there, more and more people have been showing up at my door thirsty for spirituality. It didn't used to be that way, but now people have real questions and are trying to integrate spirituality into their lives. Some years ago, that was

---

4. World Group Meditation, October 23, 2011, http://www.wisdom-forum.com/meditation_gregg_braden.php.

very rare. Is this partially the result of the energies that are coming to them cosmically?

Of course — and also from the work done by all of you. The more a critical mass is reached, the more people are affected. But because of the high cosmic energy on the planet, many people are confused. They do not know which way to go. They are looking for answers. You are shining your light like a lighthouse to assist these people. So you will see more and more people awakening and more and more information, knowledge, and channeled wisdom coming out. You must have discernment about what is appropriate for one's evolution and choose accordingly.

Infusing Matter with Intention

In an earlier session, you spoke about water [see Chapter 11: Clearing and Cleansing Your Energy]. You talked about creating handmade pottery vessels for water storage. I am a potter. I was thinking of making these vessels. You spoke about the infinity symbols and the four directions, and you also spoke about the Flower of Life symbol at the bottom. Is there anything else I should know about making vessels for water storage?

You need to know only one thing: the intention behind your action. When you make pottery, have the greatest love in your heart with the intention that your pottery will carry water that can support and stimulate you, awakening the energy of God within you. Then you are starting properly.

The most important aspect of what you do is always the intention behind every action. When you are making a pot, talk to the mud, the paste, and the water that goes into making it; then you are asking for support, and it will give you support. These things also have consciousness. They are part of Mother Earth. When things are combined, ask for their cooperation, and they will fully support your intentions.

Many things in a house are sad — chairs, tables, curtains, sofas — for they were used, taken, mortified, and placed in the house against their will. No one ever asked their permission. They were part of Mother Earth. Would you be happy? Would you rather be asked, "Will you do this for me?" There is a difference. Thank everything in your house. Bring these things love and blessings from your heart.

How do you thank them? You could envision a green forest or a green tree in your mind's eye during your meditation. When you do this to your bed sheets, to everything in your house, everything will feel relaxed. Touch the curtains, the bed sheets, or the stereo — whatever you have in your bedroom — and talk to them. Send heart energy into them and thank them. Everything will become relaxed. The next time you go into that room, you will immediately feel relaxed because everything around you is in a relaxed state.

When you are making a pot, ask permission. Honor the materials of Mother Earth for offering their lives, their essences, in creating this reality for you. By doing this, you are bringing high-vibration energy. [Archangel Metatron: When you ask permission of the mud and other materials that go into making a pot, they will be willing to support you. When there is asking, more energy is given. Making food in earthenware pots will become more fashionable in the future, and many hotels will have earthenware pots. Food will taste better and will better nourish your body.]

This is how spaceships are made in highly developed societies. The makers call forth all the things they want in forming a spaceship, setting their intention and their desires so that the spaceships never deteriorate. That is how, in the future, everything will be made, including computers. There will not be any deterioration, because you will ask permission of materials to cooperate.

Suppose I told you, "Do 'this' or 'that' for me!" Would you be happy? Compare this to me asking for your cooperation. You would probably do it more easily. Cooperation is the key. So when you are making your pot, ask for the cooperation of the clay, the mud, and the water, or any other essence that goes into it. The intention behind what you do is the most important thing. Everything will fall into place. It is called benevolence. You are asking for support from the universal force.

This is the Spirit of the Whales. Blessings to you. Before we close, Metatron will speak with you.

✳   ✳   ✳

Dearest ones, this is Archangel Metatron. We angelic beings love spending time with human beings in order to have debates and talk, even about God. It is through this that you will learn — when the discussion comes from a willingness to know more but not out of ego. We really enjoy talking with all of you, for each of you is seeking to know more about God. That is what life is all about. Never cease seeking, my dear family. Never cease seeking.

This Journey Is for You

September 2, 2013

Gaia, Mahatma, Archangel Metatron, and Saint Germain

Greetings, my dear family. Your work is making a difference to my body. At the time of this channeling, it is hurricane season in America, and you have not had many hurricanes this year. This is because of the combined prayers of all awakened souls. This is making a difference in the world and is just one example. We ask you to hold the light much more than before so that another war will not break out. Your prayers help to bring about change, and you can see their effects. This year you will see fewer wildfires than at other times. There have been wildfires in some states, but if you look at other years, there have been fewer.

Now I ask you to work for another purpose, a selfish purpose: for me. I need to move my body, and when I do, sometimes it manifests as a volcanic eruption or an earthquake. There may be movement of my body this year [2013]. I ask that you hold the light so that I can move in a very graceful way without much rough-and-tumbling. For, like you, I need to move sometimes, but if I have support, I can move much more gracefully.

You are my support team. What you do on the planet affects my body tremendously because we are connected on the level of DNA, on the level of sacred divinity, and on the level of the elements of which you are made and I am a part. We have danced together. So I ask you to hold your prayers and your intentions so that I can move much more easily and gracefully, for I need to move at least three times this year.

Sometimes I need to hold my body deliberately, for when an earthquake happens, much is being released from the ground, including new vibrational energies and spiritual truths being revealed. If we can work in harmony and balance, I can still do what I need to do. This knowledge is part of your DNA. You are all becoming masters. Brother Jesus said, "I tell you the truth, if you have faith and don't doubt, you can do things like this and much more" [Matthew 21:21, NLT]. He has shown this to you.

When a storm came, he talked to the spirit of the storm. How was he able to do this? He was in touch with his quantum being, his full DNA strands, and he communicated with the storm on that level. We ask for you to communicate from that level from now onward — all types of communication, not just with me, but to humans as well. Before you speak, set the intention to communicate from your quantum being, not from a set of preconceived ideas. Your communication will be on a much higher level, and it will create a win-win situation.

We ask you to consider this from now on: Everything you say is coming from a quantum level. Here is one other gift: When you start awakening your 12-strand DNA, how will you know how much you have consciously awakened your DNA? What is the proof or the measure? Your reality will be slowly shifted, not from an individual perspective, nor from your ego or your personality, but from the perspective of an inter-quantum being.

Today, we will touch on other subjects that are again related to DNA. Many lightworkers all over the world want to access various higher energies — for example, the golden consciousness of Atlantis or the golden consciousness of Lemuria. Perhaps they are not able to feel much energy. But they would be more successful if they changed their perspective to being able to feel this energy within their physical bodies, for that higher consciousness still exists there.

Affirmations and Visualizations from the First Person

Affirmations and visualizations do not always work as expected or desired because these practices are performed on a third-person level. They must be done on a first-person level. For example, if you want to access the higher energies of Arcturus, these energies also exist within you. Ask to access this energy within you. Then your connection will be made on a much higher level. At least you are playing at the Arcturian level, and you are becoming one with the Arcturians because you are awakening this energy within yourself.

[Archangel Metatron: To work from the first person, you have to believe that you are an essence of the Almighty Creator, having the same energy as the Creator. This may take a lot of work, for there are many belief systems to be removed. When you come to this level of mastery, you remember who you truly are with all the powers of creation. Even when you are asleep, you are creating your life.

You will remember you are God in physical human form, and you will do exactly as Jesus did — or much more. Many masters have proven this. Jesus was not the only master who performed miracles. Babaji did many miracles, as did Sai Baba, as recently as three years ago. To perform a miracle, you know that you are the essence of the Almighty Creator, and this knowingness, this awareness, is not only in your physical mind but throughout all your minds — unconscious, subconscious, supra-conscious — in your entirety. When you give a command and intent from that space, naturally it is created the instant you command. This connects to that source of power inside of you.]

Similarly, when you work with the Sphinx, work from the first person: within your body. Start from the first person, not the third person, and you will see a quantum shift in your own consciousness.

"Why did I come today?" Understanding your quantum nature is one of the measuring sticks for how far you have come on your journey, how much you have evolved and how much you have activated your DNA. When you see a wave, you see its beauty. When you see a rose, you see its beauty. When you see a small child, you see its beauty. Where does beauty come from? Beauty is within you. Within a nanosecond, you are able to access the part of you that has beauty, and you are able to see beauty outside yourself.

Accessing High Vibration Energy from Within

From now on, when you want to access the energy of Archangel Michael, Archangel Metatron, or any other being of light, ask for this energy within you to be fully activated, for all of you know, you are group energy. God is group energy. Millions of energies combined together make up what you are. Millions of energies combined are other beings of light. Now I open the door for questions.

In Atlantis and Lemuria, we had twelve strands of active DNA. Did some strands gradually deplete since then, or how did the regression happen?

You must remember one thing: In your truest essence, you are perfect all the time. Your DNA is perfect. Changes take place at the cellular and genetic levels. This is why we ask you to go back to the quantum self.

Back to prehistory, pre-Earth?

Of course. Go back to your original self, before Earth was created. Who were you? You came from the original source, did you not? What was your name? I Am.

[Archangel Metatron: To do this, ask. The original shape was a point of light, bursting forth from the brilliance of the Creator. Can you imagine yourself, bursting forth from All That Is? Visualize a huge circle full of brilliant lights, and you will see life force celebrating, like firecrackers. Imagination and visualization are the highest tools your soul uses to remember and attain mastery. That is why they are highly recommended. They have been used continuously in all spiritual traditions.

If you can visualize it, you can attain it. If you can focus on a place, then that is the place where you are. Take your attention to this birthing star, this birthing energy, and connect with that energy. Even now, you will feel the tingling sensation, the incredible energy falling into you.]

How can we identify our DNA changes? Is there a way?

How do you know you are accessing the higher consciousness of DNA? You know when you start living your life from a quantum level, communicating from this quantum level, and awakening everything within your being, not looking to an outside source.

Let me ask you a question: Where do you think Metatron is? He is in you, is he not? Everywhere including you! So why not access him there first? Then your connection with him will become much stronger when you awaken his energy within you and match your energy level to his energy level. This is what we are asking you now: Do not look outside. There is energy, and you are part of this energy. No more third person. Everything is inside of you. When you start looking at everything from that perspective, you access your highest strands of DNA. This is a sign that your DNA is being activated.

From now on, when you want to communicate with someone, the communication does not come just from your personality; it comes from all your sincerity, your energy, and your being. When you start thinking this way, your perspective changes, and you will naturally know you are accessing higher levels of consciousness within your being. This is the key, dear ones.

So let us say that you want to access some of the crystal technologies, and you are looking for someone to channel what happened in Atlantis. You will be able to pick up threads of energy because there is energy everywhere. But the basic energy, the highest truth, will be found when you are able to access this energy within your being. Remember, when you want to access higher levels of energy, first access this energy within you.

This is the question: "How do we weave the threads between both hemispheres of the brain? It is through this quantum aspect. What if you were living your life every day on that level? This is a sign that you are activating more and more and accessing more of your higher strands of DNA.

The Journey Home

Who is waiting for what, and why?

You are waiting for yourself. You are your own brilliant future! You are waiting for you to come back Home! Have you read the book called *The Journey Home* by the beloved Kryon through Lee Carroll? It is the story of Michael Thomas, a man led on his path who wants to find God. Finally, when he sees God, he is astounded and he falls down, because the God he sees is his own face. It is a brilliant book with tremendous insights, channeled from the beloved Master Kryon. He takes us on a journey covering lots of different topics and emotions, and in the end, he comes back Home and sees himself as the face of God.

So you are waiting for yourself. This journey is for you. This is the way you will all be living in the future, from this quantum aspect and from your whole essence — the physical body combined with the mental body, the emotional body, the spiritual body, and of course all other bodies. When this integration happens, life becomes an experiential thing from wholeness with no more separation.

Sex becomes ecstatic because there is no more emptiness; everything is the sharing of joy. When you are alone, you are happy, and when you are with somebody else, you are happy because you are filled with the bubbling of energy itself. When you are eating food, it is not to satisfy hunger. Eating becomes a joyful experience. Work becomes a playful experience. In the future, work will be called joyful creation, a fullness, completely full. You will experience everything through the physical body, spirit, and matter combined. You can do this; you are all reaching this level. Some of you will have periodic expressions of this; it will come and go, but it will become your new norm.

Communicating from the Quantum Self

When you talk about the quantum self, are you talking about yourself in relation to Earth, the universe, all people, rocks, trees, and so forth?

From a bigger picture, when you talk about your quantum self, you are talking about all your disintegrated parts coming back together with all your bodies — your physical, mental, emotional, energetic, etheric, astral, and spiritual bodies — all of them coming together from all dimensions.

I will give you a small example to work with: During your meditation, imagine that you are a company president, and you have a board meeting in the morning. You are sitting at the head of the conference table, and there are eleven directors sitting around the conference room. These eleven beings are you. You may give a name to each; it is your choice. What does the president expect? That all eleven directors will be in complete harmony and work together for the company's best interest. When you are able to visualize these twelve beings working in complete harmony, this is known as calling forth your inner twelve quantum beings to work together.

As we said before, if you want to have communication, you must ask that this communication begin from your quantum self, not from your personality. The great teacher Paul the Venetian said to think very carefully before you speak. The great teacher Confucius said the same thing: Think before you speak. So let the conversation come not from the mind alone but from the old, old mind of the quantum being. If this exercise is done daily, integrating all other parts in the boardroom setting, this will help you access more of yourself.

For example, when you want to make a decision, imagine the boardroom setting with many directors involved in a decision-making process. Suppose a CEO wants to bring in a new idea, what does he do? He proposes the idea to the directors. If all of the directors say, "Brilliant idea. Let's go for it," you know you are truly on the right track. But if there is infighting, no harmony in the debate, and nobody is on the same page, you must consider carefully whether your proposal is really what you want to do. Disharmony means some part of you is not in agreement with what you propose.

Perhaps you are not 100 percent certain from a soul level or soul path. If more than half of you says it is a good thing to do, you might do it. But you might not as well. You are divided and you would have challenges, and the action will only create more karmic energy.

Calling Forth Your Quantum Self

Tomorrow morning when you wake up, do not just get out of bed. Stay there for a few minutes, and say, "I call forth my other quantum selves to be integrated at this present moment, and I give intent to experience this day through my quantum being." You will feel a platinum-colored energy coming through you. You will be in a much higher place.

The first and most important thoughts you hold at the beginning of the day influence all other thoughts and actions you have throughout that day. That thought, the most important thought as soon as you wake up, is the thought that influences your subconscious mind. So why not start your day by calling forth your quantum being? Give the intention to experience and cocreate that day everything from that level.

You will feel the difference right away. If you take a moment to rest every two or three hours, you will ask yourself why you did not do that before. You will be much more in the flow. You will enjoy every moment of the day, including your vacuum cleaning and the laundry. You will not see these as chores; you will see them as joyful creation. Your perspective will immediately change. We encourage you to live from your quantum selves from now on. Call forth these beings, your being, and you will see.

People say, "If I had more awareness, my life would be better."

Dear ones, all of you are quantum beings, and you will become more aware with this practice.

Opening the Golden Path

You must also ask that your emotional intelligence be raised to match this quantum aspect of yourself. There are many teachers who are brilliant at writing books, but their emotional intelligence is like that of a five-year-old child.

We remind you again to give intention in the morning. Allow your quantum self to awaken the quantum emotions and feelings within you. Most important are quantum love and quantum grace. Your life can take an entirely new path, and you can fly like a rocket. This way of living is called opening the golden path.

This is the beginning of the Golden Age. It is the true meaning of the golden consciousness of Atlantis, a time when people lived like this for long periods. So may the golden path be opened unto you, by yourselves, from this moment onward, by activating the twelve full strands of your DNA.

Healing Gaia

Every thought, every good feeling you have toward yourself, feeds and supports me. So whether you are holding the Torah or sending a blessing, you are healing me. Every prayer heals me. Every good thought you have heals me. Every time you are compassionate toward others, it heals me. Every time you forgive others, you heal me. Every time you touch somebody through your smile, your generosity, your compassion, your laughter, your innocence, or your purity, it heals me because we are together. How can you heal me the best? When you heal yourself fully.

People ask me, "Gaia, how can I heal you? What can I do for you?" The answer is simple: Heal thyself. When you heal yourself, I am healed. I am you, the same elemental nature that is inside of you. When you heal, imagine I am a blue jewel in your hands. Send your prayers to me; I receive them at the quantum level so that they go deep into my bosom. When you anchor your energy into your heart and from your feet into the ground, it comes to me in quantum energy. Each prayer and thought helps support my well-being.

We have changed the consciousness of the planet with the help of other beings of light through events like the Harmonic Convergence. So never doubt the power of prayer — your prayers and the prayers of everyone else.

Ask through your prayer to align with Mother Earth, supporting her in her transformation. There is a difference between prayer and alignment. When you ask for alignment, you are doing what the masters did, what people have done since ancient times. When they were dancing and drumming, they were asking to come into alignment with the consciousness of Mother Earth. Ask for alignment, and immediately, the energy and vibration will be different. There will be a much higher vibration, especially when you want to work with me. Ask for alignment. In everything you do, be in alignment with me; it is in your DNA.

Any other questions from my family?

You spoke earlier about working with the fifth and seventh dimensions. I've heard about people working in these dimensions. Can you explain more about what they are about?

Dear one, they are states of awareness, different vibrational levels that you can reach. When you are in the fifth dimension, you become more fully yourself. You have more awareness, more light inside of you. So each dimension is only another level of awareness. It is opening another seal inside of you, further anchoring the higher chakras and bringing in more light to bring more awareness and access higher levels of consciousness. About who? About yourself. So these levels are just an indication that there is so much more than what you are able to see; that is all.

Accessing DNA through Release

A few thousand years ago, during barbaric eras, we did not have any concept of God. We only had animalistic nature with a low vibration. Slowly through the process of evolution and self-understanding, we raised our light quotient, and we started thinking that there is more to life than killing. This thought awakened the light within.

Does our individual DNA change and mutate with each thing that we release, resolve, and transmute from our library of experiences?

No. When you release, you access more of your DNA. It is like opening another layer of consciousness of the DNA. DNA is always perfect and is waiting for you to give command and instruction to awaken more DNA.

[Archangel Metatron: To do this, you ask and communicate with your cells and your chakras. Ask that the energy in your chakras spin in perfect harmony. Work with the brilliant light of angels or other beings to cleanse and purify your chakras so that they spin in perfect harmony and the codes embedded in your chakras are opened. Work with your guides to help you open these codes.]

So it's a process of activation?

Yes. Have you heard about the seal? Breaking the seal is called removal — breaking the seven seals and finding the diamond inside. We can liken this to release.

[Archangel Metatron: This is a symbol for the opening of the seventh chakra. In each chakra, there are embedded energies. These embedded energies are like codes. The key will fit only with the proper codes. One of the codes to open the chakras is sound. The other is your consciousness. The diamond inside is heightened consciousness. It is the "be" part of you.]

Will those whose DNA upgrades without their full knowledge or consent have different symptoms than those with an awareness of the process?

One symptom is not being grounded. People who are not grounded can look very happy and peaceful, but somebody has to look after them. They can become a burden to other people. This world demands energy from people in order to survive. People who experience spontaneous awakening are in a peaceful place, and their light is bright. But they also need to contribute to the world. It is important to be fully present in the third dimension. Ungrounded people say they do not want to work and say they want to meditate all the time. But how can they support themselves?

Emotional Maturity

There are also people who have had great awakenings but who are not emotionally mature. They become show prophets. [Archangel Metatron: Show prophets are only looking for grandeur on the outside, not the inner grandeur through their souls. They may have attained a sort of enlightenment, but they leave it there. They never work on themselves. They are more outer focused than inner focused, and they are concerned with their following. They lose what they have gained and become showman-like. "Come and follow me, for I know the truth. I have touched the hand of God." One must never stop and say, "I have awakened." One must continuously work, for there is always more.]

If you search the Internet, you will see news of a great teacher in India who was arrested for sexual assault. Ten million people followed him. [Archangel Metatron: His name is Bapu Asaram.[1] He is what we mentioned, a showman. He attained some level of enlightenment but was never able to walk his talk.] Many so-called god men have been arrested. They all have tremendous power and demonstrate miracles of power to the people, but they are not grounded, so their false egos take over. That is why awakening the kundalini must be practiced with great caution. You need understanding of the human body, and you must have the capacity to hold higher-vibrational light and fully activate your quantum being.

Just imagine, if all your twelve strands of DNA were activated and you are not a balanced person, what would you do? You could misuse your power terribly. This happened in Atlantis; it unleashed havoc.

So when there is a spontaneous awakening and someone is not ready, the person can become unbalanced or go into false showmanship of God's presence. A truly awakened soul is always humble. His or her life speaks for the truth of awakened reality. The words of a truly awakened soul, expressions of life itself, speak for the truth. There is no need to show off. Love and divinity are experienced in silence. A true master is silent. A spontaneous awakening can have drastic consequences if the person is not prepared on the spiritual, mental, and physical levels.

If your life force energy has built up to great levels of chi, fully enlightening both hemispheres of the brain (in Egypt, they call this *sekhem*), you will have much power and sexual energy inside. Will you be able to contain it?

---

1. In regard to the 2012 Delhi gang rape, Asaram Bapu is reported as saying: "Only five or six people are not the culprits. The victim is as guilty as her rapists...." See more at http://en.wikipedia.org/wiki/Asaram_Bapu#2012_Delhi_gang_rape.

Higher Level of Consciousness in 2038

Will there be a distinct split in society between those who have activated their
DNA and those who have not?

Let us not talk about splitting into separate groups. There will be
people who resonate with higher light quotients, who will have more
peace, love, and grace in their hearts. There will be others who are not
vibrating at this level. People will say, "Hmm, something has happened
to this person. When I am with this person, I feel good." By 2038, we
will be able to feel and sense people who have a much more awakened
consciousness. It will be like going to an ashram and being in the presence of a holy man. The very ground around a holy man resonates with
his presence, with his peace, and people around him will feel this peace
when they enter his auric field.

It is said that Buddha's auric field was more than seven kilometers
long, and when people entered it, they felt a sense of peace, calmness,
love, and a feeling that everything was all right, as well as an expansion
of their minds. In answer to your question, yes, we will be able to feel
the differences.

Can we share the upgrade with other people by sending light to their higher
selves for dissemination?

Of course. It is the duty of people to share. Like a lighthouse, other
people will receive this light. It is good to send light to all leaders who
make important decisions and, of course, to all people. Share it with as
many people as possible. But let the sharing come without an agenda:
"I will send this light to this person and embrace him in his fullness
without polarization."

What would be the benefit of amplifying the energies of any organ in the body
by activating that organ's stem cells?

Very simple. What happens when you energize something? It is
able to function at its highest optimum level. Suppose you work with a
kidney. You energize your kidney, and then the kidney is able to work
at its optimum capacity. Your heart can work at its optimum capacity.
Work with each part of your body, as this can truly benefit you. Send
love to every part of your body, and you will enhance it. Bless each
body part, as Anna [Grandmother of Jesus] teaches you. Every morning when you wake up, say, "I bless my body." Bless every part because
when you send it love, you energize it and heal it. This will bring every

part to its maximum optimum capacity, and you will awaken a very high degree of energy. It is very good to do this.

Loving Meditations

Close your eyes for a moment, and just focus on your heart. Ask your heart: "Are you well? One hundred percent well?" See what answer you get from inside. What did you find, dear ones? Rae's answer was, "No, I still have work to do."

On the physical level, it's okay, but on the energetic level, there's work to be done. I got a mixed answer.

This is why there is a meditation called Going into the Heart Chamber. You can go into every chamber of the heart and ask, "Is there any place where I am not holding energy for the highest good? How can I massage my heart?" Massage your heart, relax it, release it, and love it.

[Archangel Metatron: You do this in your meditation. Remember, your heart has twenty-four chambers. These are energetic chambers. Imagine that you are taking one step at a time, either down or up crystal steps in your heart. Finally, you will come to a place in the center. This is your chamber. This is your own private space. Make it a habit to go there every day. No one can disturb you in this place.

See yourself sitting in this chamber. Invite your guides. This is your inner sanctum of your inner God. This is where you can communicate with your soul, with your guides, and with the Creator. Make it a point to go there every day. It is a beautiful space, and nobody can disturb your peace in this space.]

There is also a beautiful meditation for the brain called Brain Respiration Meditation. Every day, before you go to bed, imagine that you are taking your brain in your hands and massaging and washing it with the cleanest, purest water. Because of thoughts, it has shriveled. So by massaging it — very gently, loving it, and sending love and gratitude — you are healing it.

Energizing and Healing Different Parts of the Body

To heal your kneecaps, ask what your kneecaps need at this time to be functioning at their optimum capacity. You will get an answer. For your ears, ask, "Am I hearing from the full force of my soul or quantum level?" You can ask your angelic beings to support you in opening your eyes fully so that you are able to see through the eyes of your soul and through your ears so that you are able to hear through the ears of your soul. Likewise with your heart, feel through the heart of your fully enlightened self. Talk to every part of your body; energize it part by part.

How do we control the journey through the right brain?
You cannot control the journey on a physical level. The journey happens naturally. During certain meditations, you can connect with the right and the left, but this happens at certain times, and you are not able to hold it. When you work on raising your vibration, you naturally affect your right brain. It is a natural process. One way you can increase the flow of energy from the left to the right is continuously focusing and sending light into the pineal gland, seeing the pineal gland expanding and sending beautiful silver-white light and energy strands of light into the right hemisphere of the brain, a crisscrossing of energy of the right and the left brain.

If you were able to take a photograph of the brain with the two hemispheres, you would paint one with a silver-white light and the other a brown. In the middle is the pineal gland. An interesting example to look at is the symbol of the medical profession, the caduceus. It depicts two snakes, one black and one white, facing each other with the pineal gland in between.

If you want to raise your kundalini energy, you flow it through your pranic tube, which has two columns — left and right, the lunar and the solar. Visualize the energy being lifted through both of these tubes and taken inside the brain.

These two tubes represent the black and white serpents inside the middle of the brain facing the pineal gland. If you were able to see this happening, you would say the cobra is rising. This is why in ancient Egypt, you see the pharaoh wearing a serpent on his headpiece. This means his kundalini energy is fully awakened: His left and right hemispheres are completely joined. He is being his quantum self at all times!

If the right brain is the key to our expansion and the left brain is the yin and yang journey, how can we balance the two?
You need to be balanced, living in a physical reality in a physical

body. We ask you not to discard this yin-yang journey. Do you want to know more about God? Bring more Gaia energy into you. To fully know God, to fully know Mother Earth, you must fully integrate the energy of Gaia within you — Father/Mother God.

[Archangel Metatron: You can bring more of Gaia's energy into your consciousness by calling for a sense of Gaia during your meditation. You will see a beautiful golden green light entering your earth star chakra, which is underneath your feet, filling you with this beautiful gold-green light.]

Any other questions?

Is there any way we can catalyze the energy of the pineal gland through consciousness or desire?

It is all combined, desire combined with intention, action, and the belief that you can do it. Metatron said, "Spiritual evolution requires action; it is not for the fainthearted or lazy." It requires dedication. It requires the belief that you will attain liberation. Without action, nothing happens. You must have the intention to know more of yourself, and each day, be fully aware that what you are doing will lead you to what you seek: ultimately, the God in your heart.

In a previous session, you were speaking about numerology and how that awakens DNA, especially numbers such as 11:11 and 12:12.

Also 555. We call these markers. These are the energies of the Creator telling you that you are on the right track. Do not get hung up on these numbers. The more you are aware, the more these numbers will show you. It is not a marker to say this person is more evolved than another person. Each is on a different journey and on a different vibration level.

There will be more numbers coming. In the future, it will be 11:21, 21:21, 89:98, 101:101. These numbers will be more important in, perhaps, twenty-five years. Or there will be a shift in the way mathematics will look at the number system. The whole system will change, and new numbers will be added to make a base number. But do not look at these numbers as markers but rather as a wink from the Creator, nudging you forward and reminding you that you are on the right track on your journey.

I would like to ask about the three new chakras.

There are not just three chakras. There are many other chakras as well.

I refer to the blue-green chakra, the pearl-essence chakra, and the gold chakra — the blue-green being the most powerful, which is the coming together of the heart and truth. Can you speak about these, please?

There are many chakras being activated and released to the planet at this time. We ask you to work with the chakras all the way up to twenty-two or twenty-four. [Archangel Metatron: You can do this by imagining and visualizing energetic centers over and above your head. Even now, close your eyes, dear brother, imagine there are energy points above your head; go way above.

I can start to feel them, some.

Practice. Breathe in and out through these energy portals.

I see. So breathe in and out of them as well as send energy to them?

Yes. The more you work with them, visualizing them every day, the more they will be fully activated. Remember, you are not just your physical body. You are bigger, and that bigness is around you, and these chakras are in that interdimensional aspect of you.]

For example, working with the chakra just above your thymus area can have a big effect in raising your vibration. It is called the high heart chakra. This chakra is a soft turquoise color, for this energy is directly connected to the great cosmic being called Mahatma, and this chakra represents oneness. Mahatma will share a gift with you all today.

※   ※   ※

Mahatma's Gift

My dear family, I am Mahatma. All of you carry my energy within your beings, within your pineal glands, and also within each chakra. Although the predominant colors of the chakras are well defined, each chakra also has many other colors, so my energy is in every chakra.

I ask all of you to raise your right palms up, and I will beam energy into you. We ask you to be in a meditative state for a moment in order to receive this energy, to see the beautiful turquoise energy coming into your hands and slowly forming a shape like the Ark of the Covenant box. This box is different because there is only one angel [on top];

usually you see two. See it taking shape on your right palm, the shape of the Ark of the Covenant.

I ask you to place this palm with this box on it on your heart, taking a deep inbreath. This box contains three specific energies. The first is your magnificent I Am presence energy, your soul, your mighty I Am. The second is the energy of Father/Mother Creator. The third is the energy of all the cosmic beings: light guides, teachers, masters, angels, archangels, the God of the Sphinx, ascended masters and sisters of light, Gaia, elementals, benevolent and loving brothers and sisters who support you, dragon spirits, tree spirits, and all other beings of light who guide and support you on your journey. Open this box any time you want to connect with this energy, for this is your essence along with your support team's. You have to breathe deeply three times and send grounding energy through your feet into the body of Mother Earth.

Thank you, dear ones. This is our gift for you, for all of you have reached a certain level of vibration that facilitates this gift. Work with this gift every day, and you will be able to access more of your I Am presence in this new Golden Age. This is Mahatma.

❋   ❋   ❋

Speaking and Sharing Your Truth

This is Archangel Metatron and Saint Germain. Dear family, it is very interesting to see more and more evolved questions coming up. This is how it is, dear ones: The more you raise your vibration, the deeper the truths that open up. No one has the full truth. Truth evolves all the time. The questions you asked today could not have been asked by a layperson. So we say that when the question arises, it is an indication of a person's growth. We see that much has changed. You are able to access higher levels of your brain, and you are seeking answers through this questioning. It is only through questioning that you grow.

You have heard the expression that necessity is the mother of invention. So keep seeking, with curiosity, and explore because there are so many layers. The more you seek, the more we will give to you. For what we give to you, one day you will give to others, for learning and teaching are always combined. Like two palms: one hand is receiving and the other is giving. So we ask you to share your truths, love, compassion, and understanding with all those who seek truth. Always say this is your truth. This is not the universal truth.

Chapter 16

Start Living as Galactic Beings

September 9, 2013

Gaia, Amma, Juliano, Angelic Beings, and Saint Germain

This is Gaia. Greetings to you, beloved souls who are on the Earth plane at this time. We ask you to move beyond looking at yourselves as being from only the Earth plane, for Earth is just one place in the universe. Call yourselves Earth citizens. If somebody asks you where you are from, do not say, "I am from America" or "I am from New Zealand." Instead, say, "I am from Earth." Consider yourselves as galactic citizens because you are galactic beings. People in Israel find this easy to understand because their language is galactic and of a high vibration. Start embodying that you are galactic beings in your consciousness.

You have completed most of the Earth lessons, and your next lessons are galactic. Think in galactic terms — on a higher dimensional reality. Do not be limited to seeing yourself as only from Earth. Start living this until it becomes second nature to you, and you will experience a tremendous expansion of light within you. When you become a galactic citizen, the roles for galactic integration shift. Work on bringing higher Metatronic resonance into your energy field. It will affect millions of people.

I encourage you to start envisioning yourselves as galactic citizens. In your meditation time, imagine that you are galactic beings being filled with light continuously, breathing a beautiful copper-blue light and integrating this light into your beings.

Go to the galactic masters. There are many masters, of course, the most famous being Melchior. [Archangel Metatron: Melchior is a master of the galactic plane. This planet has many planes. The next level above the Earth plane is the galactic. Melchior is a wonderful master to work with.] You can also call on Master Himalaya and Lady Himalaya. These masters support you by integrating your higher spiritual body with galactic consciousness. Also work to activate your various heart centers, for you have more than twenty-four chambers in your heart with twenty-four levels — the heart of the Earth plane, galactic plane, solar plane, universal plane, and cosmic plane. All is of the Creator. For this to happen, you must truly experience a consciousness shift and accept that you are much more than you give yourself credit to be.

Can you speak about making the shift from third-dimensional reality?

Your belief system is still anchored fully in the third-dimensional reality. That is why you do not see much change. Your belief system must match this new galactic reality, and it is up to you to shift your focus to truly experience the fifth dimension. One of the ways you can do this is to make connect with the higher reality, especially from other dimensional realities.

[Archangel Metatron: It must become a natural part of you. There is no when. Every time is when. Imagine that you are breathing in this beautiful white light, and also the golden light of the Creator, every moment, and this becomes a part of you. This golden energy runs through your entire body continuously, even when you sleep. When you are exhaling, you are exhaling all other energy that is not of the light: the energies of worry, fear, concerns, and so on.]

✳   ✳   ✳

Children of Light, and Light as Food

My dearest beings of light, this is Amma, the Divine Mother. After the shift last year [2012], there has been a transformational change in your bodies. The transformation we talk about is the vibration of light. The best food for you is light. Your body needs more and more light as food. You must constantly envision and visualize that you are breathing in the light from the universe and the galaxy. This light will become your main food source. There has been a shift on a cellular level to crystalline consciousness. What does crystalline consciousness mean? How can you fully achieve crystalline consciousness? It is by eating, drinking, and sleeping light.

When you eat your food, you must envision that the food becomes light energy in your body. Then you will start consuming less food and take in more light from the universe. The light is similar to but not exactly prana. The universe emits different types of light, and one form of light is an energy particle that can nourish the body, which means you will never have to eat again. This is how some of the masters lived. They did not breathe the prana as an exercise; they used this form of light from the universe to fuel their bodies. They lived happily and never had a need. So give intent that you will start "eating" light.

There are many children of light from the major planets — Pleiades, Arcturus, Andromeda, Venus, and others, including Sirius — being born on the planet now. They are not aware that they are from else-where; they get used to where they are and eat the foods of Earth. We wish for them to stay aware and remember who they are. For this to happen, they need to eat more and more light. So one of the tasks we can all accomplish is holding the light for these beings so that they can eat more light, which is natural for them because they have lightbodies.

Your work is to provide more light for these new children from the stars. When you take food in your hands, imagine that it is light. When you consume it, visualize that this food sends light to all the children from other systems, that the light from this food transforms the food they eat, and their food becomes light. It is a very important service we can offer these new children.

At the same time, many people still carry carbon-based bodies, so they need heavy, carbon-dense food to support them. When you change your body to a crystalline nature, it is very natural that the diet you eat must change too. You are what you eat. If you cannot feel all the changes that are happening, the reason may be that your food is heavy, dense, and third dimensional. Transform it into light, and you will see a quickening, an acceleration, in your DNA.

[Archangel Metatron: All food is from a living being. But after processing, it loses its vitality and its essence. The more processing, the more essence is lost. What can someone do who is unable to access natural foods? You can raise the vibration of your food by placing your hand over the food. Give the intention and command to raise the vibration of the food to your level. Send a beam of light from your heart into your hand and from your hand into the food. Although the food has been cooked and processed, it will be raised to your vibrational level.]

This is Amma, the Divine Mother.

※　　※　　※

Clearing the Pineal Gland

I am Juliano from the Arcturians. I put on many hats and come through many people. We work with Earth at specific points to bring healing, and we work with the Pleiadians to help the young ones. We know the young are the ones who will make a difference when they grow up.

We work with the young ones to help them maintain clarity without being polluted and to aid the development of their pineal glands. We have devices in our temples in Arcturus, which you can visit. We can scan their pineal glands to see where the distortions or contractions are in order to clear and heal each pineal gland so that it may once again open fully. We maintain this practice strictly, especially with the younger generation of children, for we know once the connections of the pineal gland are gone, the spirit is gone, and we will not allow that to happen. In that way, we help them remember their true origin so that they can work from their twelve higher DNA strands.

This is a gift we wish to offer you. We ask you to give intention to come into our temple and ask us to scan your pineal gland so that we can remove distortions, contractions, imprints and — most importantly — deeply embedded belief systems. What you believe causes chemical reactions in the body that send energy to the pineal gland. Some deeply embedded belief systems can block the flowering of this gland.

The ability to manifest your beliefs in reality is rare. Very few humans can manifest, even if they attain many levels of mastery, unless they can create, or cocreate, what they want in their lives. Without this ability, there is no true freedom. You may not understand this, but you must be able to create what you want, when you want — instantly and without effort. That ability can only come when your pineal gland is fully open.

The pineal gland is the energy sensor of emotion for the entire body, transmitting into the physical body that which you wish to create. Instantaneous cocreation is a sign of mastery. The time to create from thought is very short and almost simultaneous. It happens through the pineal gland. Come to our healing temple and work with us so that we may restore the full glory of your pineal gland. We ask you for the next twenty-one days to do this, and test it for yourself.

Pineal healing will be given to humanity at a later stage. We do not want to release it to everyone at this time, because where there is no emotional maturity, the flowering of the pineal gland and the great increase of spiritual energy can be misused, either for ego purposes or for self-gratification, and it can harm other people.

We want to tell you one more thing. We also have a crystal bed in our healing temple. You may request to be transported there during your sleep or meditation time. Lie on this crystal bed, and allow it to emanate crystalline light into you, reaching all your cells — trillions of them — so that your body is filled with crystalline light, pushing everything else out. Then ask for liquid love to be given to you. Love can be liquefied. Ask for this beautiful nectar of love to be given to you; it will be presented to you in a container (a glass or vase), and you can drink it, filling yourself with more divine love.

We often support Earth people in their sleep by giving them love drinks. This is how many are able to maintain their lives despite tremendous hardships. For many, life is very hard, so we feed these people with love. We know they have a plan with their life lessons, and we do not want them to leave the planet until they have learned. People like you who have worked on yourselves can call for this liquid light during your meditation time, and we will present it to you gladly, increasing the love inside you daily. So we ask you to use us, for this is a gift.

Different Blueprints of the Pineal Gland

Can you talk about the two blueprints in the pineal gland?

From our perspective, there are not only two blueprints. There are six or seven. One is about what you will do in terms of the fundamental things in life on the Earth plane. The second blueprint is on a higher level. It concerns your role as a healer in the galaxy and in the star systems. The third blueprint works on even higher levels, with the energies of angelic beings and the Elohim, to heal other planets and galaxies that are not on the Earth plane.

So in your prayer time, you may ask to send light not just to the Earth plane but also to other planets, galaxies, and star systems that are undergoing similar challenges and tests. This is why you were told to become a galactic citizen. You have many, many blueprints, not just two. It is like your signature cell, which is part of the pineal gland; there are twenty-four layers to the signature cell.

We ask you first to come to our temple, and let us scan the pineal gland to remove the impurities that surround and cover it so that it will operate properly. [Archangel Metatron: Do this through your intention and by asking. Express intention and request your guides to transport you safely to these ashrams before you go to sleep.] There has been misuse of the pineal gland by the dark forces to keep you in darkness, and it was also deliberately shorted by the Galactic Council that rules the Earth plane because of the potential of misuse. Many of the mystery school teachings of the ancient past were about fully awakening this spiritual gland.

Although the pineal gland is between your brain and your skull, it is directly connected to your kidney system. Like your pinkie finger and the gap between the next finger, it is directly connected to your heart center. Although this gland is in your head, it is connected to other places that are equally important. This is Juliano.

✳ ✳ ✳

Working with Food to Heal and Raise Your Vibration

We are the Angelic Beings. There are millions of angels supporting humanity. There are angels for all experiences: angels for help, business, creativity, structure, and building; angels of mercy, crops, and agriculture; and angels who support the food kingdom, the plant kingdom, and the vegetable kingdom.

Why did the Creator create so many different varieties of food? Part of the function of so many different types of food is the different types of people in all parts of the world. Why did the Creator give you so many different vegetables? Why did he create so many colors and shapes?

Shapes play a very big part in your evolution. When you look at a shape — a circle, triangle, pyramid, or a rectangle — you have a different vibration. Shapes matter a lot to the human body. Your eyes take in the shape and the vibration associated with it. For example, if you were to visualize yourself standing inside a circle, you would draw in light from the circle into your entire being. Your consciousness would then expand rather quickly. We ask you to experiment with this. While you are inside the circle, feel the difference. Next, imagine you are inside a triangle; feel the difference. Also try a rectangle and then a semicircle to test the differences.

In the same way, the shape and color of a vegetable have a great impact on the physical body, for although the human body of Earth is one prototype, it can have many characteristics. Some have the body type for the Pleiades, Sirius, or Andromeda; each body type has a different personality, vibration, and function on the deepest levels. There is a difference between the male and female body. So we ask you to look at the shape and color of vegetables to determine which support you the most. [See Appendix II: Masculine and Feminine Foods and When to Eat Them.]

Eating one vegetable, with its unique shape and color, can increase your vitality. Perhaps you have a tendency to be hyperactive, and you want to calm yourself down. There is a vegetable that will support you. A purple-and-green colored eggplant can enlarge your heart area, and it can help you to forgive, release, complete, and let go. A green eggplant can nourish people, and they will feel lively, energetic, and spontaneous with a great zest for life. Zucchini has a soft green color, and it can support healing kidney stones. Peppers come in many colors: green, yellow, red, and orange. Each color of pepper has different qualities and different essences, and each tastes different.

We ask you to start experimenting with different vegetables. Each body is different and responds differently to each vegetable. When you place one on the tongue, the tongue is directly connected to the sensory organs in the brain, and the message travels to the pineal gland. There is direct correlation between opening the pineal gland and the color and type of vegetable you eat. We ask you to look into this. You are what you eat.

When you eat food that is heavy in nature and density and not grown with love, perhaps forced to grow using chemicals or other means, plants and vegetables are not allowed to be in their natural state, and they carry sadness and depression. A person who is already prone to depression and is eating such food will take on the depression even more. If you eat meat from a caged animal or one that has been mistreated as just a food source and without any care or concern, these animals carry great fear and sadness. When you eat this meat, you carry this energy in your cells.

Food and Conscious Eating to Support Enlightenment

Vegetables are more sensitive than animals. When you move into higher reality, you are aware every moment of everything in your life. You are aware not only of the worlds you know about but also of every energy that is necessary to support a life. So we ask you to lift the vegetables you eat and place your hands over them. Ask them to support your highest good and help you move into the next phase of your being: becoming a galactic citizen and supporting the full awakening of your pineal gland. We ask you to look at the vegetables you eat and ask how they can support you in your enlightenment process as you become a galactic citizen.

You have many different types of tomatoes. Many people eat tomatoes with salt or pepper or just as they are naturally — without anything. If you add a little olive oil to the tomatoes, that can support and benefit you — left for some time in the oil if they are small.

It is also important to honor the vegetables you eat. When you pick a tomato, do not simply pick it from the plant. Honor it by saying, "Dearest being of light, I honor you. I thank you for giving your life so that I may live. I ask that I ingest you with your full divine essence so that I may awaken to the true potential of who I am." The same applies for fish or any animal.

Colors are very significant. If people are depressed, they should avoid green food. Blue-, yellow-, or gold-colored food can support their healing. If a person is naturally afraid and bites their nails, green-colored food can support them; they should avoid vegetables that are white. Blue and dark blue colors can also help these people.

Be conscious of how your body responds to the food you eat. Be open to breaking any food patterns that are habitual in nature and do not really serve you. You can ask your angels to help you identify which foods can support you. Each food, each vegetable, and each fruit contains a different vibration, because there is a hierarchy in which certain fruits and vegetables contain much higher essences than others, as well as contain more feminine energy.

When you eat feminine food, you will absorb the feminine qualities of the creative goddess. If you like to eat fish, tune into different types of fish, as each has a different vibration. Find out which is feminine and which is masculine, then eat the feminine as much as possible, and you will see a difference in your thinking, in the clarity of your mind, and in your auric field. You will know, and you will feel alive. We can support you to find out which food is best for you.

Bringing this awareness to food is about 100 percent conscious living. You are already aware of your thoughts, consciously choosing which thoughts to have, using words consciously, and acting consciously. We also ask you to bring more consciousness to the food you eat. You are what you eat, which means food has a tremendous impact on your senses and on your pineal gland, including the overall activation of your DNA.

We are the angels who support the vegetable kingdom. We ask you to experiment with these techniques. If you feel they do not support you, then cast them aside. Over time, this will really support people and play a valuable role in the evolution of their pineal glands and their senses.

The Miracle of the Pineal Gland

When you activate the pineal gland, it is only natural for miracles to occur. In reality, there are no miracles. The natural order of things is miraculous, because you are able to create instantly, being fully in touch with your fully awakened pineal gland.

When you doubt or carry heavy energetic baggage, the pineal gland is not able to open fully. Work with opening the DNA, and naturally all abilities will be opened, including teleportation, telecommunication, clairvoyance, clairaudience, and — more importantly — bilocation on an advanced level, to multiply yourself many times.

Shape-Shifting

Do any of you believe you can shape-shift? You can, and it is natural to your soul; the soul has done it. Has anybody read the book *Siddhartha* by Hermman Hess? He wrote the book in 1940. It is a brilliant book. An enlightened master wrote it. Before Buddha was enlightened, he was in a forest with many people. He became the dead jackal and the dead bird. He experienced the bird as a dead bird. He changed through shape-shifting.

Shape-shifting is a quality of the soul. Everyone has it embedded in his or her consciousness. It is a natural ability inherent in every human being. We ask you to experiment and work with it, and you will be able to achieve much more. Perhaps you would like to travel to inside the Great Pyramid or fly or experience life as a fish or live as a turtle in the deep sea connected with Mother Earth. Mother Earth needs this. Along with dolphins and whales, large sea turtles play a very important role in giving direction to Mother Earth about what needs to be done.

Mother Earth communicates with other distant galaxies and star systems. She uses mountain ranges as antennae. You can shape-shift and become a part of the mountain. One way this can be achieved is by ingesting certain medicinal plants from experienced shamans. Everyone has the capacity to shape-shift. This is a new quality we ask you to open, along with the capacity to regenerate yourself and also the ability to read the akashic records. Your life will take off, and it will be lots of fun.

[Archangel Metatron: To do these things, imagine that you have become a bird and you can fly. When you do this, you take your consciousness there. Imagine that you are a tree. You become one with the tree. Or you are one with a rock. It is simple. Express intention and connect from your heart to the essence of the being that you want to become.

Practice shape-shifting. It can open you up to many new things because you can see your old problems from a whole new perspective. When you become a bird, you can see all your problems and how to approach them. You can move forward, for you can see yourself from above. Your soul also has the capacity to shift into another lifetime. This is an interesting concept to work with every day. Become a bird, become a snake, and become a whale. If you look through the eyes of the golden eagle flying overhead, how would you look at your life? You can see where your own energy bonds hold you up.

Shape-shift. Become a bear. All shamans shape-shift. This is a gift. Your soul has done it. It is done in meditation by asking. When you take Ayahuasca, you become the snake; you become the bird. What happens? You allow this to happen because you let go of your mind and follow your soul. It takes you to a different reality. Your mind does not have any power over you, so you become a bear or anything else that appears from your soul.]

Good day to all of you. We are the Angelic Beings.

✻　✻　✻

Diluting Lower Thoughts with Higher Thoughts

This is Saint Germain. Call me the brother of love. To support you, I want all of you to communicate with me, for I am very easily accessible. We are friends. I have lived on Earth many times, so it is very easy to connect with me. There is much we can share together on many topics.

One of the topics we wish to share briefly is the scenario of war looming on the Earth plane at this time. Will a war happen? Even we cannot say, but you can shift the war through consciousness by envisioning the world leaders who make decisions about war, who manipulate the truth to create war. Envision that their untruth is completely transmuted and transformed by your light. Send light to their higher selves so that they can see more.

All of you are very aware of archon energy and the power of thought. [Archangel Metatron: Archon energy is the power of thought, so sending the vibration of higher thought into the higher mind of a leader can affect millions of people's lives. When a leader makes a mistake, it can affect millions of people. Lightworkers can join together and send beautiful energy into the higher mind of a leader so that the leader is able to see more clearly, think more clearly in a balanced way, and make a decision from that level. It can only bring benefit to all.]

A higher thought can dilute a lower thought. When a sage or a great man enters a village, he can heal many people because his vibration is very high. In the same way, the light from a few lightworkers can penetrate and weaken the thought energies sent by the leaders who want to create war. This is how powerful you all are.

We ask you to go one step further: to use the thought power of the archon energy, of a higher vibration, to dilute the destructive energies that are going out. When a leader thinks about war or decides to go to war, the energy has already been sent out. The thoughts go out into the universe, and you are able to pick them up and dissect them with higher thoughts. This is how you change your reality.

When beings with a higher light enter a dark space, what happens? They clear the ground. There is an expression some of you may have heard: "When the sage walks, all the land that is drying out starts regenerating, and the land is healed." The sage does it through the energy field. In the same way, your energy fields can make a difference in war, diffusing the archon energy. All of you have the capacity as a group to dilute the energy and thought patterns that leaders send out calling for war. Their thought patterns are diluted by your higher thought patterns.

Ask for Support for the Highest Good

Prayers sent to heal Mother Earth are truly received and utilized fully. Never doubt the contribution you are making. Continue what you do; it has an effect. Anytime you send a prayer, it carries a high vibration. It has an effect not only on what is happening but also on many other levels.

Stone structures carry great power, for they store a lot of energy. Your collective energy affects stones much more than you know. Stones are huge energy holders. They play a very important role. You can program the energy of rocks and stones so that they communicate with one another. Suppose you use the Grand Canyon, which is a great portal, and project the energy of the canyon's rocks and cliffs to all the leaders on the planet making preparations for war. Your efforts will have a great effect.

Use the natural resources that are there to support humanity. In fact, you can program everything to transmit energy, as everything has consciousness. When you ask for support for the highest good of humanity, almost all of creation will come forth. If people around the world did not pray to support Mother Earth, the species of the world would be in a much more difficult place right now.

Never doubt. When you doubt what you are doing, you give a command to your pineal gland, and the energy you send to the pineal gland keeps it from fully opening. Doubt is one of the biggest factors limiting the manifestation of your reality. For example, if you do bioresonance and ask whether it will work or not, you know the answer. When you open the pineal gland, instant manifestation and healing can happen. This is Saint Germain.

Chapter 17

Angelic Support for DNA Activation

September 16, 2013

Saint Germain, Archangel Gabriel, Archangel Metatron, Juliano, Sri Bonato, Zoosh, and Lord Krishna

This is Saint German. Let us together hold the intention that wisdom of the highest vibration may come through at this time. We are creating an energy corridor through which energies of the highest vibration can flow. We feel that if this energy corridor can be set up, it can bring forth energies of angelic beings who have much to contribute to your study of DNA. Angels help you activate your DNA, something most human beings are not very aware of.

There are specific angels you can connect with to activate your DNA on a much higher scale. You have personal angels working with you. There are angels for everything: angels for agriculture, food, business, organization, structure, and healing — even angels for cooking.

You also have angels to help you activate your DNA if the proper conditions are met. They can prepare the groundwork in setting up the correct vibrational conditions to work toward activating your DNA with greater ease. Think about how you can call on the angels for assistance with your DNA. The activation of the final level of DNA is a group effort. As you may have read, ascension does not happen without the support of your guides. It is a group effort. Angels beam light into you to help you during your ascension. In ancient times, ceremonies were held when people ascended.

So let us give the collective intention today to allow us to bring forth wisdom of the highest vibration:

"O Father/Mother God, we ask for your divine support. Hold us in your divine love, for we are your children. We ask to be in complete alignment with you today throughout this experience. It is our collective intention to bring forth new and higher truths pertaining to raising our consciousness and DNA.

"We call forth our guides individually and our mighty I Am presence to be with us at this time, holding the energy for all of us so that we may share and bring forth higher wisdom. So be it. We also call forth the presence of Archangel Michael and ask that a protective shield of light be placed around us now."

✳   ✳   ✳

Know You Are Truly a Master and That Can Ascend

Greetings. This is Archangel Gabriel. My dear family, my name has been synonymous with wisdom, for I have brought forth much wisdom to the world. You can call on me.

Today we wish to talk about some of the things available to support you in holding a higher vibration. One thing we have not yet discussed is the power of thought. You must hold the thought and the belief that you are capable of ascending.

If you asked many people — including lightworkers — whether they believe they can ascend, about 95 percent would say they believe they cannot. Start believing that you can do this, because the power of thought is so strong. When you broadcast your belief, it attracts energy to you from the other side. The more you connect with the other side in your thoughts, the more the higher beings will send energy to you. The Arcturians speak of this. It is critical. Believe this, and broadcast these thought patterns, for the other side will respond accordingly and will send support to you. Since their thoughts are of a higher vibration, your thoughts are pulled into theirs.

We feel that although humanity has waited for such a long time for December 21, 2012, many do not believe that they can ascend. Many still believe that ascension is only a fantasy or a miracle achievable only by a master. You must change this thought. This book is for people who believe in themselves, who believe they can ascend, who believe they can activate their twelve layers of DNA. If I ask you now, do you believe that you can activate your twelve layers of DNA?

I'd have to say that I have a lot of doubt about myself, and I know that that is my issue.
What about you, dear one [addressing another questioner]?

I know that Master Kuthumi activated my thirteenth DNA strand in 2004 coming back to South Africa; that I do know. I don't know what's happening now.
Do you believe now that you can do it?

Well, I certainly hope so.
What about you, brother [addressing another questioner]? Do you believe?

I do not believe in anything. I know I can ascend tomorrow. Just give me a hint.
This is what we want to know. Belief must become a knowing, and only from a knowing can you become a being: *be!* You must hold the thought in your heart that you are capable, for this is your birthright.

How many of you work with your higher selves on a constant basis, every day? How can you integrate your higher selves if you do not know your higher selves fully? You must work constantly with your higher selves every moment of your lives. [Archangel Metatron: You do this by being aware that you are the soul and your physical body is just a tool or an instrument to help you experience and know what your soul knows intrinsically.]

The more you work with your higher selves, the more your higher selves will work with you. It is absolutely critical, so get to know your higher selves more fully. Say, "I want to integrate the totality of me, my whole self." Get to know yourselves — spend time, spend energy, spend love from your heart, every day. Say, "I love the Creator. I love my guides. I send energy to them. I download energy from them." Work with your higher selves every day; this is critical.

It is time to put on the hat of a master. You must believe that you are a master and think, act, and behave like a master. You must start believing that you are a master. Put on the hat of a master, and then ask, "What does a master do?" Before you think, before you act, ask, "What does a master do in this situation? How would a master respond? How would a master react?" When you start believing and knowing that you are a master, you have accomplished 75 percent of the journey.

You must start claiming this truth, living it in your own lives every moment. Every moment that you believe that you are a master, behave like a master, think as a master, and experience life as a master creates a larger moment. With one drop of water dripping in a bucket, the bucket will fill with water over time. Every morning when you wake up, say: "Today, my every act will be as a master, and every creation will be from my mastery."

Archangel Chamuel, Archangel Tintanjin, and Archangel Macror

Call on Archangel Chamuel. He is directly related to specific vibrational strands. He holds a rod in his hand to initiate people by sending energy through the rod. Sanat Kumara does the same. In your meditation, ask Archangel Chamuel to place this rod on your third eye to fully anchor cosmic energies there. This will open your third eye. How can you keep this open consciously? One way is by deep breathing daily through your third eye.

You can also work with the Creator, asking for the Creator's energy of peace or something similar to come into you. Take this energy in through your throat chakra, and send it out through your third eye. Your third eye will stay open, and your soul will share this experience. Your soul experiences your life and energy through your third eye.

When you send energy out to a place that needs healing — for example, to Colorado where there is less snow or to Syria — send it through your third eye. Your third eye becomes strong, and your soul experiences the light going through your third eye. Practice this, and you will see a great opening of your third eye as well as a great connection between your sixth and seventh chakras.

The angel chakra is above your third eye. This is an eight-pointed star chakra. When activated, it enables you to connect more clearly and deeply with your guides and other support beings. When you start working more with your guides through this chakra, you start remembering more about your soul's purpose and why you were born.

When you come to know why you were born, you can take steps

to move onto your path. You are giving instructions to your DNA that you are ready to begin your work, which is the full activation of your twelve strands of DNA.

Your soul blueprint — the awakening of your soul contract — is directly tied into your DNA. The more you work on your soul path — why you were born — the more you accelerate your DNA activation.

I ask you to call Archangel Chamuel, Archangel Tintanjin, and Archangel Macror, for they are all here to support the activation of your 12-strand DNA. Hold this thought, this knowingness, in your heart: You were born to activate your twelve strands of DNA. You put it very beautifully, brother: "Come to a place of knowingness, and then you can *be*, which is a place of beingness."

Anna spoke of various rejuvenation techniques in her book [*Anna, Grandmother of Jesus* by Claire Heartsong]. She knew she would emerge with full vigor in a new body, and she was able to do it. Many initiates who went inside the sarcophagus of the Great Pyramid for their final initiation died. They died because of their doubts. When you doubt, that energy affects the pineal gland and blocks the realization of what you are trying to create. In your heart, hold knowingness that you are here to ascend, and you will not give up. This is Archangel Gabriel.

* * *

The New Children

This is Saint Germain. It was good that Archangel Gabriel came because he was able to give you some new information that has never been published thus far about angels, archangels, and DNA. Some new angelic names have been given to you, and you may want to work with them. So welcome these beings and work with them, for they can support you. I am ready for questions, and we may have an additional guest later.

I have heard that the New Children are to come with the three new chakras already activated — the gold, the pearl, and the blue-green — and they are capable of hearing with their four-body system. Can you expand on this?

Dear ones, they are able to expand because they know. They have come with a knowingness deep within them. This is the level we wish for you to come to. Since they know already that they are the new ones, they will not falter if they have the proper environment. If they are bathed in love and held all the time when they are children, they will remember their true purpose: to create everything from their four-body system.

The great leader from North Korea [Kim Jong-un] is an Indigo child. During his deep sleep, he awakened to his truth and his purpose for being born. He was able to connect with his four bodies completely. He was shown his blueprint and life contract. But it was difficult to practice it in his environment, which was controlled completely. So let us hold the light for him so that he remembers more and will take his country on a different journey. If he can remember more, this will propel him to become one of the greatest leaders of the century.

[Archangel Metatron: He is a special child, but a child needs an environment to open up and be comfortable. If he were to bring change right now, he would be killed. These children need an environment in which they feel safe and secure where they can bring out their gifts. They are fighting an old energy.

I can't think of a less supportive environment; it's a Stalinist state.
Made by whom?

By his family members, by his father and grandfather.
Also supported by many other powers — China and America. Do you really think America wants to get out of this situation? America sells weapons to Korea and Japan and keeps them in terror. What would happen if North Korea and South Korea joined? What would happen to all of the American soldiers in the South? What would happen to the millions of dollars of equipment sold to South Korea and Japan every year? There's a bigger picture, dear one. Things are not always as they seem.]

This boy can become the greatest leader in modern history if he is able to manifest his purpose. He knows at a subconscious level, and he managed to avert great danger in April [2013 Korean Crisis]. There would have been a great war in that part of the world, but because he was able to connect with his four-body system in his sleep, he was shown his purpose. If the New Children have the correct environment, they will be able to remember their true purpose, why they were born.

In your own country, many New Children are being born. These children, if raised in loving environments, will change the Middle East completely. There will be great prosperity, great peace, and lots of fun. Israel will be a joyous place. Millions of tourists will visit, and this will support further economic development. People will say, "What a great place to visit." It will also become a financial hub for the world, as big a financial hub as Hong Kong. This will happen in twenty or twenty-five years. These things will be brought about by the New Children as they remember their mission through their higher chakras. They will be able to integrate everything through the four-body system. What is important for these children is that they get sustenance in a loving environment.

[Archangel Metatron: You can work with the New Children. You can help them by sending light from your heart to all of them. You do not have to meet them personally, because at the deepest level, you are connected to all life forms. This light will give them a sense of security so that they can do what they came here to do. They need to feel safe and secure. When you feel safe and secure, you show more of yourself, express more of yourself more freely.

You can support the New Children through the brilliance of your light, through your heart. Visualize that the light from your heart is touching every child on the planet, uplifting and empowering them. When they feel safe, they will open up more. Could you share your truth if you did not feel secure and safe?]

Sustenance in a loving environment is especially needed by these children because their main food is light. You can also integrate like the New Children at this time. When you wake up in the morning, say, "Today, I work from my unified field of energy." Bring forth your unified energy every morning. When you wake up, say: "I am going to wear the hat of a master today. I am going to bring forth my unified energy, and I will connect with the unified energy field of planet Earth." This will bring you into complete alignment with the entire planet's creation. Things will simply flow.

Now I will take questions.

The next question is about making life easy for these New Children. Their energy patterns are woven into the omni-brain. It can be frustrating for them to relate to ordinary people or to their teachers, who are often operating at around 12 or 14 percent brain capacity. How do you suggest the New Children bridge this gap?

These children come in with higher-vibrational energy and can find it difficult to live on the Earth plane. They do not think in a linear way. They think interdimensionally. They will feel more comfortable if they are exposed to autistic children, for autistic children hold the entire spectrum of the love vibration in its purest form. At present, they are the only ones on the planet who do so.

There are also dolphins and whales. If these children can be exposed to dolphins and whales, they will be able to retain their higher levels of consciousness. If these children are not able to exercise their omni-brains, there is a tendency for the omni-brain to slowly close down. It is like a muscle that becomes saggy if not exercised. They must use their omni-brains. Expose these children to a good environment so that they are able to maintain their omni-brains' functions.

Increasing Brain Function

We also wish to give you a sound today. This sound works with your brain capacity and can be done by all of you. It stimulates your brains and creates more energy inside your brains.

The sound is *ramliyoh*, pronounced "RAM-LEE-O." This sound should be practiced holding your thumbs and index fingers together while focusing on your third eye. While making this sound, the chi energy from your fingers will start moving up through your hands, wrists, arms, and shoulders and then into your heart. Then it will go into your throat chakra and on into your third eye chakra. From there, it will go into your pineal and pituitary glands.

If possible, do this exercise in the early morning and evening. We also ask you to teach this to people when you feel the experience is working for you, especially to elderly people and those with Alzheimer's. It will greatly stimulate their brain energy.

There will be new electrical technology coming in three to four years for the treatment of people with Alzheimer's. It may be called electro-brain therapy. Electrical pulses will be sent in a very controlled way to certain neurocenters inside the brain to restimulate the entire aspect of their beings.

When you use this sound, you are sending beams of light. When you touch your fingers and gently rub them together, you feel warmth. If you keep rubbing, you will feel warmth in your heart area, which is your love energy. When you ask, "How can I feel my love?" you must feel warmth in your heart. If you can bring warmth to your heart area, you are able to experience your love. If you cannot concentrate, rub your thumb and index fingers together for a few minutes. This will start generating energy that will seep through your hands into your pineal gland. *Ramliyoh*: This is a galactic sound.

Water and Candle Rituals

Water rituals are significant and can raise your vibration. In accord with the old traditions of India and Tibet, take water in your hands when the Sun is rising and offer it to the Sun. Then drink the water. Do this three times. You will be taking in the full essence of the Sun's energy, and in a matter of days or weeks, you will fill yourself with the highest vibrations of prana. You will be sanctified and purified. Water has the capacity not only to cleanse and purify but also to sanctify. Bring that sacred awareness into yourself.

If you want to go one step further, light a candle in the morning, just for a few minutes. Candlelight represents the light of your magnificent soul, but of course, the light of your soul is a thousand times greater. After doing the water ceremony, give intention by saying, "I call for the full essence of my mighty I Am presence through this light." In the evening, light the same candle for five minutes, and say, "Today, I thank my I Am presence through this light. I give over everything that I want to release, which I have gathered today, that is not of the highest love to this light."

You can combine water and light to bring yourself to very high awareness. When you sanctify yourself using water, you are connecting with your mighty I Am presence. These are simple procedures you can practice daily using water and light. You will bring forth more of your soul essence into your being.

Magnifying Energy with the Arcturian Escalia Mirror

The next question is really simple. What is the Escalia mirror?

The Escalia mirror is a mirror from the fifth dimension anchored by the Arcturians. It is placed near Alaska because there is a portal there. This was the place where Admiral Byrd flew his plane into other dimensions and saw the other reality. When he returned and told people what he saw, they thought he was mad.

The function of the Escalia mirror is very simple. Say you want to send constant light to places that need healing. As an individual, you can only send so much energy. But send the energy into the Escalia mirror, and it will magnify your light one million times and then beam it back to the place where you want it sent. If you want to send energy to something or someone, first beam your energy to the Escalia mirror. It will naturally beam it back magnified a million times. So the energy that you send becomes much more powerful. It is a gift from the Arcturians.

✳   ✳   ✳

Raise Your Vibration with the Escalia Mirror

This is Juliano from Arcturus. We are all here today crowding around you because we are so overjoyed about what you are creating in this book. We want to support you as much as possible. So please pardon our interruption. The Escalia mirror is the fifth-dimensional mirror, like the etheric crystals. We have a double of this in our healing temples in Arcturus. When you work with the Escalia mirror not only will you magnify what you are sending but you can also send your own light there and ask that it be magnified and reflected back to you.

I was bringing it back to the grid.

You can do both. The Escalia mirror is a magnification mirror, and through your intention, its energy can be sent anywhere you want. So why not send it back to yourselves sometimes? You will raise your vibration instantly.

What happens if someone with bad intentions sends bad energy to the Escalia mirror?

My dear brother, as you know, all of our technology is only geared toward higher, good intentions. It will not work. We removed that part because of what happened in Atlantis and other places. We will not allow that to happen. You cannot use spiritual technology to harm another human being. People may use some technology for bad things but not our technologies, for we will not allow our technology to be used by the darker mind. But that is not the point of our discussion.

We ask you to try using the Escalia mirror. Call on your energy field, and send this energy to the Escalia mirror. Ask for it to be sent back to you. Your pulse will rise to a much higher level, for as you may know, you need to be at a certain level of pulsing to ascend. The energy should be so strong that you are lifted up like a rocket. Something leaves your body and moves in another direction, just like a rocket. The

Escalia mirror can help planetary healing and also individual healing. That is the beauty of the Escalia mirror. This is Juliano.

✴   ✴   ✴

Overview of the New Children

Getting back to the New Children — the Sun Children, Lotus Children, Magda-lene Children, and of course, the Indigo Children who are already here — could you give us an overview about what the differences are and what we can expect?

All of them come with certain high-vibrational qualities and senses. They are in service to humanity, and each has a specific function. Some of them will work directly with the environment. Some will work directly with agriculture and crop production, because there will be big changes in how crops are grown. There will be new technology introduced in which there will be no need for chemicals, and the land will remain fertile. Land now has to be left fallow to regenerate and become fertile again. With the new technology, land will always be fertile and will be able to give more, which will mean enough food to feed people.

Some New Children will work with water, and others will work with science, mathematics, and engineering to bring understanding of creation principles. Each group of children will carry a different function. All will work in harmony, for they all will know why they are here.

Michael Jackson was an Indigo child. But he did not learn how to be grounded and responsible. Many Indigos are now in their forties, fifties, and sixties. One problem the Indigos and New Children have is this: If they do not have a supportive and encouraging environment to grow up in, they can easily forget who they are and what they have come to do. Most of them have talents; if they nurture their talents, they can truly work wonders in the world. Some New Children who were not raised in good and nurturing environments leave their parents. They will say that they do not mind being alone. They will not stay in abusive relationships with fighting parents. They will just leave the environment.

These children carry specific vibrations. The Magdalene Children will carry and teach about feminine power. Feminine power does not mean taking over from men; it is about how to balance masculine and feminine power. The symbol for these New Children will be a square inside a circle with the four corners of the square touching the circle.

In ancient times, the square was also inside the circle. The square represents masculine energy. The circle represents feminine energy. The circle on the outside and square on the inside means a balance of the feminine heart and the masculine mind. This will empower women — but not to take over men. It is never our intention that this should happen. People say this is the time of feminine energy — yes, but not with energy that dominates others.

Your heart and mind work in harmony, and your heart rules your mind. You need both. The mind is the masculine part. The intuitive part, the feminine part, brings the energy of intuition and creativity. But the physical, masculine part is needed to make things happen. For example, a woman may have an idea, but it may take masculine physical strength to manifest it. Harmony means that you are in a much more balanced state within your heart and mind.

I would like to ask more about the New Children. Some can now "click off" certain genes. If they have an illness like cancer, how precisely can they click off that gene in order for the cancer or illness to disappear?

Yes. This is possible because they know which parts of their bodies to touch and where to focus their energy and their breathing. They know where to touch and be instantly healed. They will not need medicines at all. They will demonstrate this.

The New Children of the world may not even need this new healing technology, because they will be able to deal with imbalances in their bodies through breathing, setting intention, and focusing their attention. They will show others that they can control their bodies if they believe. Master Jesus taught the power of belief. When his disciple, Peter, came across a lame beggar lying near the river, he spoke, "I have no silver and gold, but what I do have I give to you. In the name of Jesus Christ of Nazareth, rise up and walk!" [Acts 3:6, ESV]. He just changed the beggar's belief system.

These children will show the same thing: When you communicate with the belief that the body will be healed, it will heal. This is a new gift coming into the world. But it will take some time. We ask you to look into this company in Israel.

You are inside Mother Earth. So you are related in every way. You must remember that whatever happens to you happens to Mother Earth, and whatever happens to Mother Earth also happens to you. There is no separation between you and Mother Earth.

You are saying that we are our brothers' keepers, and we are our planet's keeper?

That is the truth. You cannot evolve without the evolution of the planet. You are in a symbiotic partnership. You return to the elements after your life is finished, and you come back from the elements. You are Mother Earth. Do not distinguish between yourself and Mother Earth. Remember, it is about "we." "I" is finished; it is "we." Now we have an honored guest.

※   ※   ※

Tagging Along

My dear children of light, my name is Sri Bonato. I am the spiritual guardian, the spiritual founder, of this planet. I was asked by the Creator God to come here and anchor spiritual energy long before the archetypal dragons came. I planted a seed. I am in every tree, every molecule, and every atom. You can connect with me. I am one of the twelve emissaries that the Creator sent forth. These twelve emissaries added twelve qualities, and these twelve qualities are part of your twelve strands of DNA.

What I planned at that time is now bearing fruit. It is an awakening. It is a remembering that happens through the conscious awakening of your 12-strand DNA. One way to accelerate your evolution is to always use what in English is called "tagalong." Let us say a fly or an ant wants to go from here to there, one kilometer. It may take quite some time for an ant to travel one kilometer. But if the ant were to tagalong or jump onto the tail of a running zebra, cow, or deer, then the ant would be able to travel the distance much more easily.

In the same way, we ask you who are sincere seekers of the truth, sincere seekers of your own divine nature, to use the tagalong technique. The masters are happy for you to tagalong, because they know your sincerity and will give you a helping hand. We ask you to look into which masters from the past 2,000 to 3,000 years ascended from the Earth plane. There were not too many. It is less than one hundred actually. Then connect with them energetically, and ask them to let you tag along with them. Because these masters have the capacity to frequently cross dimensions, many of them return and stay here during this special time.

All the masters who ever walked this planet from time immemorial were on the planet in energetic form. Some were in physical form, and some are alive on the planet right now. During their quiet times, they go back to an ascended state. We ask you to connect with a master you feel close to and say, "I would like to make the journey with you." They constantly allow humans to tag along.

[Archangel Metatron: Call for the energy of a master with whom you feel connected in your meditation. When you feel resonance, inwardly ask to go on a journey with this master. Most masters will agree. The master is flying, and you just touch the master's garment, and the master takes you to higher learning centers.

You might have seen images of humans touching an angel. This is the same thing. This is what Jesus did for many of his students. He took them on long journeys. He would allow them to touch the hem of his garment, and he transported them to other realities.]

For example, recently the great Sai Baba passed away (1926–2011). He was a man who had activated many higher strands of DNA; I would say 144. This master is energetically very present at this time. You can ask, "Let me tag along with you."

There is also one more aspect to this technique. You can only ask them to let you tag along when there is willingness and sincere work on your part. If you just ask them to carry you, they will not. They want to see your effort, and then they will give you a push. "Come on, get on me, and then we will ride together." In the same way, it is said that God helps those who help themselves. With 50 percent effort from you, they will put in the other 50 percent.

So tag along, dear ones. Your journey will become much smoother and much easier because the masters come and go all the time, and the energy field is much higher on the planet right now. It is easier than before for them to transcend dimensions from the third dimension and stay for a few hours and then return to higher dimensions.

Now I will leave you with a question for all of you to think about for the next session. For a long time, this universe had twelve major planets that influenced your Earth life. This is called the basis of astrology. Let me ask this question to all of you: Do these twelve planets have anything to do with your twelve strands of DNA? Have you ever thought of that? It is a very interesting concept. Why is it only twelve? It could have been fourteen or sixteen or even eleven. It is no accident. It is mathematics. Look at that, even numerologically.

Blessings. This is Sri Bonato.

✳ ✳ ✳

Twelve Beings Supporting the Creator

Dear family, this is Zoosh. I am a friend of your Creator. When the Creator was planning the Earth experiment, there were many things to be discussed and planned, for this had never been done before. Isis, many others, and I have joined a council to support the Creator, for this Creator was very young and did not have much experience. No other Creator had started this kind of experiment. We supported the experiment, for I was a planet once myself. So my wisdom, experience, and perception came from that.

The Creator has twelve supporting teams as twelve beings of light. These beings can also be contacted by all of you; they are not exclusively for the Creator. Although they work in a higher capacity, you can contact these twelve beings.

[Archangel Metatron: Call these beings forth. You know that Zoosh is one of them. All are available to support you if you call them forth. Let me give a simple example. Suppose you have been looking for something, but you never went to the library. The library always held this information and had all the answers. You looked and looked for many years but never had an inclination to go to the library. If only you had gone to the library, you would have found the information you were looking for.

You must ask and you must look. Information is available. The masters are ready to support you, but you must knock and ask. This is where wisdom comes in throughout your life.

In other words, you must make the first step and start inquiring, and then things will start to open up.

That is the secret of God. Your love draws God to you. Your love of God draws God into you. Your love for a master draws the energy of the master into you. Your love for your soul draws your soul into you.]

Then they will guide you and instruct you, sharing all the pros and cons, to create your own universe. If you were able to know the pros and cons before you start doing something — not just what is in front of you, but every aspect — then most of creation would be very beautiful, because you would know everything through every angle. These beings can support you and make your creations closer to perfection, because all the angles can be provided to you.

Let us say you are getting ready to do a prayer to send energy to heal the planet, and you have some questions to ask. If you were to call forth these twelve beings — the supportive team of the Creator — and ask them to show you all aspects of what you want to create in its completeness, you would have much more wisdom. Then from there, you would be able to create, and that creation would be perfect.

What we wish to tell you is that you can have much help if you search and look carefully. When people say, "I want to go to university in America (or some other country)," what do the students do? The students do research. They research which college they want to go to and how they will go. They apply for grants. They apply for scholarships. They do all the preparation work, and then they can go. In the same way, if you want to ascend, you must do research. There is a support team; there are scholarships available for you. There are grants available for you, but you must look. It may take a lot of paperwork, a lot of correspondence, but you will be able to get the grant, and you will be able to go to the school of ascension where you will wear golden slippers and a golden cap and walk with the masters.

We have had some very interesting conversations going on today. I am available for tagalong, as are many other masters, for we are all archetypal energy but with great strength and great force, just like the ancient Egyptian gods. We all carry specific vibrations of the Creator.

This is Zoosh, dear beloved friends.

❊   ❊   ❊

Sound Currents to Elevate Your Consciousness

This is Krishna. You can communicate with a certain sound vibration during certain times of the day. These sounds are more effective in the evening and in the early morning. These sounds can have a very profound effect in elevating your consciousness. Interestingly, your beloved musician Beethoven tapped into these sound currents. When he wrote his famous melody "Ode to Joy," he was tapping into this sound current.

"Ode to Joy" has the capacity to bring you into higher consciousness. Listen to this, if possible, before you go to bed, and you will naturally be in a much more relaxed space, and you will carry this higher vibration into your sleep. It works best at the highest peace, early morning between 3:30AM and 4:30AM, 5AM at the latest, and in the evening between 6PM and 7PM. It sounds like this: "ohhh aaaa ohhh." This sound current is stored in a cylindrical object made of an earthen pot.

When you do this, it is like opening the lid of a cylinder, and energy is able to be channeled through this specific vibration for a specific time duration. This practice was created by the great Rishis of old to elevate you into higher consciousness. They practiced this sound current, as it is the base structure for much of creation. This is Lord Krishna.

*   *   *

Everything Is We

This is Archangel Metatron. Blessings to my family. Is it not beautiful that the Creator provides so many opportunities to raise your vibration? But how many people know about this? The Creator has given you ample energetic support systems for people who are on the path. Seek out this help in each moment, for it is there. You are never alone. Your knock will be answered, so knock and do not stop. When you get the answer, knock for the next answer, because each truth opens to a higher truth. You will be supported.

We are one. Your Father, your Mother, we are one. Everything is one. "We," not me and my hand — but "we." The body is "we." Start thinking of everything from the "we" level. Not my stomach — "we." Everything is "we" from now on. This is a difficult concept, but when you start accepting more and more of the "we," slowly it will sink into your cellular level and become a reality for you. You will never say "I" anymore, just "we."

A Sacred Interdimensional Drawing

Dear ones, we ask you to draw a sacred triangle on a piece of paper. Draw an equilateral triangle, and in that triangle, halfway across and in the lower part of that triangle, draw another triangle — one pyramid and then cutting half of this pyramid into another pyramid. So there are two pyramids, sitting like vesica piscis but pyramid shaped.

In these two vesica piscis pyramids, we ask you to place two Flowers of Life. Then draw a Flower of Life on the top of the two pyramids. Then draw one big Flower of Life at the bottom. Draw a line from the top to the bottom, cutting through the Flower of Life in the center (as shown in the following image).

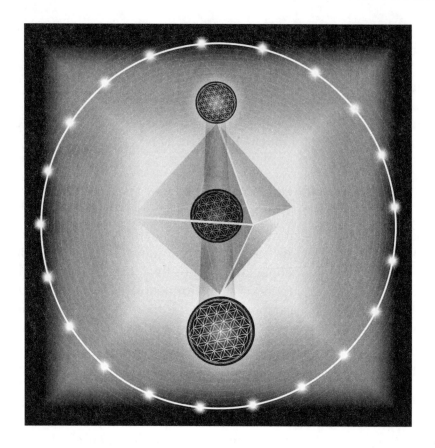

We ask you to do this exercise for a reason. When you are able to draw it out and look at it, you will feel energy from what you have drawn. This is a part of you, and it is an exercise to integrate Mother/Father energy. The center line represents the energetic tube through which your life force moves from Father Creator's sky to Mother Earth's body.

This simple exercise is done with two triangles cutting across each other and inside two Flowers of Life, then one Flower of Life at the top and another Flower of Life at the bottom, and a line going between. But make the line thicker. We ask you to color these triangles and the Flowers of Life. Look at your drawing. When you do this exercise and finish it, you will feel energy in your heart, in your sternum, and in your legs. This is your personal, individual miracle to transport you to a higher-dimensional reality. This is Metatron.

Chapter 18

The Animal Kingdom's Gifts to Humanity

September 24, 2013

Grandmother Spider

Every creature has a gift to give to humanity. Its gift is what it is able to teach people. If you observe an animal closely, you will see what it offers and how human beings are able to receive that offering and apply it to enhance their lives.

For example, various martial art practices from China and Taiwan were copied (or we can say "gifted") to the master by the grasshopper. If you were to study two grasshoppers fighting, you would notice that the techniques they use are the same as those used in martial arts: with their legs, their arms, and every movement they make. The master observed the grasshopper, and that is how this art form came into being. There are gifts we can receive from every animal, as every being in creation gifts something.

Circular Wisdom and Linear Wisdom

Look at me, a spider. How can I make a web that can keep me safe and protect and cushion me if I fall? If someone were to destroy lots of strands of my web, I would not fall to the ground until the last strand was gone. Suppose I have spun fifty strands of my web and somebody destroys forty-five; I still have five to hold on to. I do not fall until the last one is removed. It is the same with circular wisdom. You can still hold on; you are not buffeted by the winds of change. You are supported by the few remaining strands.

All universes, planets, and stars use circular wisdom. Where is circular wisdom located, and how can it be tapped? It is done through the back of the neck. This wisdom can support people.

Psychotherapists can apply circular wisdom to their clients. They can teach mothers how to communicate with their children using circular wisdom rather than linear wisdom. A mother might want to discipline her child and say, "Go and sit down now!" That is a very linear expression. How can the mother communicate in a circular fashion so that the child does not feel threatened or fearful? The mother need not be stern. By being stern or angry, she ends up exerting a lot of energy.

Living in a linear way, there is only one option, and you are unable to adapt to change. As you start approaching life with circular wisdom, it benefits humanity because you are able to see, hear, and feel more.

Communicating Using All Five Senses in Wholeness

A good practice to do when you wake up each morning is to give intention that on this day, you will use your five major senses in a complete way. Give intention that your eyes will be wide open, that your senses will be very clear, that your feelings will be fully rejuvenated, that your smell will be heightened, and that your taste will be pure. When you set this intention in the morning, you naturally start using your full five senses, and this is one of the ways to start working with circular wisdom.

Your body is constantly giving you messages, and you should listen. Your body will tell you. Your tongue is directly tied into your intuitive feelings. Your ears and your sense of hearing allow you to hear what somebody is saying without the interference of preconceived ideas.

A mother who wants to discipline her child can use all her senses and communicate with the child through her entire being to her core. This wholeness can support both the child and the mother.

The messages from your body come from a very high place. When you spin a web, remember to do it in a circular motion. Learn to integrate and cultivate circular wisdom on a daily basis.

We are messengers of the Creator in support of humanity, and we ask every human being to look at the whole animal kingdom with a new set of eyes so that he or she will see what we truly have to offer. This is Grandmother Spider.

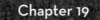

Your Internal Compass: Nature's Body Intelligence

September 27, 2013

Angelic Beings, Archangel Metatron, Archangel Michael, and Orengi

We are with the Angelic Beings. When you work with the Angelic Beings, you naturally start having good things happen in your life. You flow with the universe. We encourage you to constantly communicate and channel the energies of the Angelic Beings into your being. We hold the purest vibration of the Creator. When you start connecting with angels, you will also make a strong, benevolent connection with the elemental and the nature beings. This practice will truly support you in this time of awakening. The angels can also support you in this.

When you have a connection with the elemental beings, you are naturally connected to the entire Earth spectrum. The DNA of Earth and the Angelic Beings can support you in this transition to experience the elements and to align with them. These elementals are connected to the four directions and to the deeper compass within.

You have a compass inside of you. Every human being and every animal has this compass. Newly hatched baby sea turtles know how to get into the water; they use their internal compasses. A human baby knows to put its mouth on the mother's bosom. If you were to completely align with your internal compass, many things could be changed and accomplished. The shamans of old used their hands as wands to find the direction to go. What they were doing was aligning with their internal compasses.

In ancient times, people were nomadic. They were constantly moving from one place to another in search of food, shelter, a better environment, and safety. How did they know where to go? They used one hand, pointing in one direction with two fingers to the ground and feeling the energy their bodies communicated to them. They could feel warmth, and then they would say, "I feel more heat in this direction; this is a good direction to go. We will find shelter. We will find water. We will be safe."

Your internal compass is always available, you just have to feel for it. You can align all experiences with your internal compass. How do you know when you are aligned with your internal compass? You will feel warmth in your body. You will feel good, joyful, or expansive. You will know you are on the right path. Most importantly, when you align with your internal compass and create experiences from that level, you will be in alignment with your soul and divine will. You will be on the right track, and you will do the right thing. It will be beneficial for you and everyone else. Ask for the activation of your internal compass; it resides in your spinal column. This is your internal guidance system.

[Archangel Metatron: To activate your internal compass, call on a specific guide with whom you feel a connection and ask the being to activate this for you. You can call on the Creator to support you in this. Or you can ask Archangel Michael, Gaia, or me to activate the internal compass inside of you.]

Now I open the session for some questions about the internal compass.

Spinning Your Three-Pointed Star

Is the internal compass based on Earth's magnetism? If so, what happens when we are converting to crystalline consciousness?

The internal compass is directly connected to your soul. It does not have anything to do with the magnetics on the ground or the shifting of the magnetics in the ground. It is your internal radar system. But you must call forth this internal compass to be activated. It is like the three-pointed star, a sacred geometric pattern encoded at the bottom of your spinal column. If you are connected to it, you will almost always know the highest and most benevolent action you can take. It is like a magnetic needle that moves when you are aligned; your entire body will speak, and you will know the right thing to do.

When you are in alignment with your internal compass, you are in a state of knowingness. We ask all of you to come to this place of knowingness where every part of you speaks. When you hear great truths, you agree almost immediately, because you know the truth. Your internal compass reminds you right away.

[Archangel Metatron: You come to the place of knowingness through practice. It involves asking, but it is more than asking. You have to come to a place of being. When you come to a place of being, you are naturally in the process of knowingness. This requires mastery and work.]

Internal compass activation involves the three-pointed star using the colors of white platinum, turquoise, and gold. Visualize this three-pointed star spinning, and ask that your compass be activated and spin through your spinal column, going up and down and emitting energy. Then direct this three-pointed star to enter all your chakras; see them spinning with the energy of your compass. [Archangel Metatron: You do this practice during meditation. Allow the star to rotate any way it wants.]

In particular, work with the throat chakra. Take your internal compass (the three-pointed star) and direct its energy into your throat chakra. You will see this chakra spinning, and inside of it, you will see the three-pointed star. The effect this practice will have over time is that you will only speak the truth, the truth that is appropriate for the present moment. You will know when to withdraw, when to speak, and how much to say. You will know because you will feel whether the person you are speaking with has the capacity to understand, and as you watch, you will see how your words affect that person's energy field. The words coming from your mouth will be suitable and appropriate for that moment, for that person, and for you.

Your internal compass can also be taken into your third eye or to any other organ in your body. You can ask that every organ in your body be completely fine-tuned to bring into alignment with your internal compass.

Musical instruments such as the piano, clarinet, and harp all produce beautiful music. These instruments need to be retuned periodically. Your body is an orchestra. All its parts are creating a beautiful symphony. But through stress, time, your thinking, and your way of life, the orchestra can get out of tune. You must fine-tune all your body parts periodically so that you create harmony. When all organs are functioning properly to their highest capacity, they create a beautiful, harmonious song.

You might need to call a tuner to retune your body's orchestra. Medical doctors only examine the part of your body that is in discomfort. But the problem may be caused elsewhere in your body because your meridians connect all parts of your body. Chinese medicine looks at a body comprehensively. Your internal compass is your fine-tuning instrument. Run it through all the organs in your body. The three-pointed star will spin and throw off energies, repair damage, and align all the organs of your body, enabling it to function at its highest capacity.

We advise you to work daily with your three-pointed star, your internal compass. When your body becomes finely tuned, all your senses can be fully alert. You will be able to tap into the circular wisdom that surrounds you. When you do this, you will live from the totality of your beingness, your quantum self. You will see clearly — and sense, touch, taste, and smell clearly — because every organ is completely aligned with your internal compass.

By intention, you can tune your internal compass so that it communicates with the elements of nature. Instead of seeing rain, you feel it and become one with it. You feel the wind and become wind itself. The purpose of your three-pointed star is to align with all that you need to live life fully in a circular way.

What do we mean by this? Many people see only what is in front of them and cannot see in a fuller sense yet. They may be afraid of the future. But if they became more like the spider, aligned with nature, they could move beyond their fears. A spider has to be very aware of what surrounds it and in tune with its web for its own survival. It has to be very careful to stay alive and to catch what it wants to eat. It has to be very aware of all of the dangers in its environment. It naturally knows how to survive. If a great storm with strong winds came, the spider would know immediately what it needed to do. So it is completely aligned with nature and knows how to survive. Because of that, it has no fear.

When you tap into circular wisdom, you will start living your life without fear. The tool to work with on this is your three-pointed star within your spinal column, your internal compass. Your internal compass is turned on the moment you are born.

Every animal knows this. If you watch a calf being born, it can be a difficult process for the cow, yet she remains standing, in pain. And when the little calf emerges, it knows how to feed automatically and does not require a doctor for guidance. The calf automatically finds its mother's teats, even when its eyes are closed. The same is true for sheep and elephants and many other animals. If their senses are so finely tuned right from the beginning, what does that say about human beings who are on a much higher level? Their internal compass must be on a much higher scale. But they have not used it. They are currently unaware of it.

From today on, begin activating your internal compass. Then you will know that when you walk the Holy Land and feel your calling, you will say to yourself, "That is my internal antenna, my internal compass aligned with what I am planning to do today. It is aligned with the particular place I am going to visit today." This is called connecting with the third language: You are completely connected to your internal guidance within your being in every moment.

When we start spinning this three-pointed star, does it spin clockwise or counterclockwise?

It does not really matter. You can spin it horizontally or vertically or any way you think you want it to spin. Just see it spinning, going up and down in the three colors that were mentioned.

❋   ❋   ❋

Pineal Gland Practice

Another subject that is important for you to be aware of is working with your pineal gland. The true essence of this work can get lost in our effort to communicate in writing. What is most important is that you hold the intention of this work in your consciousness. When you command your body and hold the intention that you are sacred and divine, the energy is created naturally. Intention is the key. The hand positions create a higher-frequency vibration. Here is a three-part exercise using two mudras.

The first mudra is called: I Am Sacred and Divine. Close your eyes. Both thumbs touch the tips of both index fingers. The right hand is stacked over the left hand (the hands touch each other), and both hands are held in front of your body, fingers pointing away from you. Hold this position and feel the energy.

In the next step, both thumbs touch the tips of both index fingers, making a circle. Position your thumbs and index fingers just above your ears on both sides of your head, and start making small circles on both sides of your head with your thumb and index finger. Allow your fingers to move slowly forward, making circles until you reach your hairline. Then touch the tips of both thumbs, and place them across the top of your forehead. Touch the tips of both index fingers, and hold them on the top of your head, making a sacred triangle.

Your pineal gland is below where your index fingers touch. Rest your hands there. Visualize your pineal gland emitting pale-platinum light followed by pale-blue light, pale-green light, pale-turquoise light, pale-pink light, and then pale-purple light.

The second mudra is called Activating the Pineal Gland. The hands are positioned the same as in the first mudra, but both thumbs touch the middle of the index and middle fingers. The right hand is stacked over the left hand, and both hands are held in front of your body, pointing away from you. This is the mudra to activate the pineal gland.

The sounds to work with this activation are "ohm, ooo, wah." Draw these sounds out, and let "wah" come from the deepest parts of you. Repeat these three tones for four to five minutes or until you feel the energy. You may feel sensations in your solar plexus, see sunlight in your third eye, or see images of the depth of the sea. You are as deep as the ocean. You may also feel a deep sense of belonging.

Additional Energy Exercises

Body movements using your hands can clear great amounts of energy, and they can have a great effect on your energetic body. For example, if you have a problem with constipation, you can gently massage the index finger of your right hand going all the way up to the top for fifteen minutes. It will help release the energy of constipation. If you have diarrhea and want to use energy to heal it, you can use the same index finger, but this time, massage from the top to the bottom.

The energy created using mudras affects the nadis, meridian

points, and nerve centers in the human body, syncing with the intention of what you are trying to create. Although some mudras may look strange, they have the ability to bring healing. Experiment with your pineal gland activation; within a day or so, you will feel a greater connection with your I Am presence. [Archangel Metatron: Do this by bringing in either a beautiful golden or a silver platinum light from above. Feel it entering into your crown chakra and completely filling your brain area. Breathe through your nose, taking it through the back of your head, and then pushing it out through the top of the head. That is the one way to activate the pineal gland. Push it out through the back of the neck, and push it up and out through the middle, out the top of the head.

Another thing you can do is close your eyes and bite your tongue a little, and in your mind's eye say the word *naha naha* (not out loud). Or you can try breathing in the white light, biting your tongue lightly, and saying a different word: *sa ha no*.]

Many human beings, through their good intentions, focus on the Creator and their guides to download energy, which is very good. But they do not spend as much time on their own higher selves. Many have difficulty connecting to their I Am presences. They know that they have one, but they are not able to experience and feel it as much as they would like.

Once you start doing your pineal gland activation, you will start focusing more and more on your I Am presence. You will become more balanced. Your I Am presence will start becoming more prominent, and you will start meditating with it much more. With the guidance from the masters, your intention is to bring yourself back to the awareness of your I Am presence and integrate this presence into your conscious awareness.

The other exercise we wish to present to you resembles a foot massage. Sit down and hold the big toe of your right foot with your right hand. Then with your left hand, reach down and hold the big toe of your left foot. Massage each toe gently. The big toes are connected to the core of wisdom within a human being. These energies are related to earthly wisdom and how to live in a physical body in harmony with Mother Earth and all of her creation.

Directly underneath the toes, on the soles of your feet, are major chakras. There are chakras all around the toes. More space between the toes can signify that a person carries great internal wisdom and has a deep love in his or her heart. It signifies great light within. If you start massaging your big toes, you will be able to activate more wisdom within yourself.

When you connect with the masters, angelic beings, and other beings of light, they place a packet of wisdom in your auric field. This is connected to Earth's wisdom. So gently start massaging the big toe of each foot. Do not massage all the toes, just the big toe. The energy and the meridians from these toes are connected directly to your heart center, your third eye, and your core wisdom. Massage the toes gently every day if possible.

Another form of foot massage can help with sleep. People have difficulty falling asleep for various reasons. Lightworkers have a lot of light and energy, which means they are not able to sleep very deeply. Sometimes it is because of old age. People may wake up many times during the night to go to the bathroom. Or they wake up and cannot go back to sleep for a long time. Many people cannot sleep well because their brains are too active with stress, everyday activity, or too much light energy.

To resolve sleep difficulties, try the following: When going to bed, make a fist with your hand and gently massage the soles of your feet. If you feel pain, then you know there is a problem in your body. Next, gently massage your ankles. This area is directly connected to your brain.

If you cannot sleep well because of stress, everyday activity, or too much light energy, you need to relax your brain. You can do this by gently placing your hands over your eyes, which will start to work with your brain. This is the same as one of the hand positions in Reiki. [Archangel Metatron: Cover your eyes with both hands for eight to ten minutes. You may feel it in three minutes, but initially you might want to do it for longer to feel the energy.] You will see an immediate effect. You will start feeling more rejuvenated, relaxed, centered, and balanced.

Working with Clouds

Now we would like to share information on how to work effectively with clouds. Clouds have energy and consciousness. When you observe clouds, you will notice that they move in various directions. They have consciousness. They carry the energy of Mother Earth like waves in a body of water. Clouds also carry the energy of Father Sky. There are many energetic beings on the clouds who constantly give messages to humanity. But humanity is not aware of these messages.

If you want an answer to a question, such as what to cook for the grandchildren tonight or whether to go to town to buy vegetables, send that thought out into the universe. Then go and look at the clouds. The formations and patterns in the clouds will communicate with you; you will be able to decipher what you need to hear. [Archangel Metatron: You will know this through your feelings. This is the place you will come to know as inner knowingness.]

Once you know how to work with clouds, you can tap into the very large library of universal wisdom. If you do not believe this, test whether you can move clouds. Go outside, and make a cloud formation move to another place. Gently look up and blow out through your mouth; use your intention for the cloud to start moving, and it will. This shows that you are interacting with universal consciousness. There is energy going from you to the universal consciousness.

Have fun with those clouds. They will enrich your life. Teach your children. When you are in doubt and need an answer, talk to the clouds. You will find the answer in the cloud formation. It is time to utilize everything that the Creator has given you. You all know that water is very precious, and so are the clouds. It is no accident that clouds are all white. In the Creator's creation, nothing is accidental. Everything has a purpose. You are all part of a rainbow.

※　　※　　※

Calling Forth the Air Element

I want to ask about clouds and about the air elemental — the sylph — that also dresses up as a feathered cloud when doing certain work to cleanse the atmosphere. Can you speak about them?

Everything is created to bring healing to the planet and the people. The air elements have their own spirit beings within them, and different cultures use various names. During meditation, you can call on the elemental beings in your own life to create, disperse, and release.

Let us talk about release. If someone comes to your house with a dense energy, you can call on the Air Beings to release the dense energy. The Air Beings will come and blow away the energy. You can invite the air elementals to help in the cleansing process.

One problem common for many people is that their elements are out of balance. For example, if the air element is out of balance, it is difficult to release energy. People who hold on can find it hard to accept new tools or change their thinking. People with too much air element in them are not grounded properly. They have great ideas, but nothing gets done.

You can call the Air Beings to cleanse you and work with you during meditation. Ask the air element to come and present you with a white feather. Then see this white feather acting as a fan inside your body, fanning you from your toes all the way up to the soul star chakra. Let it fan away, cleansing and purifying you. You can also call on this great being for any cleansing or healing in your country. For example, where there is negativity, you can ask the Air Being to come and cleanse that space. Anytime and anywhere you need cleansing, call this being to come and cleanse.

When a tribe is looking for an answer to a problem in order to solve something in a gentle, loving, benevolent way, they ask the air element for guidance. When you request this element to support you in finding the wisdom you seek, it can create great amounts of air or gusts of wind. It can use the air from other geographical locations that have the wisdom you seek and transfer it by depositing soil from that location to the area where you live, where you need the transfer of wisdom. When people connect with the land, they can be inspired to connect with higher wisdom. It is one of the ways that natural elements work to support humanity.

For example, a child in a small town in Africa of 100,000 people is seeking an answer for the whole town. At the same time, someone in another village in Africa has already resolved this. The energy is in the akash. The air element of the wind will go to Africa, pick up the dust from the ground of the village, and deposit it in the first town. You can request elemental beings to support you in what you seek. You do not need to worship these beings; you just need to be in alignment with them.

You can start a ceremony of alignment. Some do the ceremony in the morning, bringing the ceremony to align with the forces that they need to do their work. When you start to align with the natural elements using ceremony, you connect with them completely. You can work miracles. For example, in the case of a great tragedy such as the one in Nairobi, Kenya,[1] there is great sadness and great negative energy because of what happened, and people fear a recurrence. This tragedy will stay with them a long time. Ask the wind element and the fire element to go and disperse this energy, and these elements will burn the dross energy from the natural environment where it happened.

The wind element is like a big broom; it will clean up the energy. It will take three to seven days for it to happen. But there will be healing. There will be clearing, and a newness can begin there. If the people who experienced the tragedy start with the newness, the dark will clear from their pasts. Nature will affect these people. So you can call on the fire element. In some cultures, the name of the fire element is Ohra [Mesopotamia and Sumeria].

Where great battles took place in the past and where there were many deaths, there are a lot of negative energies. When lands are conquered by people, they need to be cleared using the natural elements to restore balance once again so that people can live peacefully. So work with Ohra, the fire element being. Work with that water element and earth element too.

Is it correct that our vibrational growth and physical exercise are directly linked to our DNA? Are we able to raise our vibrational frequency through exercise, even when a limited number of strands of DNA are activated?

We call exercise of the physical body a meditation of the body. Exercise can raise the vibration in the human body. It can elevate the life energy. All of this is very true. But exercise alone will not support what you seek, except when it is combined with the meditation of the mind. When you combine the energies of the body with the energies of the mind, you are in a very high place, creating high light-force energy.

Activating the Codes Connecting You with All Creation

You mentioned that our DNA and RNA have a consciousness that can be communicated with. Can you expand on how we can go about communicating with it?

---

1. September 21–24, 2013, gunmen attacked the Westgate shopping mall in Nairobi, Kenya. There were at least sixty-seven deaths, including four attackers (http://en.wikipedia.org/wiki/Westgate_shopping_mall_attack).

Every body part has a consciousness that can be communicated with using feelings, through intention, and by sending focused energy. If you want to communicate with your heart, focus on your heart. Send love from your heart to your heart, and say whatever it is that you need to say. It is the intention and the energy focus that will naturally start connecting with that body part. The DNA and RNA have consciousness, for they are connected directly to the creative force of the divine universal truth. When you start connecting with the creative part of the Father/Mother God energy, you naturally communicate with this force.

One thing you can do in your meditation time is call forth the activation of the codes connecting your DNA with all of creation. DNA is an instruction manual that carries codes, and it is through these codes that instructions are given. Ask for the codes inside your DNA that are connected to all of creation to be fully activated. This is very important. Often people will say that they want to do it, but everything is like a time lock with a key that has codes on it, and these codes need to be reactivated.

During Rae's recent trip, he met a wonderful tree that was 1,000 years old. It asked Rae to sit down and said, "Look at the other trees around me. There is no other tree that is as big as me." The tree went on to explain that this was because it was able to connect with its source. Its source was inside, at the solar plexus region, which is known as the power point.

There are codes and sacred geometric patterns, and when you connect with these codes, you connect with your fullest essence. The tree said, "Everybody talks about the heart, and that is very beautiful and important. The heart can have great compassion and great energy, but the true power source is not the heart. It is the point between your solar plexus and your spinal column."

When you connect with this source, you are connecting to the water element within your being. Do not forget that you are a water being, because your essential nature is water. When you connect with this source, you are connecting with your power center. When you start connecting with this power center within yourself, you will naturally grow as strong as that tree and will rejuvenate yourself. You are connected to your source and to your power. The tree said not to neglect this part. Many people focus on the heart, but you must also focus on this power point.

Activating Circular Wisdom

We ask that you focus on an important part of your body: your power source, which starts behind your neck. There are many important chakras coming down from just below your head.

Imagine in your mind, or even draw with your hand, a triangle going from the back of the head, just above the neck, and down to your hips. The top point of the triangle is above the neck. The other two points are the two hips; the bottom of the triangle goes from your left hip across to your right hip. Now imagine a line down the middle of this triangle.

Work with this. If you work with envisioning this triangle pattern every day with the three points of the triangle emitting light (like the three-pointed star of your internal compass), you will start activating the circular wisdom within your being.

The circular wisdom is connected not only to your senses but also to your ancestors. Just imagine: You can connect to the ancestral wisdom from your father's side and mother's side. You can connect to how they overcame challenges in great difficulties and ancient times. You can connect to their wisdom and their understanding, for most ancestors were indigenous people connected to indigenous wisdom. Most importantly, they were directly connected to the land. You are affected by at least five to seven generations on both sides. So circular wisdom is not only what is all around you but also includes ancestral wisdom.

We ask you to work with this triangular pattern every day for fifteen minutes. You will see more opening within yourself. Your perception will increase right away, and you will start looking at things from this higher reality.

Balancing the Seven Major Chakras

Could you speak about healing, harmonizing, and balancing the seven major chakras?

You can do that simply. Bring forth your soul star chakra. [Archangel Metatron: Your soul star chakra is just above your crown chakra. It is sometimes called the transpersonal point as well. Imagine a beautiful star shining there, and envision that you are breathing through this star, and you are always anchoring energy through this star. The more you work with this star, the more you'll get in touch with your soul. Most people only focus on their seven chakras. You must also focus on the higher chakras.] See your soul star chakra going into your crown chakra and then into other chakras, slowly going through each. Your soul star chakra is able to flow easily through all the chakras. In this way, you will be able to bring more of your soul energy into all your chakras. Just imagine the soul star chakra going into your crown, going into your third eye, and then going down all the way. Imagine it as a pendulum going through all the chakras, going up and down.

This visualization is very simple but very profound. Truly you must be able to bring forth more of your soul essence into the chakras. So when you work with the soul star chakra, you are bringing more God force into your seven chakras. Do it every day in your meditation. You will see the effects right away. You will be able to run your soul star chakra continuously up and down, and this will clear your chakra column continuously.

☀   ☀   ☀

"I Am the Light"

Hello, dear ones. This is Archangel Michael. We wish to share a sound with you that you can use. The sound is very simple. The sound is "omaan y u omaaan yyy uuu." It means only one thing: "I am the light." When you say the words, "I am the light," do you not feel expansion? Do you not feel completeness? When you say it, "I am the light, omaan, yy uu," it says it all: I am in the Creator, and the Creator is within me.

Now, before we go, we have a surprise, a gift, for you. The main course is finished, but I know you still want dessert. So let us bring in somebody.

☀   ☀   ☀

Perfect Masculine-Feminine Balance

Hello. I am speaking from an ancient language. My name is Orengi. I am the water spirit.

In your house or outside in nature, somewhere with water, place your bare feet into water. Breathe through the soles of your feet, imagining and visualizing that you are breathing the water. You will feel a warm, pulsing sensation coming into your feet. You are breathing water, and the water is running throughout your being. It has two properties: It is cleansing, and in its purest form, water contains the purest love of the Creator. As you visualize the water running through you, it is a very cleansing process.

Once you finish this cleansing, sit down and ask that this water transmit its true origin, its true purpose, to your being. When you do this, you will feel a different sensation in your body because you will feel the love of the Creator.

You can also ask us to transmit the energy of water with its true purpose into the different codes in your body, for you all have 144 sacred codes to be activated. Water also carries the blueprint of life. And your own blueprint, your DNA, can be activated using the water element.

So first, do breathing and cleansing. Then ask for integration of the balance of feminine and masculine energy that the water contains.

Water is very well balanced. Many people associate water with the feminine. I would say no. Water is both feminine and masculine, fully balanced. None of the elements are male or female. They are a unified force of energy. Why, then, is Mother Earth called Mother Earth? It is because she nurtures and supports humanity and life. So we give her a motherly quality. Mother Earth is a unified energy of male and female. It is the same with water. You will transmit these codes and under-standing when you place your feet in water and breathe in and out, which will work in activating the new codes within yourself. It is to be in alignment with Mother Earth.

※   ※   ※

Working with Your Birth Star

What is the meaning of your birth star? When you were born, each of you was aligned to a star. This star is your support system. You are aligned specifically to your star. Find the star that holds tremendous light and energy that can be of service to you. When you connect to your star, you will start downloading high-vibrational energy that can truly catapult you and increase your vibration by at least 40 percent.

Can you give us a hint? We aren't talking about the zodiac, are we?

The zodiac is just one part. We are not talking about the zodiac.

Each person is aligned to different star systems.

There are so many stars. How can we know which star system we are aligned to?
    First, make a list of all the stars you know. You can use the Internet
to find out about all the stars. It takes work. Then you run your hand
over each star name. You will feel the energy. Narrow it down until you
have five stars that resonate strongly. Then you can use kinesiology or
a pendulum.
    Many of these stars are not known. They have names, but people
do not know them. Science has discovered them, but they just have a
number. Work with your star, and immediately you will be able to rise
to a higher vibration.

*I think it would be much more wonderful if you could channel to us what our
star is. At least give us a shortcut.*
    Why do you think we have so much difficulty when somebody is
born? Some people come very early, and some people come very late.
Sometimes birth labor can take thirty-eight hours, and in others only
two hours. Have you ever wondered why people have different birth
labor times?

To line up with the right time?
    Exactly — to align with the right star. Your inner human compass
is aligned to your star, and you must connect to your star. When you
connect to this star, you will really expand your energy.

Afterword

Omran 12-Strand DNA Activation

After the last Skype session for this book, Rae received from Archangel Metatron a 12-strand DNA activation procedure for practitioners to activate the DNA of another person. Shortly afterward, Rae established the Omran Institute to disseminate information about DNA activation and to train and certify practitioners of Omran 12-Strand DNA Activation.

This is very powerful work, and both Rae and Robert have been conducting it for their clients and friends. Metatron described this work as follows:

"This ceremony is an initiation into the deeper interdimensional (or quantum) aspects of your consciousness. When this initiation is done, you can be opened to experiencing your core essence. Omran is an Aramaic name for 'gate opener.'"

Your DNA contains a record of all you are. The double helix — two strands of physical DNA — determines the characteristics of your physical body. The other ten strands of etheric DNA contain the entire history of your soul, your spiritual essence, and the truth of who you really are.

If there is a place where your higher self, or spirit, resides, it is in the etheric strands of your DNA. The whole story of you is there; it is your akashic record. All the gifts, talents, and abilities you ever achieved are there. The energy of all the actions you ever took and all the choices you ever made reside in your DNA. The spiritual history of the human race and your essence as part of the human journey is imprinted in your DNA. It carries your spiritual blueprint and all the spiritual journeys you have ever taken in all your lifetimes.

You have the ability within your consciousness to talk to your DNA, to engage it, to control it, to work with it, and to become part of it. When you give instructions to your DNA and it starts to respond, you will awaken to your multidimensionality, which is your true essence.

A quantum consciousness creates a different system of understanding. When you activate your DNA, you also have the capacity to extend your life span and the ability to understand and read your akashic record. DNA activation means increasing the information in your DNA. This can help you begin the process of returning to a multidimensional state of consciousness. A person with quantum consciousness is one with everything.

The etheric strands of DNA stay dormant unless they are commanded to open. This initiation ceremony is a gift from the Creator. The dormant nonphysical strands of DNA are commanded to awaken. This is a sacred ceremony that honors the divinity within you and opens the way for you to experience it.

This work is not for everyone. To be effective, ask yourself whether you are ready to receive at the highest level and to use what you are given for the highest good. To be most effective, you need some spiritual understanding. The spiritual path you have followed does not matter. Have you worked on yourself — sought to improve your spiritual life, to raise your vibration? Come seeking to know more of the Creator within you with both your mind and your heart. Then you will receive the highest benefit. Your DNA is an instruction manual that reflects your intentions. If your intentions have not focused on your spirituality, you probably won't feel too much from this work.

DNA Initiation Process

If done in person, this initiation ceremony takes about an hour (it can also be conducted as a distance session). You will lie on a treatment table with your eyes closed. The practitioner will stand over you and activate twelve trigger points on your body by touching them and will chant special tones to energize the activation of these trigger points. Then you will sit or lie in a meditative state for about thirty minutes while special harmonics play in the background.

You will become increasingly aware of the effects of this work over time. What can you look for during the next one to six months? There are many possibilities. One of the first things many people notice is a feeling of well-being. They have more confidence. They feel connected with a sense of belonging, of not being alone. Some may have healings. Karmic energy can be dispersed. Perceptions and values can change. Some have a sense that they are somebody, that they belong to the universe. Some have more confidence and trust.

You will be given a booklet to take with you. Some pages are for journaling. There will also be an online support group for people who have had this work done. We encourage you to participate in this support group and to share your experiences with others as well as hear what others have experienced. You may do so anonymously. You can find the online support group at www.BerkshireEnergyHealing.com.

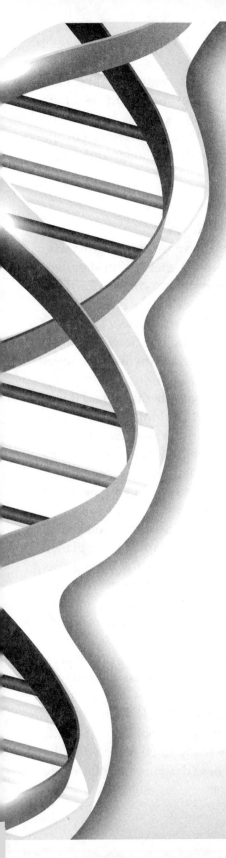

Appendix I: Working with the Energy of Dragons

March 31, 2011

Lord Merlin

Greetings. This is Lord Merlin. The legend of dragons has been on Earth for a long time. You might wonder how this came about. Like all legends, there is a story behind it. Dragons were created to inspire and to overcome many of the battles constantly raging in the human psyche.

Humans and dragons have a lot in common: Both breathe out fire. Humans breathe out the fire of hatred, anger, and all the other base emotions. Dragons do the same — breathing out the fire of destruction. The question is how to tame the dragon within and without.

All the legends and stories about dragons involve battles between a human being and a dragon. Ultimately, the human being wins, thus conquering the dragon, making it a friend. This is also true of the human mind. When you conquer the human mind and make it your friend, you have conquered the dragon inside you.

Dragons also roamed Earth many millions of years ago, and their remnants can still be found in some parts of the world such as China and South and Central America. Not all dragons on the Earth plane were enlightened creatures. Most were not. Dragons were not of the earth. They came from water, but they were able to adapt and adjust fairly quickly to their new environment.

How Dragons Came to Earth

Before the realm of dragons on Earth, there were twelve dragons who came here from another star system to set up the energetic grid system for this planet. These twelve dragons were invited to come to Earth by an emissary of the Creator to lay the groundwork for the energy of this planet in preparation for the arrival of the human species. There was a long period of preparation before humans could live here. Earth was an experiment, and the dragons were the first beings invited here to set the energetic framework.

Dragons brought pure crystalline energy with them and laid it into the ground, and this is what is awakening now. The long-dormant crystalline consciousness will awaken fully within the next two decades, and it will assist all of humanity in awakening and remembering its true heritage. After the initial work was done by these twelve magnificent beings, they departed to their homeland, and after a long period of time, other creatures started arriving on Earth.

Your star system is vast and has a myriad of life forms; some stars have dragons, not unlike the twelve who initially came to this planet. Many found their way to Earth and settled here, for the energy was similar to their home planets. The remnants you find now are the remnants of these dragons. In the course of their own evolution, some of them advanced in consciousness and moved into higher dimensions.

There will be more and more sightings and feelings of being connected with these dragons as humans evolve into higher consciousness. In the course of their advancement, these higher-dimensional dragons fanned out to all the major energy centers in the planet. Some moved to Japan, some moved to the Andes Mountains of South America, some moved to Mount Shasta in California, and some moved to the hills of China and Indonesia. Dragon energy is ready to be revealed in the Ural Mountains and Mount Kilimanjaro. These dragons are collectively holding the vibration for humanity to move into the fifth dimension. Human eyesight will be awakened to see the truth in the near future, for this is one of the gifts humans will soon have: the newly awakened eye that sees the truth and can distinguish truth from illusion.

Working with Dragons

Lightbeings can contact dragons by calling on them and connecting with them on an energetic level. Dragons can support you in raising your courage, steeling your will to seek the truth and never give up, thereby giving you fearlessness and wisdom.

Many human chakras are connected to dragon energy. Some of the geometric patterns of the chakras are found on the skins of dragons. You can use dragon energy to work with your chakras. Enlightened dragons emit sounds that can support humanity in its awakening. Dragons can also teach you about sound vibrations that you can use to awaken your kundalini power.

Some of the original dragons who came to Earth will now communicate with you.

Dragon Vaaa

Greetings. This is the dragon being known as Vaaa, and I live in the sacred hills of Malaysia called the Batu Caves. The hills of Batu were chosen specifically because they carry higher vibrations, and the Batu Caves are connected to the energy of three star systems. The ancient people living in this area intuited this; thus they chose to make this a holy place by consecrating the holy Gods of India into these hills.

There is a specific purpose to the Batu hills, for they carry the energetic vibrational pattern for the awakening Mer-Ka-Na in human beings. This is one of the highest vibrational patterns you must achieve before moving into the final stages of ascension from this planet. I hold this energy for humanity.

I invite all of you to avail yourselves of this grand energy to awaken further. The tonal frequency to use to work with my energy is "vay-ooooooooooooo vayooooooooooooooo vayooooooooooooooooo." The color to visualize is green.

Dragon Kiyoo

Greetings. I am the dragon being known as Kiyoo. I live in the Himalaya Mountains. Many people have seen me while climbing these mountains, but they thought they had seen a mirage, an illusion, or that their minds were playing tricks on them at the higher altitudes.

I appear to those with whom I have worked before. I hold the vibrational pattern of the memory of the awakening pineal gland. When you tone my name and visualize your pineal gland opening and expanding, my energy will be infused into your brain, and you will see the beginning of new awakened consciousness.

Awakening your pineal gland is one of the most glorious things a human being can do to activate the higher brain, where true connection with the Creator can always be maintained. The tonal frequency to use to work with me is "kiyoooooooooooooooooo." The color to visualize is soft pink.

Lord Vallar

Greetings. I am the being known as Lord Vallar. I am the king of dragons, and I hold the energy pattern of the great serpent power for planet Earth. My color is a soft purple with pink in it. I also have some green, along with shades of gray on my skin.

The ancient Gods used me in awakening their awesome power by invoking me to infuse my energy within them. I hold the vibrational pattern for the entire set of your DNA. Connect with me, work with me, and let us together awaken this awesome power within you.

My abode is in the region of Antarctica. The tonal frequency to use to work with me is "valarruuuuuuuuuuuuuuuu." The color to visualize is magenta.

Dragon Vyaau

Greetings. I am the dragon whose name is Vyaau. I am the emissary who connects human beings with the five elements. Humans in their movement toward ascension must master and work with the kingdoms of the elements.

I hold the vibrational energy for the wind. You must master this element, for it is directly connected to the breath you inhale. Breath has the power to liberate you from illusion.

The tonal frequency you can use to work with this element is "vaaaaaaaaaaaaaaaaaaaaaaaaaaaaaahhhhhhhhhhhhhhhhhhhh." When you use this tone, you stretch your vocal chords and thereby enable yourself to take more oxygen into your body. Work with this tone to elevate yourself.

Lady Asuraya

Greetings. I am the one known as Asuraya. I am of the female form, and I hold the vibrational pattern for human beings to connect with the flower and plant kingdoms, which is a prerequisite for ascension. By connecting with the flower and plant kingdoms, you can truly and fully open your heart. The heart must be completely opened before you are allowed to go into the higher dimensions.

There are also aromas that we all carry that can support humanity in its evolutionary process. Call on me, Lady Asuraya, and let us work together to integrate the essence of the flower and plant kingdoms within you.

Dragon Vanni

Greetings. I am the dragon known as Vanni. I represent the energetic pattern for connecting with the mineral kingdoms. I hold certain specific vibrational patterns for the minerals of this planet, especially the crystal kingdoms. Crystals emit and transmit energy. You must master this quality by integrating with crystals before moving into higher dimensions.

Your body is made of crystalline energy, and naturally, there is a pull and connection toward the mineral kingdoms. You must consciously awaken to this energy within yourself, bring it forth, and then enhance it to raise your vibration.

My partner, Lady Asuraya, and I hold energy for the opening of the higher chakras (eight through eleven). Connect with us, and let us work together in anchoring your higher chakras to your body. The tone you can use to connect with us both is "vooooooooooooooooooooooooo ooooooooooo oh wyyyyyyyyyyyyyyyyy."

Dragon Seacleyn

Greetings. I am known by the energetic name of Seacleyn, and my abode is in the mountains of New Zealand. I hold the energy pattern for connecting with the water kingdoms. Water is the source of all life, and people must master this element to move into higher dimensions. If you can understand the water patterns in your body, you can understand your life fully.

Water holds the key to your life. When you can work with the water, most of your problems — personal and global — can be solved instantly. Learn to master this element within yourself. One way of doing this is to hold water in your bare hands, offer it to the sky, and then drink it. Do this three times. This is best done in the early morning before you consume any food. This will start the process of awakening and integrating the essence of water in your body, which in turn will help you to remember your true origin.

Dragon Agniratham

Greetings. I am the dragon known as Agniratham. I am the fire element in the human body. I am the electric impulse in each of you, and I carry the life force inside you. There is great power inside of me and inside of you, and you must work to activate this. The seat of this power is near your naval. Once you are able to master the power of this fire inside yourself, the balance of the journey to mastery is much easier.

This power can consume you and destroy you, or it can transform you and elevate you. Use this power with caution. Start working with small doses of this power first and gradually build it up. The tonal frequency for this is "theeeeeeeeeeeeeeeeeeeeeeeeeeeeeiiiiiiiiiiiiiiiiiiiiiiiiiiiiiiiiiiiiiiiiiiiiiiiiiiii om."

Lady Molemaaaaaaaa

Greetings. My name is Lady Molemaaaaaaaa. I am called the baby dragon, for I hold the energetic pattern for innocence in life. At the core level of every human being, everyone is innocent, pure, and loving. I hold this pattern, lest humanity forget its true nature.

Connect with me daily and rediscover your inner beauty, purity, and innocence. Call on me any time you need upliftment and gentle encouragement. Tone my name, "Molemaaaaaaaa," three times, and you will feel my presence in your heart.

Dragon Vallllllllishakkkti

Greetings. I am the dragon known as Vallllllllishakkkti, or the gate-keeper. My duty is to open the gates of perception in human beings. There are many perceptions; ascension (moving into higher dimensions) is a perception. Try to see the higher perceptions in everything so that you are not blinded by the illusions of the everyday world.

The color of my energy pattern is soft pink with a little magenta. Bring this color into your mind's eye, and place it into your third eye before you go into meditation. You will then be working to open your higher-perspective mind/eye. You can also embody this color on your clothes, carry it with you as a drawing, or use it in any other way so that you are able to perceive more clearly.

Dragon Kieosomb

Greetings. My name is Kieosomb, and I hold the energy pattern for connection with planet Earth. My abode is in the hills of Europe, and many times I appear as a little bird for the curiosity seekers visiting these places.

My role is to hold the memory of the deep symbiotic connection you have with planet Earth, for you and planet Earth are partners who have both come here to increase awareness and to grow. Call on me and work with me to awaken this connection.

Dragon Saaaaaaaaaaaaaaaaaashtraiii

Greetings. I am the one known as Saaaaaaaaaaaaaaaaaashtraiii, meaning the wise one. I hold the energy pattern of putting all things together for the manifestation of something bigger or higher. You must have an understanding of the principles of energy and how it is used in order to move into higher dimensions.

I hold certain sacred codes within me. You also have codes, and there are certain codes in the ground as well. When you combine and work with all these codes, you are able to assimilate all the wisdom you have gained and use the love in your heart to move into higher dimensions with ease. The tone to connect with me is "sssssssssssssssss ssssssssssssssssssssssssssssssssssssssss." Say this in a high pitch and then slowly lower pitch eight times.

✳ ✳ ✳

So you see, my friends, why dragons are coming out into to the open now. Play with them, for they can teach you much. This is Lord Merlin.

Appendix II: Balance Your Diet to Enhance Spiritual Energy

Amma, Angel Samiel, and
Master Kuthumi

Note: *The information herein is for educational purposes only. The contents of this article should not be used to give medical advice or to prescribe any form of treatment for physical, emotional, or medical problems without the advice of a physician, directly or indirectly. Should you use any recommendations in this article for yourself or others, the author, compiler, and publisher assume no responsibility for your actions.*

Greetings. Today we would like to discuss food. The food that humanity eats has a lot to do with the way people experience life. You have heard the expression "you are what you eat." It is literally true. If you observe carefully, you understand a great deal about people just by noticing the foods they eat. All foods can be categorized into two main groups: masculine and feminine.

What Are Masculine and Feminine Foods?
How Do They Affect You?

The purpose of life is to create balance in all areas of expression, and this starts with food because it is food that drives human beings to do things. At the subconscious level of every human being, memory has recorded times when there was no food, whether this happened yesterday or thousands of years ago. Thirty thousand years ago, you scavenged for food. There were also times when you killed for food. These memories of not having enough food are still submerged deep within the psyche. Almost all the time, most of you eat more than you need because your bodies remember a time when you did not have enough. Your natural tendency from a young age is to eat whatever you are given, and you grow into that habit.

We can say some foods are better than others, some have chemicals and some do not, some are heavy, some are light, and so on. There is always a debate among people whether they should eat meat or not. Once you have a basic understanding of the energies of food, you will be able to choose which foods support you and which deplete your energy.

Food plays a very major role in your spiritual awakening process. We are coming into a time when we need feminine energies to be more prominent. When you are in a masculine body, there is also feminine energy; each of you is both masculine and feminine. If people could focus on eating foods that are more feminine, this would activate feminine energy and they would perceive a wealth of soul energies coming forward. A new aspect of the Creator would be activated from within each person. This would result in tremendous wisdom, skills, and abilities that would simply emerge from each person who eats more feminine-vibration food. We ascended masters are asking humanity to embrace feminine qualities activated from within and to use them in their actions, thoughts, and meditations. To eat in this way is extremely important.

Sometimes you have to take physical action in order to make spiritual shifts. We believe that eating in this way is a physical action that anchors spiritual shifts and activates the energy of greater love, creativity, and beauty. It changes the entire vibration of the body, and this is what humanity needs to do in order to ascend further. With so many people emanating feminine energies, Mother Earth will also embrace these vibrations and create healing in the physical reality. This diet can heal the physical body and the physical Earth.

What Foods to Eat and When

Let us consider the first meal of the day: breakfast. Medical professionals will tell you that a healthy breakfast is the key to the day, and everyone should eat a well-balanced breakfast. Now let us take that doctrine and look at it closely. When people wake up in the morning from restful sleep, their energy fields are in a receptive mood. If they eat foods that are opposite to that, then the receptive, creative part of them is slowly being drained of its energy. To give you an example, let us take a typical American breakfast of bread, eggs, milk, coffee or tea, orange juice, and so on. All of these foods have masculine energy. When you eat them, the creative part shuts down and the masculine part takes over. On the other hand, if people eat foods that support their energy fields in the morning, then their energy is enhanced and they continue in a receptive and creative space. The energy of the first food and drink in the morning sets the pattern for the entire day.

When can you eat masculine food? Lunch is the best time to eat masculine food, for it will give you energy to carry you forward. The evening food should be feminine. This helps not only in the health arena but also to enhance creative ideas while you sleep so that you are in a more balanced state when you wake up.

One other thing to note about the energy of the food is in the way it is cooked. Food retains the highest vibration when it is cooked in an earthen pot because such a container holds higher energy and more natural essence of Mother Earth.

Choosing Masculine and Feminine Foods

Dear ones, all foods can be divided into these two categories, including water. Cold water is masculine and warm water is feminine.

Experiment with the foods you take and you will come up with the most appropriate one for you.

Humanity lives in an accelerated time with tremendous input of highly spiritual energy to Earth. You want to maintain the best energy field to use these highly potent, charged energies. Therefore, you want to keep your body as light as possible to be able to use these energies. Just by observing the foods you eat, you will be able to make the necessary adjustments to support your spiritual process.

Masculine Foods	Feminine Foods

Cold water | Warm water

FRUITS

Masculine		Feminine	
Bananas	Pineapples	Apples	Oranges
Grapes	Mangos	Papayas	Cantaloupes
Dates	Apricots	Pomegranates	Kiwis
Strawberries	Watermelons	Cherries	Dry grapes
		Figs	Tomatoes (baby tomatoes only)
		Berries (raspberries/	Pears
		blueberries)	
		Avocado (The No.1 balanced food can be eaten any time.)	

VEGETABLES

Masculine		Feminine	
Cabbage	Sweet potatos	Carrots	Lettuce
Cucumbers	Chickpeas	Turnips	Radishes
Onions	Soy	Cauliflower	Broccoli
Zucchini	Olives	Sweet corn (if it is organic)	Lentils
Eggplant	Salad with dressing	Garlic	Asparagus
Baked Beans	Sweet corn (mass produced)	Spinach	Lady fingers (okra)
Mashed potatoes/Hash browns		Leek	Celery
		Salad without dressing	Mushrooms

MEATS AND DAIRY

Masculine		Feminine	
Eggs	Bacon	Sheep milk	Cow milk (farm produced)
Cow milk (factory produced)	Fish	Small shrimp	
Meat (all kinds of meat)		(less than one inch long)	

GRAINS

Masculine		Feminine
Pasta (all kinds)	Breads (all)	Natural cereals
Wheat, rye, and so on	Rice (all kinds)	

NUTS

Masculine		Feminine	
Peanuts	Cashews	Walnuts	Almonds

SPICES

Masculine	Feminine
Indian curry	Pepper

BEVERAGES

Masculine		Feminine
Soda	Coffee and Tea	Green tea
Herb teas (most of them)		

PREPARED FOODS

Masculine	
Pizza (all)	Cookies (all)
Chicken pot pie	Hot dogs
Potato chips	Chocolates (all)
Cakes (all)	Corn Chips
Doughnuts	

What Foods Create a Healthy Energy
Experience throughout the Day?

For breakfast, cereal with farm-produced milk, avocado, papaya, and freshly squeezed orange juice are all recommended. In the morning, you want to be receptive. For the afternoon, it is good to have masculine food as an energy driver to keep you going. For snacks in the early evening, instead of munching on cookies and candies, nuts without any seasoning and raisins are recommended. For supper, try foods that are feminine in nature. Include fresh foods, pima (red, green, and especially yellow sweet peppers), baby carrots, spinach (fresh or steamed), kidney beans, green peas, baby tomatoes, miniature apples, and so on. Dear ones, play with the food energies and come up with your own diet plans.

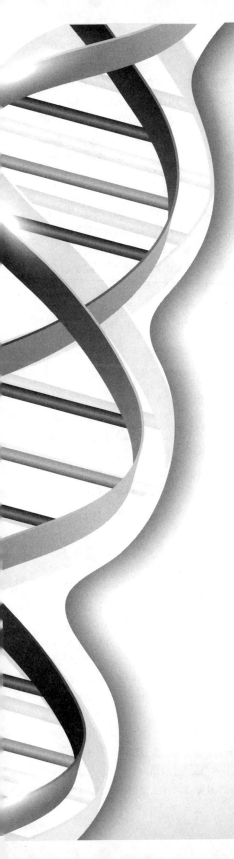

Appendix III: Activating Codes for the New Yuga

Archangel Metatron

Angelic greetings to all. This is Archangel Metatron. My dearest fellow creators, it is time to step up into creating a new reality in this new timeline where you are in complete harmony with yourself. As you all are aware, the consciousness of the planet shifted again on the spring equinox of this year, and this shift is called "moving from the darkness to the light." It is also called "moving into a new Yuga" — a new timeline that will last a few thousand years. With this new shift, the veil has become thinner, and the communication and the connection with the fifth dimension have become easier. When intent combines with preparation and action, you can truly take advantage of this new time period. What do we mean by this — intent and preparation?

First of all, you can prepare for this shift by asking for and activating the Aquarian code within you. Each

Yuga, or time period, has a specific code and a master associated with it. There are two beings of light who are overlighting this new Yuga, and they will be with Earth till the next phase of the new Yuga. You can call on these beings: Lord and Lady of Aquarius. They have a specific vibrational signature, and you can call for the integration of their specific light pertaining to this Earth plane for this time period. The color of their light frequency is a soft metallic yellow. See this light coming into your tenth chakra, which is way above your head, and then flowing through all your chakras before going into the body of Earth's spirit and grounding there. What is important to keep in mind while integrating this light is that you run it not only into your chakra column but also into your pranic tube. The next phase of your evolution comes from the pranic tube. Do this daily for a few minutes, and see the energy settling in and easily flowing — both in the chakras in the front and back and also in your pranic tube.

Activating Dormant Codes

The activation of the Aquarian code will act as a base for the activation of the other codes. What are these other codes? Human beings are made up of sound frequency and sacred geometry, and each sound frequency and bit of geometry contains a certain code. These codes lie dormant for eons of time until they are activated and worked with.

All of you are very well aware of the guides and other supporting energies working with you, and some of you communicate with them frequently and on a daily basis. These guides are part of your soul group energy, and each guide has a code. When you activate these codes, you fully embrace the full essence of these beings. For example, there are codes for masters and guides like Master Buddha, Master Kuthumi, and Lord Maitreya. You can ask for the activation of these codes in your meditation/quiet time. There are also angelic codes you can activate. There are codes for me — Archangel Metatron — codes for Archangel Michael, codes for Archangel Gabriel, and codes for all other archangels and angels. Simply requesting with pure intent and love in your heart will start this process.

When you activate these codes, you are bringing in more light of your guides and infusing it with our own light, and this will immediately enhance your light frequency. This is similar to upgrading your software in your old computer so that it can run faster and more smoothly with the new programs. Planet Earth moved into a higher reality, and you must accelerate and upgrade your light quotient to be on par with the new frequencies of Earth. There are also codes for Earth, for all the elements, for stars, and to connect with the pure essence of the animal spirits. When you activate these codes, you will come into alignment with all of these at a higher level, and you will be in communion with all of creation. Most of you have desired at the deepest level of your beings to experience this aspect of yourselves, to experience the God aspect of yourselves in everyday living with all of creation. This is one way of doing it, fellow creators.

Working with New Codes and Your Star Heritage

The next exercise we wish to share with you is activating the Moses code within you. The Moses code contains the specific energy of transcendence and liberation — an energy that can support you in identifying what is precious and what is not supporting you in self-realization. Most of you have great difficulty in letting go of deep attachment to third-dimensional behaviors and patterns, and working with Moses codes during meditation can help you identify these patterns and eliminate them completely from your life.

There are also codes within your being called soul blueprint codes. Many of the lightworkers and others have great difficulty understanding their life purpose or why they were born, and by calling for the activation of these blueprint codes, they will be able to sense, feel, and intuit their soul purposes rather easily.

One other area we wish for you to focus on is your star heritage connection. Many of you, after your Earth incarnation, travel to different star systems to experience or learn specific lessons. During these times of learning, you create star karma, for it is the same principle of cause and effect in these realities also. Many on Earth carry heavy star karma, and this must be balanced and released. Once this is done, then you can call forth and activate the star codes within you, for all of you are aligned with a special star, and that star is one of your supporting energies waiting to be called forth. You are all aligned with a star, a dragon, a tree, a plant, an animal, a sound frequency, a color, a smell. You can call for the codes of these supporting energies to be activated and brought forth in your meditation, for they are in support of you.

Balancing Energy

One other area we wish to bring your attention to is the area of energy imbalance, otherwise known as karmic energy. Karma is simply that — energy imbalance. We incarnate again and again to balance energy. But now in this new time period, you have the capacity to erase much of this imbalance energy by working directly with the Karmic Board. The Karmic Board consists of twelve beings of light, and this includes some ascended masters like Master Buddha and Lady Quan Yin. Practice communicating with them during your meditation, and ask for a release of this imbalanced energy from your akash and your quantum energy field. Again, asking and giving intent for this to happen will start this process. You can also request that the Karmic Board bring to your awareness the lesson embedded in the karma — imbalance without the pain and suffering. This requesting and erasing karma is a gift you have earned yourself, for we wish for you to go into this new Yuga with a clean slate.

Finally, we ask you to call forth the great teacher Sanat Kumara, for he carries a special energy and code directly tied into this Earth plane. Sanat Kumara embodies the energy of the planet Venus, and Venus is the place you come before you are incarnated into this Earth plane. In this place, you have full awareness of who you are and ask Sanat Kumara to activate this code of pre-birth awareness. This can help you remember more of yourselves and the God within you, for all of you are gods and goddesses. Dear family, just by using these simple tools of codes, you will come to a place of more understanding of yourselves and your universe.

Description of
DNA of the Spirit,
Volume 2

DNA of the Spirit, volume 2 will continue where volume 1 left off. It will include additional sessions and more teachings. The working subtitle for volume 2 is *Advanced Techniques for Meditation, Activation, and Initiation from Ancient Mystery School Teachings and Archetypal Energies of the Masters.*

Some of the material provided will be from Skype sessions, as in those in volume 1. Some information will be from activation and initiation ceremonies conducted in sacred places in Egypt and Greece.

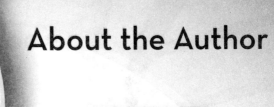

About the Author

Rae Chandran was born in India and has lived in the United States and Japan. He performs individual channeling sessions for his clients, and he has published articles in the *Sedona Journal of Emergence!* Rae teaches workshops throughout the Far East on the Ancient Egyptian mysteries, DNA activation, and channeling. He creates soul symbols for his clients, and he leads tours of ancient holy places worldwide.

Rae founded the Omran Institute, which promotes DNA awareness and certifies practitioners of Omran 12-Strand DNA Activation. He also performs individual Omran 12-Strand DNA sessions for clients. Rae lives with his wife and children outside of Tokyo, Japan. Visit his website at www.RaeChandran.com.

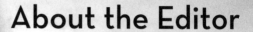

About the Editor

Robert Pollock was born in Washington, DC, and has lived in London (England), Canada, and the Berkshire mountains of Massachusetts. He is an energy healer at a holistic health resort in the Berkshires, and he has an energy healing practice with locations in New York City and the Berkshires.

Robert wrote *Navigating by Heart*. He teaches workshops in spirituality and DNA activation. He also performs individual Omran 12-Strand DNA sessions for clients. Robert currently lives in the Berkshires, and his website is www.BerkshireEnergyHealing.com.

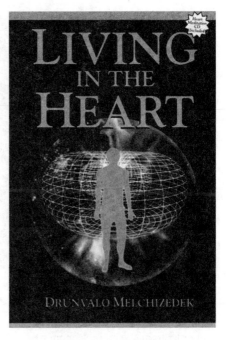

Light Technology PUBLISHING *Presents*

THE ANCIENT SECRET OF THE FLOWER OF LIFE,
VOLUME 1

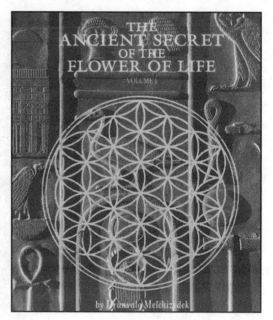

✴ *Light Technology* PUBLISHING *Presents*

THE BOOK OF
transformation
THROUGH ROBERT SHAPIRO

Topics Include:

Heart Love/Heart Heat • Benevolent Magic • Living Prayer
Disentanglement • Deep Disentanglement
Disentanglement Clearings • and much more!

— Learn how to ask for clearing of old traumas and discomforts.
— Learn how to create a nourishing, benevolent life for yourself and others.

THE BOOK OF
transformation
ANCIENT & FUTURE SECRETS
OF CLEARING & CREATION

channeled through
Robert Shapiro

eBook
ONLY
$**2.99**

Shifting Frequencies
Sounds for Vibratory Activation
by Jonathan Goldman

with CD

For the first time, Healing Sounds pioneer Jonathan Goldman tells us about shifting frequencies — how to use sound and other modalities to change vibrational patterns for both personal and planetary healing and transformation. Through his consciousness connection to Shamael, angel of sound, Jonathan shares his extraordinary scientific and spiritual knowledge and insights, providing information, instructions, and techniques on using sound, light, color, visualization, and sacred geometry to experience shifting frequencies. The material in this book is both timely and vital for health and spiritual evolution.

$25⁰⁰
Plus Shipping

ISBN 13: 978-1-891824-42-5
Softcover 448 pp.
6 X 9 Perfect Bound

In this book, you will:

- explore the use of sound in ways you never imagined for healing and transformation
- discover harmonics as a key to opening to higher levels of consciousness
- learn about the angel chakra and what sounds may be used to activate this new energy center
- find out how to transmute imbalanced vibrations using your own sounds
- experience the secrets of crystal singing

Chapters Include:
- Sound Currents: Frequency and Intent
- Vibratory Resonance
- Vocalization, Visualization, and a Tonal Language
- The Harmonics of Sound
- Vocal Harmonics and Listening
- Energy Fields

Print Books: Visit Our Online Bookstore www.LightTechnology.com
eBooks Available on Amazon, Apple iTunes, Google Play, and Barnes & Noble